# Teaching Religious Education 4–11

## Second edition

*Teaching Religious Education 4–11* is an accessible, practical guide for primary teachers, and covers the teaching of religious education at the Foundation Stage, Key Stage 1 and Key Stage 2. This second edition has been extensively updated to take account of recent changes to religious education.

The book is divided into three sections: 'Setting the scene'; 'Planning the teaching'; and 'Background'. It maps out and considers the implications for teachers of:

- the changing aims and objectives of RE;
- the legal framework;
- the broadening understanding of the notion of religion;
- concern for spiritual development;
- emergence of citizenship as an additional component of the curriculum;
- introduction of formal guidelines to the content of RE;
- tackling important topics and contemporary issues;
- planning RE across the primary school;
- planning a unit of work;
- using different teaching approaches;
- monitoring and assessing progress;
- teaching Christianity and other world faiths – Buddhism, Hinduism, Islam, Judaism and Sikhism.

The book is full of practical examples and ideas for use in the classroom and also contains a helpful resources section.

**Derek Bastide** was formerly Principal Lecturer in Education at the University of Brighton, UK and is now a Religious Education consultant.

# Teaching Religious Education 4–11

## Second edition

Derek Bastide

Routledge
Taylor & Francis Group

LONDON AND NEW YORK

First published 1987 by Falmer Press

This second edition published 2007
by Routledge
2 Park Square, Milton Park, Abingdon, Oxon OX14 4RN

Simultaneously published in the USA and Canada
by Routledge
270 Madison Ave, New York, NY 10016

*Routledge is an imprint of the Taylor & Francis Group, an informa business*

© 2007 Derek Bastide

Typeset in Palatino by Keystroke, 28 High Street, Tettenhall, Wolverhampton
Printed and bound in Great Britain by Bell & Bain Ltd, Glasgow

*British Library Cataloguing in Publication Data*
A catalogue record for this book is available from the British Library

*Library of Congress Cataloging in Publication Data*
A catalog record has been requested for this book

ISBN10: 0–415–28781–2
ISBN13: 978–0–415–28781–4

To Billy, Annabel, Sophia and Milo
who are just beginning their religious education

# Contents

# Acknowledgements

Anyone who produces a book of this nature is indebted to various individuals and groups of people over a number of years. There are, of course, professional colleagues of various subjects and persuasions, both in the university and the diocesan education team, who have willingly shared ideas. There are cohorts of students who have asked searching questions and come up with creative ideas. There are also the pupils taught in school from whom again one has learned so much.

At the present time any writer on religious education is indebted to the National Framework for Religious Education produced in 2004 for the Secretary of State for Education. This has perhaps the lowest status but highest influence of any document in religious education – of low status because it is advisory (and so could be ignored) but of high influence both because of its clarity and because of the overwhelming support it received in the consultation process.

Beyond all this I am also immensely appreciative of the understanding and loving support of my wife, Judith, in this as in previous similar ventures.

# Setting the scene

# 1 Introduction

The first edition of this book, then titled *Religious Education 5–12*, was published in 1987, a year before the Education Reform Act of 1988 came into effect. In many ways this Act changed the face of education in England and Wales, perhaps especially in primary schools, by introducing so much that is now taken for granted: the National Curriculum, the key stages, the numbering of year groups from YR to Y13, SATs, OFSTED, to name but a few. As the book predated the Act none of these, not surprisingly, appeared in it.

The Act contained some valuable directions on the content of religious education, chiefly that it should 'reflect the fact that the religious traditions in Great Britain are in the main Christian whilst taking account of the teaching and practices of the other principal religions represented in Great Britain'.

This clearly laid out the framework of a subject content although it did raise many issues which needed to be solved over the succeeding years. This development is charted in Chapter 2. Although the first edition of the book came before the Act, its philosophy and approach to RE was essentially the same and this is largely because the Act did in fact enshrine in law what had already become good practice in RE over the 1970s and 1980s.

A very significant milestone in the development of RE was the publication in 2004 of a 'National Framework for Religious Education'. Prior to its appearance in final form, the framework was subjected to widespread consultation and was overwhelmingly welcomed with enthusiasm. Like the Education Reform Act in its time, the framework reflects best practice in the subject across the country. It is at present a non-statutory document and therefore without force of law but it is intended as advice to local authorities in the five-yearly revisions of their agreed syllabus. Although a few local authorities may decline to follow its advice, it is highly likely that most will use it as a basis for their future work. The framework is therefore set to be a crucial shaper of future RE. The approach of this book is closely in line with that of the National Framework for Religious Education.

The underlying principles of the approach of this book can be summarised under six main headings.

First the book assumes that religious education in schools is different from religious nurture which is the work and privilege of the appropriate religious community. It also assumes that in voluntary aided schools pupils will be given religious education as well as religious teaching of a nurturing nature.

Second, Christianity should occupy half of the RE teaching time over each key stage and that over the years of compulsory schooling pupils should become acquainted with the other principal religious traditions in Great Britain: Buddhism, Hinduism, Islam, Judaism and Sikhism.

Third, to avoid 'mishmash' and trivialisation, pupils in Key Stage 1 should study aspects of Christianity and (only) one other religion, and in Key Stage 2, Christianity and (only) two other religions. This does not exclude reference to other traditions but it does mean that the identified religions should be the focuses. How these are taught will depend upon the age and stage of the child. Which religions these should be will normally be determined by the local agreed syllabus.

Fourth, a religion should be studied as a *living activity*. It is *living* because for countless millions religions are highly important, giving values, shaping lives, providing support and offering a coherent framework of meaning. It is an *activity* because religion for most adherents is concerned with doing: celebrating festivals, engaging in worship, going on pilgrimages, initiating the young, hearing and retelling stories significant to the faith. Even the sacred books which are usually of ancient origin are studied so as to enlighten the present. Religions should not be presented as the relics of a past age.

Fifth, there should be two main focuses as attainment targets: *learning about religion* and *learning from religion*. Pupils need to have a knowledge of the beliefs and practices of the principal religious traditions, but a knowledge which transcends just facts and which incorporates both understanding and empathy, so that they learn both the 'what' and the 'why'. In the end RE is not about knowing lots of facts about religions but about developing a sympathetic understanding of them. This study should be undertaken in a respectful way recognising that for large numbers of people across the world these faiths are their holy ground and should not be trampled on. This ties in closely with the concern in the National Framework that RE should be an agent for inclusivity in society. Pupils also need the opportunity to develop their own ideas and understanding about meaning and purpose in life (learning from religion). This also matches closely with the concern in the National Framework for pupils' own spiritual development.

Sixth, RE should be seen as a normal school subject. It should have its own policy and scheme of work, it should be monitored and evaluated, it should figure in the school improvement plan and there should be assessment (see Chapter 16).

This book is written principally for teachers in primary schools and for students in training who as class teachers will teach RE along with all the other required subjects. It is not an agreed syllabus for RE nor does it try to be one. Rather it tries to meet the need that many teachers feel for a deeper understanding of the aims of religious education and for some information on and understanding of religion and religions if they are going to work successfully in RE. They also need an understanding of how to approach RE in the classroom – and this involves an interrelationship of the aims of the subject, the age, stage and development of the pupils, and the subject content. Early in the book there is a detailed consideration of the nature of religion and the aims and expectations of RE. At the end of the book there are two chapters with material at adult level, one containing brief accounts of the six principal religious traditions and the other on Christian festivals. Material at adult level appears throughout the book especially as background to particular units of work. (A look at the contents page will give a flavour of the approaches in RE explained in the book.)

A particular feature of the book is the provision of detailed teacher accounts of successful RE work done in schools as illustrations of the different approaches.

The overall hope of this book is that teachers and those in training will give thought to the teaching of RE so as to make it exciting to children, to help them to understand the beliefs, values and practices of their neighbours with traditions other than their own, to treat these with respect and tolerance and, at the same time, to have the opportunity to nourish their inner beings.

# 2  Where is RE now?

## The legal position

Ever since schools were founded in England, religion has had a place as a normal part of the curriculum. The first schools in the country were largely established by the churches and so religious teaching was central to the education provided. In 1870, the date when Parliament approved the plan to provide compulsory education for all, it was decided as a national policy that existing schools provided by the churches should remain and that the new schools, provided by the School Board set up in each locality, should fill the gaps in the existing voluntary provision. While it was clear that in Church of England schools, for example, the form of religious teaching should be Anglican, it was less clear what form it should take in the new Board schools which were paid for out of taxes and had no allegiance to any of the churches. An agreement was reached (called the Cowper-Temple clause) by which religious teaching should not be given 'by means of any catechism or formulary which is distinctive of any particular religious denomination'. This early principle remains with us today and from this came the long tradition of Bible/scripture teaching, the Bible being of great significance to all the Christian denominations, which dominated RE in English schools for a century.

### The 1944 settlement

The 1944 Education Act, often called the Butler Act, was the next great step forward in RE – or to be more precise RI (Religious Instruction), as it was called then. This Act made the following references to religion:

- that religious *instruction* should be given in every county school;
- that each school day should begin with an act of worship;
- that in each school there should be a right of withdrawal both for teachers and for parents on behalf of their children;
- that each local authority should formulate its agreed syllabus for religious instruction (or adopt that of another LEA).

Although the 1944 Education Act did not lay down what it considered should be the aims of religious teaching or give guidelines for its content, there seemed to be an implicit assumption that the teaching should be, to use a technical term, *confessional* (that is, it should attempt to lead pupils into a commitment to the Christian faith). Evidence for this is provided by the term *instruction* and by the right of withdrawal on the grounds of conscience for both teachers and parents on behalf of their children. For the forty-four years from 1944 to 1988, the requirements of the 1944 Education Act were in place. During that time, however, much happened which began to change the ways in which RE was both understood and taught. Of these, two movements seem to be the most significant.

### Changing times

First, in the 1960s there was a considerable research focus on the way children's understanding of religious concepts developed. Of these researchers Ronald Goldman was certainly the most influential. Goldman agreed that the apparent lack of success with religious teaching in school was caused partly by much unimaginative teaching and partly by a focus upon Bible stories which were often too complex and difficult for younger children to make proper sense of. The net result was the misunderstanding by significant numbers of children of many religious concepts. Goldman's interviews with pupils from aged 5 to 15 revealed different levels of understanding occasioned by limitations of thought and experience of younger children. For example, one Bible story he discussed with children was of Moses and the Burning Bush. In the story, Moses sees a bush burning on the mountain side which burns but never burns away. God speaks to Moses from the bush and Moses, overawed by the event, is afraid to look on God. When asked why Moses was afraid to look on God, children aged 4–6 years tended to be limited in their thinking by egocentricity and monofocalism: one child responded, 'God had a beard and Moses did not like beards'! Further quotes from Goldman's collections from his interviews with children of this age include:

> 'God is the man in the moon. He has a round head and he has bent ears. He lives in a round house.'

> 'God is in the sky and you can't see him. He flies around. Sometimes he stops behind a cloud to have something to eat. He goes down to land at night to see shepherds and talk to them.'

Goldman's research indicated that children's understanding developed as their thinking and experience developed. Thinking became less egocentric and monofocal, so an 8-year-old would not be concerned about Moses and beards but would be more likely to speculate that 'it might have been because the bright light from the bush was frightening him'. This response is clearly more logical but, as Goldman noted, still limited by concrete thinking.

Goldman argued strongly for a shift away from Bible-centred RE to child-centred RE and he recommended the exploration of topics such as bread, water, families, light, sheep and shepherds which were much closer to children's own experience and would therefore be more appropriate for pupils, especially younger ones, to explore religious ideas and concepts implicit in these topics. Goldman's ideas have almost certainly brought both benefits and disadvantages to RE teaching but they had considerable impact on that period and made very many teachers – and agreed syllabus writers – think very carefully about the appropriateness of much of the content of traditional religious teaching.

The second movement was a change in the religious composition of the country. This was in part a loosening of the connections of many people with the main churches. Some of the traditional indicators of religious practice – churchgoing and baptisms, for example – were declining and it was becoming much more acceptable to admit publicly to agnosticism. At the same time other religious traditions were beginning to appear in Britain. In the 1950s and 1960s, there was large-scale immigration into the country from the Caribbean, Africa, Cyprus and the Indian sub-continent. Practically all those who came from India, Pakistan and Bangladesh practised religions other than Christianity. The result was that mosques, temples and gurdwaras began to appear in many towns and cities and many teachers found that they had in their classes children from different religious traditions.

These factors, which will be explored in more detail later in the book, led to considerable changes to the aims and content of RE in the county school and it was this approach to RE which was widespread in 1988 when the Education Reform Act was introduced.

## RE in the Education Reform Act (1988)

Contrary to many reports in the media at the time of the publication of the Act, the requirements in RE were not an attempt to put the educational clock back to the period of the 1944 Act, but rather they reflect and enshrine in law the thought and practice which had developed in the intervening years. In its attempt to give coherence and balance to the overall curriculum, the Education Reform Act has given RE a firm, if slightly idiosyncratic, place in its plans. In general, the Education Reform Act continues the religious settlement of the 1944 Education Act but introduces some helpful clarifications and modifications.

### *The basic curriculum*

The Education Reform Act introduced the notion of a basic curriculum to which all pupils are entitled. The aim of this 'balanced and broadly based curriculum' is to promote 'the spiritual, moral, cultural, mental and physical development of pupils at the school and of society' (Section 1:2). This provides the overall framework in which RE and the ten foundation subjects which form the National Curriculum (English, mathematics, science, technology, history, geography, music, art, physical education, and in Key Stages 3 and 4 a modern foreign language, plus Welsh in schools in Wales where Welsh is not spoken) are placed, and it is intended that they should all make their contribution to the rounded development of individuals. None of those defined aspects of development is the preserve of any given subject. It would be a mistake to think that spiritual development is the responsibility only of RE; it would be hoped that English, science, art and music and others too would have their contribution to make.

Unlike the foundation subjects of the National Curriculum, RE has no prescribed national attainment targets, programmes of study or assessment arrangements, so from this it is clear that RE has a unique place in the basic curriculum. The (then) DES Circular 3/89 expresses it:

The special status of religious education as part of the basic curriculum but not of the National Curriculum is important. It ensures that religious education has equal standing in relation to the core and the other foundation subjects within a school's curriculum, but is not subject to nationally prescribed Attainment Targets, Programmes of Study and assessment arrangements.

This means in effect that the Secretary of State has little power over religious education. In reality the RE curriculum, rather than being national, is local – the responsibility of each local education authority.

That RE is not part of the National Curriculum seems to arise for a number of reasons. First, it is no doubt partly due to the long-standing responsibility which LEAs have held for the content of RE through the agreed syllabus. Second, the existence of a conscience clause enabling parents to withdraw their children from RE would mean that some children might not be able to participate in part of the National Curriculum – and that would be odd. Third, the fact that a significant number of schools are voluntary aided and can therefore teach RE according to their trust deeds would mean that they would be ignoring the content of the National Curriculum. It is reasonable to suspect, too, that the government feared that to reach agreement on national programmes of study and attainment targets for RE could be a very controversial process and therefore one best avoided if possible! The traditional responsibility of the LEAs for RE in their boundaries was therefore a very attractive solution. While it did solve one difficulty, it did create another. An underlying principle of the National Curriculum is that children, wherever they live in the country, should have an equal educational entitlement which should not be subject to the vagaries of the LEAs or of individual schools. Because of its essentially local character, this principle could not apply to RE. This is an issue which is still being addressed.

### The content of RE

Although the Education Reform Act deputed the RE curriculum to each LEA to devise in the form of an agreed syllabus it did provide a very important framework in which these syllabuses should be drawn up. This framework is contained in one sentence in the Act, which states that all new agreed syllabuses must: 'reflect the fact that the religious traditions in Great Britain are in the main Christian whilst taking account of the teaching and practices of the other principal religions represented in Great Britain'. Before the implications of this sentence are examined, it is important to note that the law for the first time lays down a requirement about the content of RE – that over the period of compulsory schooling pupils should have the opportunity to study a range of religious traditions. LEAs are free to draw up their agreed syllabuses but they must fit within this framework. This would mean, for example, that an agreed syllabus which included only Christianity would not be within the law and neither would one which attempted to exclude it. This is a most definite development from the 1944 settlement and one which reflects very clearly what has been happening in the teaching of RE over the intervening years.

It is important to note that the sentence from the Act above refers to religious traditions (in the plural) and while it acknowledges that Christianity is the main one, it is still one among a number. The religious composition of Britain is therefore seen as *pluralist*. This has implications for the aims of RE in county schools. While it is never stated explicitly, there is the implicit assumption that RE is more concerned with developing awareness and understanding of religion and of religions than it is with any confessionalist or missionary intent.

The Act is very clear about the criteria for the selection of the religions to be included in agreed syllabuses: they should be the other principal religions represented in Great Britain. This geographical context is extremely important and has implications in two directions. First, the religions to be studied are those which children will come across in moving around Great Britain. Therefore schools are not licensed to teach little-known religions from the remoter parts of the world but those which are significant in this country. Second, each local authority is required to draw up a syllabus which reflects the fact that the religious traditions of this country are in the main Christian whilst taking account of the teaching and practices of the other principal religions represented in Great Britain. This means that all local authorities, including those in which the presence of other religious traditions is not significant numerically, must base their agreed syllabus upon the religious composition of Great Britain.

Although this provides extremely important guidance to LEAs in the drawing up of their agreed syllabuses, there are a number of issues which are not dealt with. Nowhere does the Act specify which are 'the other principal religions represented in Great Britain'. Despite early fears that this might be an area of high controversy, these seem to have generally been accepted as Buddhism, Hinduism, Islam, Judaism and Sikhism. Nowhere does the Act give guidance upon the amount of time to be given to the different traditions apart from the general implication that Christianity, because of its position as the main religious tradition, should have the most.

It was not clear whether it meant that Christianity should receive a larger time allocation than any other religion or whether it should have more time than all the other religions put together. This is an issue upon which the government has resolutely refused to rule; it is seen to be within the remit of each local authority to make a decision according to its own local circumstances.

However it is interesting to note that the model syllabuses, produced by the Schools Curriculum and Assessment Authority (SCAA) as informal guidance to LEAs in the drawing up of an agreed syllabus, worked on the basis that Christianity should be awarded 50 per cent of the RE curriculum time. While these model syllabuses have absolutely no legal standing, they have proved to be highly influential. Most agreed syllabuses now accept this reading of the Act and give 50 per cent of the RE syllabus to Christianity.

It is important to note that the Act does not lay down any requirement about when different religions should be taught. Initial fears that children, even as young as 5, would have to study several religions in the same year have proved to be groundless. The legal requirements are for the content of agreed syllabuses and these cover the teaching of RE from the age of 4 through to 16 and, in some cases, 18. Although no guidance has been given formally, again the model syllabuses have spread their influence. In their planning they look to two religions, Christianity and one other, as the focus in Key Stage 1, and three religions, Christianity and two others, in Key Stage 2. Although these syllabuses have only an advisory function, they are again proving influential.

It is worth noting that the Education Reform Act did formally change the name of the subject from *religious instruction* to *religious education*. This was a timely change as the former term had virtually disappeared from usage. This use of the term religious education acknowledged the broadened role of RE in the school curriculum, a broadening process which the Act itself continued.

### The role of the SACRE

The Education Reform Act requires that each LEA establish a Standing Advisory Council for Religious Education (SACRE). Its *chief function* is to advise the authority upon matters connected with religious worship in county schools and the religious education to be given, in accordance with an agreed syllabus, as the authority may refer to the Council or as the Council may see fit (ERA, 1988, 11.1(a)).

The matters of concern referred to are likely to focus upon such items as teaching methods, the choice of teaching materials and the provision of inservice training for teachers. To fulfil this function the SACRE is required to publish an annual report on its activities and this report should be distributed to schools, local teacher training institutions and the Qualifications and Curriculum Authority (QCA). This report should describe the matters upon which the SACRE has advised the LEA, the advice which was given and any issues upon which the SACRE agreed to advise the LEA even though its advice was not sought. In addition to this advisory role, the SACRE does have two very specific responsibilities. First, it can require the LEA to review its agreed syllabus. If such a requirement is made, then the LEA must constitute a standing conference to review the syllabus. Second, the SACRE can consider requests from schools for a variation in the legal requirement for the act of worship. These applications would come from schools where a significant number of pupils are from religious backgrounds which are not Christian and, if approved by the SACRE, a school would be granted a determination for five years exempting it from the legal requirement to provide acts of worship which are 'wholly or mainly of a broadly Christian character', though this would not allow a school to discontinue worship. As this book is about RE rather than collective worship, this responsibility of the SACRE will not be developed here but it is referred to as it is one of the few powers invested in the SACRE.

The Education Reform Act is very clear about the *composition* of the SACRE. It lays down that a SACRE should be made up of four representative groups (or three in Wales): Christian and other religious denominations, the Church of England (except in Wales), teachers' associations and elected councillors. It is interesting to note that these four groupings were those which the 1944 Act laid down as the constituents of the standing conference which was to draw up an agreed syllabus. It is important to note too that in the first named group, Christian and other denominations, there is a useful clarification in the wording. In the 1944 Act this was referred to as the 'other denominations' group for the agreed syllabus conference and there was always controversy as to whether this referred only to Christian denominations other than the Church of England. This new wording removes the ambiguity and now non-Christian religious traditions can belong to SACREs on equal terms with those of Christian denominations if, in the opinion of the SACRE, they 'appropriately reflect the principal religious traditions of the area' (11.4(a)). This clarification is significant because it underlines the intention of the Act that RE should take account of the teaching and practices of the other principal religions represented in Great Britain.

Under new guidelines, membership of the 'Christian and other religious denominations' category must reflect the relative size of the different denominations, and it is up to the LEA to determine the size of membership of the different denominations within its territory, which is no easy task. Any denomination can request representation and membership and this would have to be considered by the LEA.

In addition to this membership it is also possible to coopt additional members. A particular issue has been the membership of Humanists on SACREs. Although not religious in the conventional sense, Humanists frequently have a strong interest in the approach to RE based on knowledge and understanding and have been active members of a number of SACREs. Where they are members, they have usually been offered membership under the 'Christian and other religious denominations' group. However, this is no longer allowed by the Department for Education and Employment, as Humanism is not strictly a religious denomination, although as a movement it does share a number of similar features. Humanists who are members now have to be coopted and, as they do not belong to one of the four groupings, they do not have voting rights. SACREs also have the right to coopt representatives of any grant maintained schools within their area.

In one LEA, which is not noted for the multicultural or multiracial composition of its population, the 'Christian and other religious denominations' group consists of representatives from the Baptist Union, the Methodist Church, the New Churches, the Orthodox Churches, the Religious Society of Friends, the Roman Catholic Church, the Salvation Army, the United Reformed Church and representatives from Buddhism, Hinduism, Islam and Judaism. The rest of the SACRE is made up of three representatives of the Church of England, five county councillors and representatives of the main headteachers' and teaching associations. The different size of the groupings does not matter in terms of voting and decision making as voting takes place in groups – members of SACRE disappear into four different rooms or corners of the main room and each grouping comes to its own decision.

### Agreed syllabuses

It has been noted already that each LEA is required to draw up an agreed syllabus for religious education within its jurisdiction, or, failing that, to adopt that of another local authority. The fact that it is called an agreed syllabus suggests that it must be agreed – and agreed by those who are presumed to have a special interest or concern for RE. This means in practice the general public (through their elected councillors), the teachers and the various religious traditions – the same groupings as constitute the SACRE. It is sometimes claimed, erroneously, that it is the SACRE which draws up an agreed syllabus. To draw up a syllabus the LEA must call a standing conference representing the interested parties; this is very often very similar and sometimes identical in membership to the SACRE but it is not the same as the SACRE – it has been set up for this one highly specific purpose.

It is laid down in the Education Reform Act that syllabuses for RE should lie within local control. This is discussed earlier in this chapter. The freedom of each LEA in this sphere is limited to some extent by the requirement that 'all new agreed syllabuses must reflect the fact that the religious traditions in Great Britain are in the main Christian whilst taking account of the teaching and practices of the other principal religions represented in Great Britain'. Within that, however, the standing conference can decide which religions should be taught in which key stages, the key aspects of those religions which should provide the focus for the teaching, and the proportions of the RE curriculum time which should be awarded to the different traditions according to the perceived local need. An agreed syllabus should contain sufficient factual content within it so that it can be a useful guide and enable any reader to gain a clear insight into its flavour. An agreed syllabus should form the basis of RE in community and voluntary controlled schools. Voluntary aided schools may follow their trust deeds, though they can (and sometimes do) adopt the local agreed syllabus. The agreed syllabus should provide the basic guidelines within which a school draws up its own scheme of work. Each LEA is now required to review its agreed syllabus every five years.

### The model syllabuses

Reference has been made several times to the model syllabuses. Produced by the Schools Curriculum and Assessment Authority (SCAA) in 1994, these two model syllabuses were set out as guidance to SACREs and agreed syllabus conferences when they were devising or revising their own agreed syllabus. Although both were set with the same aims and objectives, they had different starting points, one working out from the religions towards the child and the other working from key religious questions and issues to the religions themselves. Although they have no legal status and are offered entirely as guidance to those involved in the revising of syllabuses, it is likely that they are already proving to be influential and may well have the effect of bringing a range of diverse agreed syllabuses, all originating locally, into much closer agreement.

A particular strength of the model syllabuses is the process by which they were drawn up. All of the major faiths in Britain – Christianity, Buddhism, Hinduism, Islam, Judaism and Sikhism – were invited to set up faith working parties, backed up by consultants, to make recommendations about what they felt it was important for pupils to learn about their particular tradition. Prior to that, the subject content of the various religious traditions had been selected largely by 'outsiders', educationalists and teachers with little reference to members of these traditions. For the first time the faith communities were talking for themselves. These recommendations were included in the same package as the model syllabuses and are a very useful resource which agreed syllabus are in fact making good use of.

### Qualifications and Curriculum Authority (QCA)

The Schools Curriculum and Assessment Authority (SCAA), which produced the model syllabuses, was succeeded by the Qualifications and Curriculum Authority (QCA). This body has produced guidance for teachers which has been highly beneficial to RE.

In 1998, QCA produced the booklet *Exemplifications of Standards in Religious Education*. Its purpose is to help teachers to consider what are good standards in RE, to identify continuity and progression in teaching and learning through the key stages, and to illustrate some teaching, learning and assessment strategies. The booklet, which considers work drawn from all four key stages, offers many examples of children's work, giving a commentary on each.

In 2000, in *Religious Education Non Statutory Guidance in RE*, the QCA offered guidance on assessing RE, on learning across the curriculum and on the often misunderstood attainment target 2 of RE, learning *from* religion. This publication has become particularly significant because it proposed an eight-level scale for assessing pupils' progress in RE.

Especially helpful to primary teachers has been *Religious Education: A Scheme of Work for Key Stages 1 and 2* (2000). This is a document which gives much sound advice on planning for RE across a primary school. Perhaps its most helpful feature is the development of thirty-two units of work ranging from the Reception class to Year 6. There is no doubt that teachers find these units very helpful, and when they are used they normally lead to an improvement of the quality of RE in a school. Inevitably the units are uneven in both quality and appropriateness but, this acknowledged, they have made a tremendous contribution to the teaching of RE by more specialist class teachers in primary schools.

### National Framework for religious education

It has been noted already that the local control of RE can be both a strength and a weakness. That it allows local education authorities to reflect the special conditions of their area in their agreed syllabus is a strength, but the considerable variation in quality between different syllabuses is a weakness in an education system which is focusing strongly upon the raising of standards across the board. Because of the increasing popularity of RE as a public examination subject in secondary schools and also because of the potentially important role that RE can play in developing understanding in a multiracial and multi-faith society, the Secretary of State for Education and Skills requested the Qualifications and Curriculum Authority to develop a framework for RE which, although non-statutory, would be a powerful guide and steer to agreed syllabus conferences when reviewing their agreed syllabus, a task which has to be undertaken every five years. The framework underwent extensive consultation with interested parties and received very positive and widespread backing. Essentially the framework provides detailed guidance on how RE can be taught so that pupils not only learn about religion but can learn from it too. It sets out ways in which pupils can develop their knowledge, understanding and skills and suggests levels of attainment that they should achieve.

At the launch of the National Framework on 28 October 2004, two powerful contributions which RE could make to the curriculum were noted:

> Religious education can transform pupils' assessment of themselves and others and their understanding of the wider world. It is vital in widening inclusion, understanding diversity and promoting tolerance.

> Religious education has a vital role to play in providing pupils with a range of experiences that enable them to develop a realistic and positive sense of their own beliefs and ideas.

Here we have confirmed and included all the developments which have been noted over the years. In these quotations we have the two attainment targets with a special focus for each: for social inclusion and for spiritual development. Good practice in RE in England very simply reflects all these.

The publication of this framework was a milestone in the development of RE. As it is non-statutory it can be ignored by local education authorities. Given the widespread support shown for its contents, though, this is unlikely to happen except in a very few places. Anyone writing on RE since its publication would be very unwise to ignore it and this book certainly makes frequent reference to it.

# 3  What are we trying to do?

## Some aims and objectives

A number of primary school teachers attending courses at an inservice meeting were asked the following question: 'What do you think ought to be the aim of religious education in school?' Here is a sample of their replies:

(a) To get the children to know something about God. Hardly any of them seem to go to Sunday school these days so it's the only opportunity they'll have to learn about Him.
(b) I don't know. I never teach it myself. I'm not religious.
(c) To give the children some knowledge of their religious background. After all they've got to know something to understand Milton and Shakespeare.
(d) To help the children to have some understanding of how other people live and what they believe. To make them more tolerant I suppose.
(e) To make children Christian.
(f) To make better behaved, I guess – though it doesn't seem to work!

This wide range of answers shows how much confusion there is about the aims of RE. Views certainly do differ, though it is possible to detect three broad – and differing – approaches:

1  The 'confessional' approach.
2  The 'giving them the facts' approach.
3  The 'understanding religion' approach.

*The 'confessional' approach* sees the aim of religious education as leading pupils into Christian commitment – replies (a) and (e) above fit neatly into this approach. This approach assumes the truth of the Christian religion and would seek to initiate pupils into it over the period of compulsory education. In practice, this aim is little different from that of the church or the Sunday school. Sometimes it has been called the 'missionary' approach. It is interesting that reply (b) might also subscribe to this view of the aims of religious education – although she does not agree with it!

*The 'giving them the facts' approach* rejects the 'confessional' approach with its desire to teach children to be Christians. It adopts a completely neutral view of whether religions are true or false; they are around and children ought to know about them. Reply (c) fits well into this approach.

*The 'understanding religion' approach* rejects both these approaches. It starts from an uncommitted position but does not feel that just giving children information is sufficient. Children need to be helped to understand religion. Reply (d) fits partly into this approach.

## How did all this come about?

Historically in England there has always been a close link between school and church. Most schools before 1870, the date when compulsory education for all was agreed, were founded by religious bodies and transmitted their religious teaching. Most of the schools built as a result of the 1870 Act continued the practice of giving religious instruction, although of a non-denominational kind. In the 1944 Butler Education Act, when religious instruction was made compulsory, it was only making mandatory what was universal practice.

The religious clauses of the 1944 Butler Act are looked at in more detail in Chapter 1. Suffice it to say here they *implied a confessional approach*. The term religious *instruction*, the daily act of worship, the fact that provision was made for teachers to opt out and for parents to withdraw their children, both on the grounds of conscience, all pointed very firmly in that direction. Agreed syllabuses written at this time make this abundantly clear. Here is an example from the Surrey syllabus of 1945:

> The aim of the syllabus is to secure that children attending the schools of the County . . . may gain knowledge of the common Christian faith held by their fathers for nearly 2000 years; may seek for themselves in Christianity principles which give a purpose to life and a guide to all its problems, and may find inspiration, power and courage to work for their own welfare, for that of their fellow creatures and for the growth of God's Kingdom.

This approach to religious teaching reflected the sort of society at the time. Most people identified in some way and at some level with the Christian religion. A large majority turned to the churches for the rites of passage – for baptism, for marriage and for burial – though the majority were not regular church attenders. There were, of course, groups within society which clearly rejected the Christian religion, bodies like the British Humanist Association and the National Secular Society. They were persistent campaigners for the removal of this sort of religious teaching from the schools but they made little headway with the vast majority of parents and teachers.

However, changes were afoot both in school and in society. During the 1950s and 1960s there was immigration into Britain on a large scale from the Caribbean, Africa, Cyprus and the Indian sub-continent. Practically all those from India and Pakistan practised religions other than Christianity. Mosques began to appear in Bradford, Hindu temples in Manchester and gurdwaras (Sikh temples) in Middlesex. These new residents had children who attended local schools alongside indigenous children and it was not unusual in many of our cities for teachers in a primary school to find that they had within their classes adherents of four or more religions.

This, of course, raised the question of whether it was right, given a class containing practising Muslims, Sikhs and Hindus, to present Christianity as *the* religion. Some people saw no difficulty with this but many others did.

In a wider way, too, within the population as a whole the grip which Christianity held was loosening. The decade of the 1960s saw, for example, a decline in church attendance. People felt freer about admitting religious doubt – certainly in public opinion polls on religious allegiance the number of professed agnostics and atheists increased, although still a small minority. The signs were clear, though, that the country's religious complexion was becoming increasingly diverse. The change was inevitably reflected in the teaching profession and a number of teachers felt unable to teach religious education in this way: 'How can I teach RE if I don't believe in God – it would make me a hypocrite.'

Within schools, too, there were changes. Visitors walking around primary classrooms noticed that teachers spent less time standing in front of their classes and talking to them and more time moving around the children as they worked. Children were being encouraged to learn from practical activity, to discover things for themselves. In mathematics they were being encouraged not to accept things merely on authority but to question and then to challenge and to think for themselves. The confessional approach to RE did not seem to fit in. Although religious education as it was conceived seemed to be out of joint, there were still persistent and massive demands for its continued presence in schools. In surveys of parental opinion, around 90 per cent were in favour of RE in schools. Commentators put this down to many causes – guilt, a desire to offload on to the school an unpalatable part of parenthood (rather like sex education), a feeling that it might encourage good behaviour. Whatever the reasons, the demand still seemed to be there.

All this led many of those involved in religious education to seek out a different approach. Religion would still figure in the school curriculum but its *aims* would be different.

One approach which appeared attractive to many was the straightforward *'giving them the facts'* approach. The argument for it goes thus: children live in a world surrounded by religion: the church on the corner, brothers and sisters baptised, aunts and uncles married, monarchs crowned, the Bible permeating much of literature. They need to know all about this as part of understanding how the world works. This can be developed: on their TV screens children see and hear about mosques, Muslims, Sikhs in turbans and so on. They should have some knowledge of other religions and ways of living so as to enlarge their understanding of the world and – with some luck – learn greater tolerance through knowledge. The teachers' role is clearly not to foster belief or to encourage commitment to any particular religion, or even to commend a religious view as opposed to a non-religious view of life. They are there to provide information that will help the child to make more sense of the world in which he or she lives.

On first sight this view seems ideal. It respects the diversity of society; it is seen by most people as a valuable exercise; teachers of any religious persuasion or of none can teach it without conflict of conscience. They can make statements like 'Christians *believe* that Jesus is the Son of God' or 'Muslims *believe* that the Qur'an is the Word of God' – factual statements which any teacher can convey to any class of children – they are not required to evaluate them or to examine them for truth.

It was this very openness and neutrality, this insistence upon keeping to the *facts about* religion, to being always descriptive, that led to numbers of people becoming concerned about this approach to the teaching of religion. It could be likened to certain approaches to the teaching of music, in which pupils learn about the lives of great composers, the name of every musical instrument, where each one is positioned in the orchestra, but never hear a symphony or play a note of their own music. In what sense could this approach be called a musical education? In the same way the 'giving them the facts' approach to religious education was seen as arid and as avoiding the heart of the subject. There was no real place for *appreciation* or *understanding*.

Advocates of the third approach, that of *'understanding religion'*, reject both the confessional and the 'giving them the facts' approaches, the confessional on the grounds that they do not want to persuade children to commit themselves to a particular religious stance, and the 'giving them the facts' approach because it avoids the central questions of religion. The key term they use is to *'understand'* and by understand they mean to *empathise*. They want, as far as is possible, to get children to step into the shoes of other people and to see things from their standpoint. So, understanding in this sense involves appreciation. For example, it is a fact that devout Muslims fast during the hours of daylight in the month of Ramadan. Children can be told this as a simple fact but if they are to have some understanding of it they need to have some glimmering of *why* devout Muslims fast. In this way they can begin, even if only in a very small way, to enter inside a religion. In this sense it is often said that religious education should transcend the informative.

Alongside this emphasis on looking with sensitivity at religions, and to a small extent from within them, comes the notion of *personal search*. This underlines the idea that children (and many others too for that matter) are on a personal quest for meaning, trying to make sense of such insistent questions as 'Is this all there is to life or is there more?' or 'What happens when we are dead?' It is to these deeper questions that religions address themselves, and this approach to religious education can be helpful in this personal search. It might be argued that this is more of a concern for the teenager than for the 5-year-old or the 9-year-old. As an emphasis this is almost certainly true but it would be a mistake to overlook younger children's less sophisticated attempts to make sense of some of these religious questions for themselves.

**The two attainment targets**

These two aspects of RE, the learning about the various religious traditions and the notion of personal search, which we have just seen emerging have now become enshrined in two widely acknowledged attainment targets entitled very simply in the National Framework 'learning about religion' and 'learning from religion'. In some agreed syllabuses they have more elaborate titles, for example, 'Investigating the religious traditions' and 'Exploring and responding to human experience' – but essentially they are the same.

*Learning about religion (AT 1)*

By this is meant the study of the prescribed religious traditions from the standpoint of Smart's dimensions of religion which provides most agreed syllabuses with their theoretical framework. Pupils would, therefore, normally learn about the features of the religions studied including their beliefs, rituals, social institutions, stories and so on and would begin to learn a vocabulary of technical terms. A key element of this approach, though, is understanding – *why* as well as *how* should be an essential ingredient of the approach and understanding and empathy should be at the centre of pupils' learning about religions.

When I was studying the Hajj with my Year 5 class, I found a lovely book on it full of dramatic photographs. As the Hajj is one of the five pillars of Islam I thought we might do it in some detail, referring to pilgrimage in other religions as well. Although the unit of work began well with a discussion about how the pilgrims would actually get to Makkah, it soon became a bit of a chore. I had reached the fourth day of the pilgrimage when one child asked 'Why on earth do they want to do all this?' The pupils were getting bored with their diary of what happened but when we began to talk about why it was so special interest revived considerably! Thank goodness.

(Teacher, Year 5 class)

Generally teachers in primary schools are confident with teaching to this attainment target. It is the second one which some teachers feel less positive about.

### Learning from religion (AT 2)

Learning from religion is related to the earlier notion of 'personal search' and is seeking ways to assist children to enrich their own inner experience. In order to do this, pupils need to be encouraged to engage at a personal level with the aspects of the religion being taught so that it is more than just a study of other people and their beliefs, practices and values. Pupils need to be challenged to think of their own approaches to the issues involved.

Here are two examples from Key Stage 1 of teachers engaging their pupils in a discussion of a story told so as to enrich both their understanding and appreciation of the story itself and also their own understanding of the issues.

> In preparation for Christmas, I told my Year 1 class the story of the birth of Jesus in the stable. In order to get them to go beyond a 'stained glass window' understanding of the story, I encouraged the children to talk about their experiences with babies (many had young siblings). It was very helpful discussion because it made the birth of Jesus much more 'real life' to them but it also made them think much more about family roles and their place within them.

> At Easter time I was talking to my class (Year 2) about the arrest of Jesus in the Garden of Gethsemane and how all his disciples fled and Peter even denied knowing him. I led the children into a discussion of what it feels like to be let down by one's friends and this led to a much greater awareness of (and sympathy for) how Jesus must have felt as well as an enlarged appreciation of themselves and their relationships. An increase in empathy!

Here are some examples from Key Stage 2. Probably because of the greater experience these pupils have than those in Key Stage 1, they have been able to move further away from the immediate context of the teaching and to deal with more developed issues. Note that the second example raised one of the great 'frontier' questions – why be good?

- A Year 5 class was studying a unit on Sikhism with special reference to the Khalsa, the Sikh brotherhood, and the role of Guru Gobind Singh in its establishment. The class teacher told a number of stories of the Guru which emphasised his skills in leadership. This led on to a very successful discussion on the nature of leadership – good, bad, successful, unsuccessful, military, ideological, spiritual – which raised questions of which qualities and values should be admired.

- A Year 6 class was undertaking a unit which focused on the ethical rules and principles which the followers of different faiths urged one to follow. The teacher opened a discussion which invited pupils to consider possible implications of some of these. This led rapidly to a discussion of what we mean by good. What is a good action? What might be a good life? Why be good? The teacher skilfully led this as a focused discussion over two sessions and encouraged pupils to illustrate their points by making reference to work which they had done earlier.
- A Year 4 class heard the stories of the charismatic Hebrew figure Samson and his strength, as part of a unit on 'Heroes'. They were excited by his exploits and by the way he was able to defend the faith against those who would harm it. However the stories also helped the pupils to consider the use and misuse of strength and to reflect on this in their dealings with others.

**The aims of religious education**

It is important to set the aims of RE in the context of a summary of the legal requirements:

- Central government delegates to each local education authority the responsibility of creating or adopting an agreed syllabus for local use.
- All agreed syllabuses must reflect the fact that the religious traditions in Great Britain are in the main Christian whilst taking account of the teaching and practices of the other principal religions represented in Great Britain.
- Although these 'other principal religions represented in Great Britain' have never been defined legally, most agreed syllabuses take them to be Buddhism, Christianity, Hinduism, Islam, Judaism, Sikhism.
- Most agreed syllabuses now accept that Christianity should be taught in each key stage and represent 50 per cent of the time given in school to RE.
- Most agreed syllabuses recognise that teaching all six religions during the same year would be very confusing, especially to younger children. Therefore most suggest:

Key Stage 1    Christianity + one other
Key Stage 2    Christianity + two others.

Some agreed syllabuses lay down which these additional religions should be, others leave it open. It is important to check this up in the syllabus.

- Recommended teaching time is 5 per cent, i.e. one hour per week. Collective worship is an entirely different activity and should not be included in the RE time allocation.

Within this structure RE should assist pupils to:

- Acquire knowledge and understanding of the central beliefs and practices of Christianity and of the other principal religious traditions in Great Britain.
- Develop an awareness of the ways in which religious belief affects the values and behaviour of individuals and communities.

- Make informed judgements about religious and moral issues.
- Enrich their spiritual experience.
- Search for meaning, purpose and a faith to live by.
- Explore fundamental questions of life in a religious context.
- Reflect upon their own beliefs and values in a positive way.
- Develop empathy with people holding different religious beliefs and to respect and value those beliefs.

# 4 What do we mean by religion?

Defining religion is no easy task. A group of students offered the following definitions:

(a) It's trying to lead a good life (8)
(b) It's believing in God (6)
(c) It's believing in the supernatural (1)
(d) It's a form of mental illness (1)
(e) It's the opiate of the people (1)
(f) It's going to church (or to the temple) (3)

Here there is a variety of views, four of which attempt to be definitions. Two of them are not: (d) is a psychological assessment and (e) is a comment on the function of religion in society, borrowed from Karl Marx. Of the four definitions offered, there could easily be concerns about adequacy. Religion certainly *is* about trying to lead a good life but is it not also about believing in certain things too? Religion is very difficult to fit into succinct definitions.

The following two approaches to the matter can be helpful:

1 Religion as a personal search for meaning and value.
2 Religion as a six-dimensional activity.

## Religion as a personal search for meaning and value

This is an approach which sees religion principally as an individual's, or as a group's, attempt to make sense of experience. Underlying this is the notion that there are certain fundamental questions which certainly puzzle most people and which often also baffle and distress. These questions would include 'Why are we here?', Is there a purpose in life?', 'Is death the end?', 'How can I know what is right?', 'To what extent am I responsible to other people?' and so on. These interrelated questions are ones which most people ask at certain points in their lives and attempt to provide answers to. Religions tend to fulfil this function as they do give a coherent answer to these insistent questions though they may not always be identical answers. In traditional societies where there is little change over generations and where there is a widely held religion, it is likely that the young will be inducted into that religion and imbibe the answers without necessarily asking the fundamental questions listed above. In a society like Britain where there is a variety of options, Christian and non-Christian, agnostic and atheist, it is much more likely that young people will have to engage in their own search for meaning.

This approach to religion inevitably raises objections, notably:

1 A number of believers from different religious traditions would be loath to see their religions from this angle. For very many (if not most) Muslims, Islam's truth comes from the revelation of God. People, they would agree, would know little of God if he had not chosen to reveal himself through Muhammad and through the Qur'an. It is this revelation which demands faith. Very many Christians would adopt a similar stance: that Jesus Christ is the vehicle for God's fullest revelation of himself and the Bible bears record to this. To see religion as a search for meaning would seem to place too much emphasis upon the individual and not enough upon God who out of loving kindness has shown something of himself and of his ways to the human race.

2 Seeing religion as a search for meaning could seem to imply that any form of meaning could be termed 'religion'. What, for example, should be said of Marxism which is certainly a framework for seeing meaning in human history and in the fulfilment of the human race. Marxism sees history as moving towards a goal, towards the victory of the proletariat and the eventual disappearance of the state in the perfect society. This provides answers to the fundamental questions and forms a coherent system. In the definition of religion as being a search for meaning Marxism could be seen as a religion. The same point could be made for Humanism. Again, Humanism is a faith system which gives answers to the fundamental questions and provides a framework for meaning. Yet to call both Marxism and Humanism religions is likely to enrage both Marxists and Humanists who normally regard themselves as people who have rejected religion! It also seems out of joint with most people's understanding of religion which is normally associated with the supernatural.

These two objections, both seriously and strongly held, are going beyond the point and imputing significance which is not intended. An important element in the appeal of religions is that they do offer a view of the world which is both coherent and comprehensive. This does not mean that they explain everything – the place of suffering is a serious difficulty within the Christian faith – but they offer a general view. Just as young children will work hard at making sense of their experiences of the physical environment (stone is hard, wool is soft), so most mature humans will try to make sense of the variety of their experiences both emotionally and physically.

Now this desire to make sense of things may result in different outcomes. Some may find that they can see no coherence, others may lose interest, others may find it in submission to one of the world's religions, others in Humanism and so on. This does not make Humanism and Marxism religions, it means rather that they have things in common with religions. This is why they have often been called 'quasi-religions' or, to use more modern jargon, 'non-religious stances for living'.

The most important point emerging from this section is that the desire to make sense of these fundamental life questions is an important source of *motivation* in the religious quest and therefore something for teachers to develop and to extend. To do so is to engage the students in a process without prescribing the outcome. Clearly the teenage years are the ones when these questions are most agonised over, but younger children do ask these questions in different guises which teachers would do well to listen to carefully and to encourage.

Religion, therefore, is likely to begin with a search for meaning, though not all outcomes will necessarily be religious. This brings us back again to the question at the beginning of the chapter, 'what do we mean by religion?'

## Religion as a six-dimensional activity

It was noted early in the chapter how difficult it is to define religion. An alternative approach is to try to describe it. There is a considerable amount of activity going on in the world which is commonly described as being religious. Countless millions claim to belong to one religion or another and most of the globe is covered with places of worship and religious devotion. To look at the practice of religions in the world might be a much more fruitful way of looking at the breadth of religion. This was the approach adopted by Ninian Smart and the results of his analysis of his observation of religion were summarised in his six dimensions.

There is nothing sacrosanct about Smart's account, others might well do it differently. It is discussed in detail here because many have found it a very helpful tool in understanding religion and it has also been used as a basis for certain approaches to religious education.

Smart's six dimensions of religion are:

1   Doctrinal
2   Mythological
3   Ethical
4   Ritual
5   Experiential
6   Social

These could also be seen as the different facets of a jewel. Each one can be studied separately but they are all facets of the one gem and as such are interrelated and interconnected indissolubly.

It is important to note that Smart subsequently developed seven dimensions of religion. Essentially the only difference is that he created a 'material' dimension, taken out of the ritual dimension. For our purposes here, the six dimensions form, on balance, a more serviceable *foundation* for teaching RE.

### Doctrinal dimension

Every religion has at its centre a set of doctrines or beliefs which form part of its foundation. These doctrines, which would be about a religious vision of ultimate reality, may be elaborately worked out in philosophical terms, as they are in some religions, or they may be expressed in vague and less coherent ways. In Christianity, the central doctrines are expressed in the official creeds of the church, notably the Nicene Creed, and focus upon the two basic doctrines: the Trinity (God in three persons, Father, Son and Holy Spirit) and the Incarnation (the entry of God the Son into humanity in the person of Jesus

Christ). Within Judaism there is great stress upon the oneness of God and his loving kindness. In Hinduism there is a central belief in Brahman, the life force, and in the millions of 'gods' (or images) who manifest the 'One'. Within Islam there is a strict emphasis upon Unity and upon the uniqueness of God. These doctrines are binding upon the believer. Five times each day the devout Muslim confesses 'There is no God but Allah and Muhammad is his prophet'. In baptism, the Christian rite of initiation, the follower confesses belief in the divine Trinity. There will inevitably be different levels of understanding of the doctrinal systems between, say, educated and simple followers, and there will be different interpretations of the doctrines, some being more literal or more symbolic than others. Nevertheless, doctrines are a crucial dimension of any religion and are an analysis and codification of what is expressed in the mythological dimension.

### Mythological dimension

The mythological dimension, often called the story dimension, is the means of conveying the teaching of a religion through stories, poems, legends, hymns and so on. Mythological can be an unhelpful term, developing as it does from the noun 'myth' which in common understanding has come to mean an untrue tale. However, in its more technical sense it derives from the Greek 'muthos' which means literally 'story'. To describe the sacred stories of the world's religions as mythological is therefore no comment upon their historical truth. The term is quite neutral.

These 'stories' would certainly include the accounts of the lives of the founders: the stories of Moses, of the Lord Buddha, of Muhammad, of the Ten Gurus, of Jesus. Within the Hindu tradition, there is a vast amount of material from the Vedas. The significance of the mythological dimension is that it is another vehicle for expressing the teaching of a religion. For Christians, for example, an essential part of the year is the keeping of Holy Week and Easter. From Palm Sunday, through the week to Maundy Thursday, Good Friday, Holy Saturday and finally to Easter Day, the believers go through in mind Jesus' entry into Jerusalem, his teaching in the temple, his last supper with his disciples, his betrayal in the Garden of Gethsemane, his arrest, trial, crucifixion, death, burial and finally his resurrection. This is done lovingly each year because in these stories is laid out the central mystery of the Christian faith, the reconciliation of God and humanity. Whether or not these stories have attached to them legendary accretions is not of first significance – what matters is that they both express and also feed the experience of believers.

Often there is dispute among believers in a particular tradition about the historical status of a story or series of stories. A case in point is the Nativity stories in the Gospels, especially with reference to the virginal conception of Jesus. The stories are about the entry of 'God-made-man' into human affairs and hence are of great significance for believers. For very many believers these stories are an historical account of what actually happened. This was the way that God chose for Jesus to enter humanity. Others would say that the story of the virginal conception is an example of a symbolic story or a myth – a story written to convey the understanding that here was someone entering the world who was quite different from anybody who had done so before. In one sense both groups of believers are expressing the same conviction, though they generally do not approve of each other's approach!

### Ethical dimension

All religions lay upon their followers a way of life which ought to be followed. Judaism, for example, has always placed great importance upon the Torah, the revealed law of God. When a Jewish boy reaches adolescence he has his Barmitzvah, his coming of age, when he becomes (literally) a son of the law. This means that he takes upon himself the responsibility of the law. The Torah centres upon the Ten Commandments which are binding upon all Jews. Islam, in the Qur'an, also lays down detailed requirements of Muslims which include even styles of dress. An important requirement is one of hospitality. Within Christianity the law of charity (or love) – loving God, and your neighbour as yourself – is supreme and Christians are pointed to the life of Jesus as an example for living.

Most religions have an important place for 'saints', people within the tradition who by their life and works have given an example to others and are often described as 'lights'. The study of such people has played an important part in much religious teaching and still has a special place today.

In the modern world, religions are increasingly being challenged to develop and express ethical attitudes towards such matters as nuclear weapons and ecology. In some senses this is not a new problem, as all living religious traditions have the constant task of applying their ethical principles to the issues of the day.

### Ritual dimension

The ritual dimension encompasses all those actions and activities which worshippers do in the practice of their religion. It ranges from the closing of eyes in prayer to participation on a once-in-a-lifetime pilgrimage. It includes services, festivals, ceremonies, customs, traditions, clothing, symbols. In many ways the ritual dimension is the shop window of a religion. The following would come within the limits of the ritual dimension: Muslims removing their shoes outside the mosque, Sikhs and Jews covering their heads before worship, Sikhs wearing the five symbols of their faith (the five Ks), Christians being present at a celebration of the Eucharist, the celebration of the coming of age at the Barmitzvah, the making of pilgrimage to holy places, whether it be Jerusalem, Makkah or Amritsar, the celebration of festivals: Diwali, Christmas, Passover, Guru Nanak's birthday and so on.

The ritual dimension is very closely associated with the stories of a religion. Very often rituals are enactments of the stories. In Judaism an historical event of great significance is the rescuing of the people from Egypt in the Exodus. This is very deep within Jewish feeling. The Passover meal, celebrated annually in the home, is a re-enactment of the original meal and in the course of the meal the ancient story is recounted. The Christian Eucharist is a re-enactment of Christ's death and resurrection and is seen as making it real in the present.

There is a danger in talking of ritual of serious misunderstanding. In much common language, words like ritual and ritualistic are used in a pejorative sense. Ritual is seen as something which is empty or fussy or formal, something which is devoid of any real meaning or significance. Certainly anything can degenerate into this state but in this context ritual is merely a descriptive term for the activities in a religion which are significant to its followers. Rituals provide the framework for both the sustaining and deepening of the worshipper's faith. They reflect too the devotion of worshippers – look at the faces of pilgrims on the Hajj or at Lourdes – and also often enhance that devotion ('I felt uplifted . . .').

The ritual dimension is much more akin to religious feelings than to religious doctrine. Of course the rituals reflect the doctrines, but they really work upon the emotions of believers – and upon others too. I remember being present with a small group of Western tourists of differing religious views amongst the vast crowds of worshippers in the Russian Orthodox cathedral in Smolensk. The sound of the choir, the smell of the incense, the visual beauty of the building, the devotion of the congregation were all intensely moving and all the members of the group felt to some degree that, to quote the Orthodox themselves, they were in heaven.

### Experiential dimension

At the core of religion is feeling and the experiential dimension bears witness to this. Most, if not all, believers would claim that at the centre of their religion is an experience to some degree or other of the divine. In some individuals it comes in dramatic forms. In the Old Testament, Isaiah's searing vision in the temple would certainly come in the first rank, as would, of course, the visions of Muhammad. The experiences of most believers are not in this league. For most, the experience of the divine would be much less dramatic, though not less significant: a feeling of being in tune with creation, a feeling of being given strength in times of difficulty, a feeling, as John Wesley put it, of the heart being strangely warmed. This dimension is important because it is this one which provides the motivation for the others and makes the practice of religion worthwhile. It is this experience, this feeling, which makes, for example, the performing of rituals a living and significant activity rather than a participation in an historical curiosity. The experiential dimension is closely related to the ritual dimension in that it provides the incentive to participation, but the festivals, pilgrimages and ceremonies also in turn feed, enrich and enhance the experience of believers. Pilgrims (as opposed to tourists) to Lourdes make the journey with some degree of expectation, visit the holy domain there, are present at mass in the grotto, join in the Procession of the Blessed Sacrament, mingle with the sick, and return home with their commitment deepened and their spirits 'uplifted'. Their religious feelings motivate them to partake in the pilgrimage and the doing of it deepens those same feelings.

One of the problems with the experiential dimension is that it is very difficult to describe religious experience in words. Naturally any attempt to do so must rely heavily upon such devices as symbolism, simile, metaphor and analogy. Isaiah's vision in the temple and Moses and the Burning Bush are both well known biblical examples of this. The problem is compounded where the religious education of younger children is concerned because on the one hand it is very important that children should develop some notion of religious feeling, but on the other there is concern that the symbolism of many of the well known stories may be a barrier to this being achieved. There can be no doubt that young children do experience, in other than 'religious' contexts, the sort of emotions which are important in religious feeling – awe, wonder, an awareness of mystery, a sense of belonging and so on. These feelings should be fostered and this can be done in a number of ways.

### Social dimension

The social dimension of religion is concerned with the expression of that religion in society. Clearly it is closely related to the ethical dimension which gives guidance on how the faithful should live in the world. The social dimension is more concerned with the corporate nature of religious institutions. For example, in Judaism it is important to look closely at the organisation of the synagogue and its relationship to the home. In Christianity, the church is obviously of central importance and within that the role of the bishop in the unity of the church and of the priest in the work of the individual parishes. Religious communities, with the monks and nuns who constitute them, are highly significant in most religions. All the time here one is stepping over into the ritual dimension, but this is only to be expected, as they are constantly interrelated and intertwined.

There is another aspect to this dimension. Many religions have a vision of how human society should be organised and how people ought to view each other and the world in which they live. In Christianity, for example, as in other religions, there is a strong belief that men and women are all brothers and sisters and children of God. There have therefore been movements within Christianity to resist oppression because it offends against this vision: for example, Wilberforce to free the slaves, Martin Luther King for equal rights for black people, and Desmond Tutu against apartheid.

### Two implications for teaching children aged 4 to 11 years

Within this there are two major implications for teachers which will be considered in greater detail later in the book.

1　Religion is partly a personal search for meaning which most children (and adults too), even quite young ones, engage in. While it is much easier for older children to identify issues and to formulate their questions, younger children are just as interested in making sense of themselves, discovering who they are and attempting to grapple with many of the mysteries which surround them. Often, though, their questions and comments need rather more unravelling by a teacher or parent than do the questions of older children. The adult needs to listen carefully, to ask questions (if appropriate) carefully and to help, in a very sensitive way, children to continue and progress in their search for meaning. The teacher's role is not to give answers because there are no answers which are universally agreed. It is rather to help the children to move along in the process of finding their own meaning.

2　The six dimensions of religion, covering as they do such a vast and complex activity as religion, naturally include aspects which are highly cerebral and intellectually sophisticated and others which are essentially emotional and visual. From what we know of the development of children's religious understanding, some dimensions are clearly more suitable for younger children than others. Most teachers who have worked in this area and with children in the age range 4 to 11 years would pinpoint the most appropriate dimensions as:

> social
> ritual
> mythological

To this list may be added some aspects of the experiential dimension, though there are problems about this which are referred to earlier in this section. The ritual and the social dimensions are appropriate for younger children mainly because they are concrete and visual. The mythological dimension appeals to children's love of stories. The two dimensions which have been omitted, the doctrinal and the ethical, are both difficult for younger children.

The doctrinal is essentially intellectual and tends to raise questions which children of this age tend not to ask. Ten-year-old children are, on the whole, not very much interested in asking questions about the relationship between the divine and the human in the incarnate Jesus (doctrinal dimension), though they usually love to hear the Christmas stories (mythological dimension) and are often quite interested in learning about the Christmas ceremonies (ritual dimension). The ethical dimension can be difficult with younger children because it is not until they move into what Piaget calls the heteronomous stage that they are able to reflect about, rather than just accept, rules and this tends not to happen until the end of this age range (4–11).

Most religious material selected for study by children in the age range 4–11 years will therefore be drawn from the ritual, social and mythological dimensions of religion. This does not mean that children in the age group are not made aware of beliefs or ethics. The dimensions are not sealed from each other. All are interdependent, so although a unit of work or a topic may be focused in one dimension, the work will inevitably move into other dimensions too. A study of the life and work of Mother Teresa in Calcutta, for example, would fit most naturally in the mythological/story dimension but it is also a splendid illustration in concrete terms of Christian ethical teaching lived out by a person in the world. Here the mythological dimension links with the ethical. A unit of work on prayer in Islam, although it may be sited in the ritual dimension, must inevitably deal with Muslim belief about the nature of God. Here the ritual dimension ties in with the doctrinal dimension. These dimensions which are often more difficult for younger children are best approached in this way.

# 5  Spiritual education

The Education Reform Act (1988), as has been noted, talks of a basic curriculum consisting of the foundation subjects and RE, which is the entitlement of all pupils and will be provided in all maintained schools. The Act then goes on to require that this basic curriculum 'shall be a balanced and broadly based curriculum which promotes the spiritual, moral, social, cultural and physical development of pupils in the school and of society'.

### What is spiritual development?

The terms spiritual development and spiritual education have proved very difficult for many teachers over the years mainly because very many people are not quite certain what they mean. This is further complicated by the fact that, traditionally, spiritual development and the broader notion of spirituality have been seen as largely the preserve of the great religious traditions. In most of the great world religions there is a basic belief in a supreme being who created humanity, to whom humans can relate and whose will provides the framework for human living. While this will provide a basis for spirituality for those with a religious faith it is of less value for those who do not possess one. To be of general value to all teachers and pupils our understanding must be broad and open, incorporating those issues which are generally accepted as being related in some way to the spiritual.

Here are four definitions or descriptions which frequently appear in the literature on spiritual education:

1  'The development of an awareness that there is something more to life than meets the eye, something to wonder at, something to respond to. . . .'
2  'Spiritual development deals with what is supremely personal and unique to each individual (rather than how we deal with others).'
3  'Spiritual development is an aspect of inner life through which pupils acquire personal insights into their personal existence which are of enduring value.'
4  'Spiritual development draws attention to aspects of human nature which give meaning and purpose to human existence.'

These quotations all point to aspects of spiritual development which are recognised as its essential ingredients. The first highlights the fact that spiritual awareness recognises that there is something beyond the immediate, *beyond the material*, and something which is *greater than the individual*. The second quotation emphasises that spiritual awareness has to do with what is essentially *personal to the individual* – not concerned with relationships with others but special to oneself. The third takes up the same element, the personal and unique, and talks of the *inner life* (a term often used in writing about spirituality) which is essentially personal and private and also *of lasting value*. The fourth brings into the arena those deep questions about life the answers to which are fundamental to the development of individual spirituality. These are questions about the meaning and purpose of life (is there any point in it?), good and evil (why on earth should we be good?), life and death (is death the end?), the origins of the universe (is there purpose and is it personal?), beliefs about God or the Divine, and values such as justice, honesty and truth (what basis do we have for holding these dear?). It is in response to these that an individual, consciously or not, builds a philosophy of or framework for life which necessarily includes a set of values.

Finally it is important to note that all four quotations see spirituality as *enriching*, as *enlarging*, as *enhancing life*. The purpose of spiritual education is to extend pupils' experiences of themselves as unique individuals and so to help them to come to terms with the mysterious and complex world in which we all live. There are certain situations which lend themselves perhaps more readily to the development of spiritual awareness. These include:

- An awareness of beauty which takes the breath away.
- The experience of love, both to love and to be loved.
- A sense of awe and wonder which makes individuals see themselves in relationship with the immensity of the universe.
- Times of celebration bringing with them both joy and a sense of belonging and community.
- A sense of grief, loss and transience which raises questions of purpose in life.

### What is spiritual education?

Spiritual education is not synonymous with RE. RE by its very nature is bound to be a key contributor to the process but all subjects in the curriculum have a contribution to make.

A key feature of spiritual education is *reflection* so that pupils have the opportunity to attribute meaning to their experiences. This reflection can be individual, as in collective worship, for example, when pupils in a time of quiet are asked to think how the story just told might have implications for them. Reflection might also take place in a group, in circle time for example, as discussion and sharing can deepen an individual's perception.

A second feature is the *valuing of a non-material dimension to life*: to recognise and to esteem the world of experience which lies beyond immediate material objects. Here, for example, the beauty and power of music, of art and of poetry can vastly enrich an individual's enjoyment and understanding of life.

A third feature is the *hint of an enduring reality*. A person who has been overwhelmed by the sight of the Grand Canyon or the Himalayas may, when faced with the majesty of these great features, see themselves as a small and transient figure on the face of the earth.

Their transience is emphasised by the vast age and permanence of these features. This feeling of smallness and transience in the face of all this is a spiritual experience: they see their own place in the whole scheme of things. Some would go even further and see these majestic and ageless features as images of and pointers to the Divine which lies behind it all. However it is not necessary to take this final step; without it the experience is still profoundly spiritual.

## Spiritual education in the curriculum

It has already been noted that spiritual education is a cross-curricular activity and that ideally all subjects should contribute to it. Many primary schools have developed a Spiritual Education Policy in which they identify where spiritual education is planned to take place and more specifically in what subjects in which year groups over the year. This is a very helpful way of ensuring that pupils have the opportunity to develop in this area.

An example of this is a unit of geography/science work with Year 4 pupils which a school identified in its policy as contributing to spiritual education. The work centred around the ecology of a woodland and the teacher was drawing out and emphasising the intricate balances at work which enabled the woodland to thrive. She was clearly fascinated by the impressive way in which the ecosystem worked and this excitement began to infect the children who became equally fascinated and excited by the interrelationship and interdependence in the life of the woodland. This led on to considerable discussion about design, purpose and plan. Had this simply evolved naturally or could one detect something deeper at work? So in a planned way this brought children round to asking questions of meaning. Here was something to wonder at and to hint at questions of purpose and design in the universe. Such an important area of human experience cannot, of course, be restricted to certain parts of a school's curriculum. It will bubble up in all sorts of places often without warning. The role of teachers, then, who may be on the scene is to exploit it as best they can. Here is one such example:

> A group of Year 5/6 pupils from a deprived area of inner London were taken for a week's camping trip into the countryside. For most of them the countryside was a new experience and seeing sheep, cows and horses roaming in fields was almost like going to the zoo. The initial day was fortunately warm and cloudless so the tents were erected with great excitement. That evening, after the meal had been prepared and eaten, everyone settled down around the camp fire at dusk. Songs were sung and jokes told as dusk turned to darkness – and being in the heart of the countryside it did get very dark. As the camp fire died down to its last few embers and just before the teachers switched on their torches as the signal for bed, one of the children chanced to look straight up to the sky – and simply said 'Cor! Look!' Everybody did and everybody was suddenly silenced. The great roof of the sky was above them with a million stars as pinpricks of light. It was awesome. Someone said 'It makes you feel so small'. The children, living as they did in a city with polluted air and perpetual street lights, had never experienced this overwhelming vastness before. This experience could never have been planned – it just happened – but this gave the children a taste of awe and wonder in the face of the immensity of creation. The following day the teachers had the responsibility for helping the children to reflect together on this experience!

**Religious education and spiritual education**

Although RE is only one of the many subject partners in spiritual education, it would be surprising if the subject did not have a particularly significant contribution to make, as in many ways they are seeking the same ends. RE is, for example, concerned to help pupils to reflect upon the meaning and purpose of life and to discover for themselves a faith or code by which to live. It seeks to assist pupils to explore beliefs and their effect upon the lives of believers. It endeavours to introduce children to the central beliefs, values and practices of the major religious traditions. Any attempt to provide a cognitive content to spiritual education is likely to include the following:

- Knowledge of the central beliefs, ideas and practices of major world religions and philosophies.
- An understanding of how people sought to explain the universe through various myths and stories including religious, historical and scientific interpretations.
- Beliefs which are held personally and the ability to give some account of them.
- Behaviour and attitudes which show the relationship between belief and action.
- Personal response to questions about the purpose of life and to the experience of, for example, beauty and love or pain and suffering.

Seen in this way, RE has a very definite contribution to make to the development of spirituality in children.

# Planning the teaching

# 6  Some preliminary considerations

Over the last quarter of the twentieth century, RE was broadening its subject base considerably. All these developments which we have seen already were confirmed in the National Framework for Religious Education which identified two prime focuses:

- Widening inclusion, understanding diversity and promoting tolerance.
- Providing pupils with a wide range of experiences to enable them to develop a realistic and positive sense of their own beliefs and ideas.

At one time, world religions were taught so that white British pupils could gain an understanding of the main faiths which had settled and were growing in Britain. Now the overall aim is that groups can understand each other so that, for example, Hindu pupils can begin to understand the Christian base of British society and also develop an awareness of Buddhism, Islam, Judaism and Sikhism, as well as looking afresh at their own tradition, Hinduism. The hoped for outcome of this is that all pupils will feel that they belong in this society and that, through the awareness and understanding of this diversity, there will be greater tolerance of difference. This in turn should lead pupils, through knowledge and understanding, to be confident in what they themselves believe and value.

## Avoiding mishmash

Although six religions are to be taught, educational considerations were brought into play when it came to planning how this might happen. Given the usual timetable allowance of one hour per week and so roughly forty hours per year, and with Christianity normally occupying half of that, it would be completely unfair to the great religious traditions to allocate them four hours per year each, as well as creating that phenomenon, *mishmash*, the mess of many undifferentiated stories, facts and beliefs, in pupils' minds. To avoid these pitfalls, there has been a strong national steer on agreed syllabuses to require that in Key Stage 1, pupils should study Christianity and one other faith, and in Key Stage 2 Christianity and two other faiths. As each agreed syllabus determines which religions those should be, often from their own local situation, it means that there is considerable diversity across the country. Many, however, appear to nominate Judaism for Key Stage 1 and Hinduism and Islam for Key Stage 2. In an authority which has this pattern there is no embargo on doing some further work on Judaism in Key Stage 2, nor for that matter on making reference to Buddhism and Sikhism, perhaps in connection with a festival, but Christianity, Hinduism and Islam would be the principal focuses.

If pupils are to learn about different faiths, subject content is vitally important but so also are all those qualities that RE is expected to foster: empathy, interest in other people's situations and cultures, understanding, tolerance and respect. Content alone is not enough, as religions can be taught in a negative way which can create and reinforce prejudice. On the other hand, understanding, empathy, tolerance and respect cannot be fostered unless there is knowledge about the different faiths and the knowledge is taught in such a way that the adherents of those faiths are content with the teaching.

## Stepping stones not stumbling blocks

If the teaching is to be successful, then teachers have to think very carefully about the age and stage of their pupils. What they are teaching must relate or attach in some way to pupils' current experience and this to some extent will depend on the situation. It is, for example, much easier to teach about world faiths if the school is multifaith in composition, as the pupils naturally have first-hand experience of other faiths which sparks off their curiosity. It is also probably not a good idea to teach 5-year-olds the Christian doctrine of the Trinity nor to talk to them about the Buddha's diagnosis of the human condition in the Four Noble Truths, as there is little in their experience which is likely to foster understanding. They might use the right words but these will be hollow. On the other hand young children experience birthday parties and Christmas and these are excellent ways to move into an understanding of festivals and special occasions. The selection of teaching material should be designed to act as stepping stones to a positive and developing understanding of religions and not stumbling blocks. It became popular in recent years to develop a topic in Key Stage 1 called 'Festivals of Light'. This topic included the three autumn and winter festivals in which light is a powerful feature – Diwali (Hindu), Hanukkah (Jewish) and Christmas (Christian). Stories were told, lamps were made and a good time was had by all. However, from an RE point of view the topic often proved to be less than satisfactory. Pupils often became very confused about the boundaries between the festivals and the faiths from which they were drawn and were left with a welter of confusions and misconceptions. Not a stepping stone but a stumbling block.

## The role of the teacher

Whether a teacher is committed to a religious tradition or not does not matter as far as teaching RE is concerned. The teacher is there to be a guide and help to the children so that they can fulfil the two main attainment targets of RE: to learn about and understand the major religious traditions in Great Britain, and to have the opportunity through that to begin to formulate their own approach and path and to learn tolerance and acceptance of other people's differences. The teacher's role is not to try to commend any one path or no path at all. It is bad practice to say '*we* believe in . . . but *they* believe in . . .'. It is good practice to say 'Christians believe . . . Muslims believe . . .' and so on. This is part of the professionalism of the teacher.

In that sense, teachers are neutral. However teachers cannot remain neutral if they hear pupils mocking the religious faith of others or acting in a prejudiced way towards particular religious groups in the school. Such behaviour needs to cease and the virtues of tolerance, acceptance and inclusiveness need to be emphasised.

**Organising RE in the school**

Schools have to consider the question of how RE, and other subjects too, can best be organised within the curriculum. As far as RE is concerned there have been two main approaches: *integrating RE* within topics or planning RE as a *discrete subject*.

Integrating RE into the class topic can make planning easier for the teacher, but as the only approach it would make the job of meeting the requirements of the agreed syllabus very difficult. At its worst the relationship of the RE in a topic has often been only at the level of word association. Noah's Ark has appeared frequently in primary schools in topics which can range from water, to boats, to animals, to weather. However the story of Noah's Ark is not really about any of these things. Integrating RE into the class topic works more successfully if the topic is, for example, journeys. In that case the school could plan a sub-topic on pilgrimage (religious journeys). This would make for better RE. However, even with such more suitable examples, it is hard to see how the necessary coverage and depth can be achieved in RE if it is always an adjunct to the class or school topic. A number of primary schools have decided therefore to plan their RE as a discrete subject with an identified slot on the timetable. The only danger here is a possible one of subject isolation, but this is unlikely as RE is closely tied in with a number of cross-curricular themes such as personal, social and health education (PSHE), spiritual, moral, social and cultural education (SMSC) and citizenship. The great advantage of planning and teaching RE as a discrete subject is that pupils have an experience of RE which is both regular and coherent.

**Teaching religions – single strands or themes**

Religious tradition can be presented in different ways in planning and in the classroom. One approach is to develop units of work which focus upon an aspect of one religion. Examples of this could be 'The Qur'an' or the 'The role of the synagogue in Judaism'. Another is to take a theme which crosses a number of faiths and look at this particular aspect in all of the traditions. Examples of this could be 'Pilgrimage' or 'Holy books'. The advantage of the former approach is that pupils begin to develop a knowledge and understanding of a particular faith and so are spared the possibility of 'mishmash'. Cross-faith themes are best avoided with younger children but they have a place with children in the 9–11 year range as level 4 of the attainment targets requires pupils to 'describe some similarities and differences both within and between religions'. Cross-faith themes can provide opportunities for these comparisons to be made.

**Planning RE across the school**

All schools are required to plan for RE and the centre of planning for maintained schools must be the agreed syllabus for RE of their local authority. The only exceptions to this are voluntary aided schools, whether Anglican, Roman Catholic, Muslim, Jewish or Sikh, which are not required to follow the agreed syllabus but can teach religion according to their own trust deeds. The non-statutory National Framework has no authority in schools; it is essentially guidance to the local authorities to help them when they come to revise the agreed syllabus every five years. However, over the next few years its influence is likely to be very significant because of the support it received nationally when it went into wide circulation.

As with other subjects in the school curriculum schools will need to plan RE in three stages: long term, medium term and short term. Effective planning is the major factor in ensuring that the experience that children receive is of good quality. Of course, for good quality RE there also need to be informed teachers, but without an overall plan even inspired teaching is likely to be haphazard and spasmodic.

## *Long-term planning*

A long-term plan is effectively a broad outline of what will be taught and when during each year group over a whole school. Its purpose is:

- To provide for coverage of the local agreed syllabus.
- To ensure balance and progression across the key stages each year and to avoid repetition.
- To define broadly a pupil's entitlement to RE across the appropriate key stage.
- To make appropriate links with other subject areas.
- To outline the year's work for each teacher.

## *Medium-term planning*

Medium-term planning (sometimes called the scheme of work) is concerned with taking the units within the long-term plan and developing them. An effective plan for the development of one of these units would normally include:

- Identifying learning intentions.
- Providing an outline of content.
- Identifying teaching strategies and learning activities.
- Identifying focuses for assessments.
- Identifying resources.
- Identifying curriculum links (where appropriate).

## Short-term planning

Short-term planning is normally undertaken by the class teacher (occasionally with support from the RE coordinator). This is the normal lesson planning that any teacher is used to in this phase. This includes:

- Identifying clear learning intentions/objectives.
- Making provision for differing abilities in the class.
- Identifying assessment opportunities.
- Planning the pattern of the lesson.
- Identifying any special groupings of pupils.
- Identification of resources.

## Long-term planning

This is normally undertaken by the whole staff, or in the case of a large primary school, by a sub-committee of the staff usually led by the RE coordinator. It is rather like creating a map for RE across the age groups in the school.

Long-term plans will differ from school to school because the RE policies of individual schools will vary to some degree as they will reflect different compositions of school staffs and also different school planning frameworks.

Here is an account by an RE coordinator of the principles which underlay her school's long-term plan.

> We based our long-term plan on our local Agreed Syllabus and our RE policy, which took some time to hammer out. In the end I was pleased with the result; it was not exactly what I would have decided but it was near enough to that and it did reflect the views and interests of the staff, and it is a stable staff.
>
> The principles which lay behind our long-term plan were:
>
> - The two religions to be focused upon in Key Stage 1 are Christianity and Judaism and the three in Key Stage 2 are Christianity, Hinduism and Islam.
> - While we intend to focus on these very strongly, we are not prevented from making reference to aspects of other religions.
> - On the whole the staff is concerned about causing confusion in children's minds, what one called mishmash, so on the whole we prefer RE work to focus on one religion at a time rather than have a thematic approach (although there are some themes in the plan).
> - As a continuation of this, we decided in Key Stage 2 to have Christianity in each year group but to block the other two religions namely Hinduism in Years 4 and 6 and Islam in Years 3 and 5.
> - We recognise the importance of providing pupils with the opportunities to enrich their experience so that religious ideas and concepts will have a richer meaning. There is therefore a balance between our two attainment targets.
> - We tried to plan for progression and this is perhaps most noticeable in the provision for the annual celebration of both Christmas and Easter which we wanted to be both progressive and varied.

### Medium-term planning

Once the long-term planning is in place, it becomes necessary to develop the individual units in order to give them more substance. This may be done by the class teacher but it may well be that the coordinator has to work with class teachers to develop the individual units appropriately. Together all the units so developed will make up the RE scheme of work.

There are no rules as to how a scheme of work/medium-term planning has to look, and this will vary from school to school, but it should give an indication of learning intentions, outline of content, some intimation of teaching strategies and activities, and some opportunities for assessment.

Below is an example of one of the units, 'Pilgrimage in Christianity', proposed in a Year 5 class.

Development of the unit

PILGRIMAGE IN CHRISTIANITY

Year 5
Number of hours: 8

*Learning intentions*

- Begin to understand the notion of a sacred place.
- Know the customs involved in making a pilgrimage.
- Develop an understanding of how pilgrimage can deepen spirituality and heighten awareness of community involvement.

*Outline of content*

- Discussion of why some places are special/sacred in Christianity.
- Look at case studies drawn from Jerusalem (especially the Via Dolorosa), Lourdes and Walsingham.
- What is involved in making a pilgrimage, extracts from *Canterbury Tales*.
- Discussion of pilgrimage as symbol of the journey of the human soul to God.
- Talk by a pilgrim to Lourdes.

*Teaching strategies and activities*

- Discussion.
- Video of pilgrimage.
- Visiting speaker.
- Produce booklet of imaginative writing on being a pilgrim.

*Assessment*

All pupils are expected to produce a booklet which will enable them to 'describe the customs and feelings involved in making a pilgrimage' (end of key stage indicator of attainment).

### Short-term planning

The above unit on 'Pilgrimage in Christianity' will, before it is presented to pupils, have to be organised and arranged into a series of lessons, each one of which will need to meet the criteria as laid out earlier in this chapter. Normally short-term planning would be the responsibility of the class teacher, though RE coordinators are often involved when the subject matter is felt to be particularly difficult.

## Varied approaches in the classroom

RE has often been bedevilled in the past by a very simple pattern of lesson: the teacher tells or reads a story, followed sometimes by some discussion, and then the children write it out or draw a picture. Whereas this may be appropriate on some occasions, if it becomes the regular pattern then it can be a very ineffectual way of teaching and learning. There are many different approaches which can be adopted which can make the teaching more lively and the learning more effective.

### Story

Despite what has been said in the previous paragraph, story is very important in RE, especially in the primary school. Teachers are very familiar with the power of stories both to explore meaning and to express it.

Basically there are three broad groupings of stories which are appropriate to RE.

- Stories from religious traditions. Often these are about important people within the tradition such as stories about Jesus, Muhammad, Khrishna, Guru Nanak.
- Ancient stories and legends which have attempted to explain why things are as they are. Examples of these, such as 'Pandora and the whispering box', can be found in Chapter 11.
- Other stories, not from religious traditions, which deal with themes which are relevant to RE. Popular here are books like *The Lion, the Witch and the Wardrobe* (by C. S. Lewis) which deals with the battle of good and evil, *Grandpa* (by John Burningham) and *Badger's Parting Gifts* (by Susan Varley) which deal with death and separation, and *I am David* (by Anne Holm) which deals with the boy David's personal journey to discover who he is (see Chapter 14).

As indicated above, the selection of the stories is highly important. Curriculum time is limited and there are many, many stories. Why have these particular ones been chosen? Do they give an insight into the teaching of a particular key figure or do they illustrate a piece of ethical teaching? The treatment of the story is also very important. Is it just told to the children or is there sufficient discussion to explore its meaning? The other, secular, stories, listed above, are only appropriate for RE if the teacher explores the themes with the children. *Badger's Parting Gifts*, for example, is only appropriate to the RE curriculum if the teacher (gently) explores the theme of death and separation with the class. If it is so treated it can be very powerful RE as young children are exploring with their teacher one of the great 'frontier' questions of life.

### Dialogue

Dialogue is not new to primary education – it is often used in the English curriculum – but it has been introduced to RE in recent years through the work of Julia Ipgrave and is described in her occasional paper published by the Warwick Religious and Education Research Unit, *Pupil-To-Pupil Dialogue as a Tool for Religious Education* (2001). The approach, dialogical RE, is not seen as a new form of RE but as an enriching process which draws upon existing RE work. Ipgrave worked in multiracial primary schools in Leicester and established in her classes dialogue groups consisting of a small group of children with a teacher/facilitator. Questions were devised which were presented to groups. In one example given, a group of Year 4 pupils (one Hindu boy and two Christian boys) along with Julia Ipgrave as facilitator were responding to one of the questions prepared by a Year 6 group, 'How many gods do you think there are?'

It is clear from this that dialogical RE draws upon pupils' existing understanding of religions built from home, friends, the media, RE lessons and so on. Placing pupils in these dialogue settings brought them up close to different religious traditions and encouraged them to think about these experiences and to build them into a coherent framework. Dialogue settings provide the necessary opportunities for pupils to talk thoughtfully and respectfully with each other so as to understand the religious viewpoints of others, to reflect upon their own beliefs and attitudes, and to make adjustments and developments. This is quite a different activity from either the sort of discussion based on ignorance which can so easily occur in RE lessons, or the unthinking presentation of opposing views.

Clearly the great challenge for dialogical RE is establishing the right atmosphere and relationship in a class which will enable this openness and sharing to take place. For this to happen there needs to be trust in the dialogue groups so that pupils feel able to make their contributions. There also needs to be a willingness to accept that each individual's contribution is of importance and that all in the group must be included in the activity.

The dialogical RE described here took place in schools in which a variety of religious traditions were represented. This is a situation in which the dialogue process works most effectively. However it has worked in other settings. Dialogue can take place among pupils of the same religious tradition as most traditions have elements of diversity. The project also linked by email the Leicester schools with schools in other parts of the country which were not so rich in religious diversity and this enabled dialogue by email to take place.

### Visits to places of worship

First-hand experience is of great importance in RE, as it is in the rest of the curriculum. Children remember their visits and many would see such visits as one of the most important parts of RE work. There is a more detailed discussion of visits to places of worship in Chapter 17 but here it is important to note that visits should be built into the planning. Clearly the geographical situations of schools vary and some will have a range of places of worship from different religious traditions on the doorstep while others will have a more limited choice. All should have at least a church in close proximity. Ideally a visit to a place of worship should involve meeting people there who are associated with it. Care needs to be given to timing: a visit to an empty unheated church on a cold wet Monday morning might not yield the experiences hoped for!

### Artefacts

Artefacts have become a natural part of RE over the years. Although there can be issues about their treatment, teachers have come to rely upon them to give pupils first-hand experience, through both seeing and handling of important elements in the practice of the faiths being studied. All schools should have their collections of artefacts geared towards the content of their schemes of work. There is a discussion of the use of artefacts in Chapter 17.

### Information and communication technology

There are many videotapes and DVDs available now which are relevant for RE and which can provide important second-hand visual experience. The internet too is a rich source of curriculum support. If teachers are not able to take their children to visit a mosque, then it is possible to have a tour on the internet. There is now so much religious material on the internet from different sources that it is very important that teachers make a careful check of content and style before using any with a class.

# 7 Religious education in the Foundation Stage

## The Foundation Stage

One of the more encouraging of recent developments in educational practice in this country has been the establishment of the Foundation Stage as a distinctive educational phase. The identifying of this age group (3–5 years) as a distinctive stage gives clear recognition of the crucial importance of this age and stage in the development of children.

It is a stage which, perhaps more than any other, sees a tremendous development in children. Children are making sense of things. Young children need plenty of first-hand experiences; they need the opportunity to play and have enjoyable playful experiences. Not only are they learning about the nature of things but through play they are learning to control their impulses, to establish rules, to develop social skills and empathy.

The Foundation Stage, therefore, is concerned with the interplay of learning and physical development:

- Children need to be provided with choices so as to promote independence and active learning.
- They need frequent changes of activity as periods of concentration are short.
- They need to have frequent breaks and the opportunity to move about.
- The most effective way to work with young children is in a one-to-one situation or in small groups; whole class activities, except perhaps in singing or story, are often less effective.
- Opportunities to play outside are particularly important because of the need for plenty of oxygen for the children's growth spurts.
- Outdoor learning is additionally important as it provides opportunities for children to be imaginative, messy, creative, and for playing games with rules and for adventures.

Above all, teachers in the Foundation Stage need to plan and resource a challenging environment, building in the considerations listed above. Much evidence suggests that formal instruction for young children does not pay off in lasting benefits. Leading young children too rapidly to textbook learning can be a way of damaging their natural intellectual curiosity.

This is the philosophy which underlies approaches to the Foundation Stage curriculum. In a very important sense it is one curriculum, but – mainly for the sake of adults who have to plan a balanced experience for the children – it is given a theoretical structure made up of six 'early learning goals':

- Personal, social and emotional development.
- Communication, language and literacy.
- Mathematical development.
- Knowledge and understanding of the world.
- Physical development.
- Creative development.

### The contribution of religious education

Religious education must be taught to all registered pupils in maintained schools. This does not apply to pupils in nursery classes in maintained schools so some children in the Foundation Stage are required to have RE while others are not.

However even for those for whom RE is not legally required it may well be that RE can provide valuable educational experiences for children at this stage. RE can make a contribution to all six areas of learning but it has perhaps a stronger contribution to make in four of them:

- Personal, social and emotional development.
- Communication, language and literacy.
- Knowledge and understanding of the world.
- Creative development.

Before we consider some examples of RE work in the Foundation Stage we need to look in a little more detail at the nature of the Foundation Stage as a whole and also what might count as religious education in a broad sense.

As its name suggests the Foundation Stage is intended to provide a foundation to assist young children, in ways which are appropriate to their age and stage, to develop skills and attitudes essential to their later education. It is by definition not subject-based but skills are being developed which undergird later subject development. Presumably all artists had to begin by learning to grip and use a crayon or paintbrush!

When we consider RE at this stage there will be examples of pupils having contact with what has been called 'explicit' RE, that is, contact with religious material such as hearing a story about Jesus, handling a religious artefact or visiting a place of worship. However there is much more that is going on in the Foundation Stage which is crucial to a developing understanding of religion. This has often been called 'implicit' RE and consists of skills and attitudes being fostered in the Foundation curriculum which are essential for pupils to have if they are to develop an understanding of religion. It may be helpful to see these as pre-RE activities. These include:

- A positive awareness of themselves, their needs and their feelings.
- The capacity to reflect upon relationships.
- Empathy.
- Thinking about notions of right and wrong.
- Having respect for the culture and beliefs of others.

These skills and attitudes not only undergird an understanding of religion but are also the foundation of a wide range of other learning and will permeate the curriculum. Much of this will be the result of careful planning on the part of teachers. A topic such as 'Who am I?' is widely popular. But others can happen unexpectedly and without planning:

> Children in a Reception class had all planted their seeds in their separate flower pots and all had started to grow except for one, that of a small boy who was becoming increasingly despondent as his frequent checks brought no good news. Then one morning as he hurried over to check once again he saw the unmistakeable hint of green pushing through the soil. His joy and excitement were more than he could contain. In a completely unplanned way he had experienced that feeling of awe and wonder which is an essential ingredient to the lives of so many religious believers.

### Two examples

Here are two examples of extended work on RE in the Foundation Stage, both by teachers in Reception classes. Neither is an RE specialist. Both have developed the work from their own research and with support from the RE subject leader in their school. Both projects are described by the teachers in question and both accounts are quite lengthy.

#### EXAMPLE 1: OUR NEIGHBOURS

Since childhood I have been interested in the different religions and cultures there are in the world and I have felt how important it is to have some knowledge and understanding of them. I think that this awareness has increased considerably on a global scale since 9/11. I wanted my class of reception children to begin to extend their understanding of this. I also wanted them to develop an awareness of their own position. I have found through my teaching that I must not underestimate their understanding: I was amazed how much these children aged four and five had already picked up from both experiences they had had and questions they had asked. The class consists of twenty-nine children of whom two belong to ethnic minority groups, one from a Hindu family and one from a Sikh family. This mix is about normal for my school. Obviously having children in the class from different faith traditions is a great advantage for the work I plan to do. I call the work 'Our Neighbours'.

My learning intentions were to encourage the children to:

- Explore how people live their lives.
- Ask questions about religion and culture.
- Be curious about religious buildings and artefacts.
- Reflect upon their own experiences.
- Respect the beliefs, customs and traditions of others.
- Begin to develop a religious vocabulary.

To fulfil these learning intentions I planned work around:

- A visit to a place of worship.
- A variety of religious artefacts.
- Stories from various religious traditions.
- A visitor from a religious tradition.

The visit to the *place of worship* was in fact a visit to the local *parish church*. This had the advantage of being both close enough for us to walk and quite 'visual' with stained glass windows, statues and plenty of colour. Clearly a visit to a church is very rich in learning materials across the whole curriculum so I identified very carefully what I wanted to focus on, always allowing for the unexpected. As one of our learning intentions was to encourage respect for the beliefs, customs and traditions of others I talked about appropriate behaviour in church – no running or shouting – which shows respect for other people's 'holy ground'. At the beginning of the visit I wanted the children to sit quietly on the pews for a short time in order to feel the stillness and calm of the building. Then we identified some key features of the church – the altar, the font and the lectern. We pointed out the cross on the altar and explained why it was such an important symbol in Christianity. The children then looked for other crosses around the church – in decorations, in the stone work, in the windows – and found a large number! Finally we looked at two of the stained glass windows, one of the nativity and one of Jesus teaching the crowds, both stories we then looked up in the big church Bible on the lectern. Some children also picked out a statue of the Virgin and Child. Finally some of the children observed how 'clean and shiny' the church was so I explained that looking after the church so well was a sign of the congregation's love and respect for God. We took a digital camera with us on the visit which the children used to make a photographic record of what we had seen – which was then used extensively back in the classroom. The visit, which the children found both exciting and memorable, led to considerable oral work, writing and art work.

I used *artefacts* which I borrowed from the school's central collection in order for children to be able to handle them and to raise questions about their use. I created an artefacts table within the classroom and placed artefacts a couple at a time upon it. I explained to the children that these were very special to people from that religion and that they must be handled gently and with respect. Each one was carefully labelled and children were frequently at the table feeling the artefacts and talking to each other about them. Every so often I would talk to the children, either in a group or with the whole class, about one of them linking it with a story if possible. Particularly attractive to the children were the *kara* (the steel band worn on the right wrist) and the *kangha* (the comb which holds the uncut hair) in Sikhism, the *cross* and *rosary* (prayer beads) in Christianity, the image of *Hanuman* (the monkey warrior who helped Rama and Sita) in Hinduism, the *tallith* (the prayer shawl) in Judaism and the *Qur'an* and *Qur'an stand* in Islam. This last one I would not leave on the artefacts table. I explained to the children that in Muslim eyes the Qur'an is so special that when it is not in use it must be wrapped up carefully in cloths and kept on a high shelf away from the dirt and dust of the floor. This information provoked considerable interest and some discussion on why it is so special.

Over the period of the year I selected a number of *stories* from the religious traditions which I always prefaced with 'This is a story which is very special to Christians/Jews/Muslims' etc. These stories were chosen to reflect significant events, such as festivals, over the year and stories associated with important people in the different religious traditions. The stories were interspersed with 'ordinary' stories and as they were often connected with festivals they spread over the year. In a sense too the work planned here permeated the year.

I told the story of Rama and Sita which underlies the Hindu festival of Diwali and we also lit little Diwali lamps to welcome Rama and Sita back from their exile. I told the story of the Passover and the escape of the Hebrew slaves from Egypt. Christmas and Easter were covered along with the rest of the school. I also told some delightful stories of Guru Nanak.

A real highlight of the work was the *visit* of Jasbinder Kaur, the mother of Gurdeep Kaur, the Sikh girl in my class. She came to talk about the child naming ceremony in Sikhism but it did not stop there as the children were full of questions – why did Malkit Singh (Gurdeep's older brother in Year 3) not have his hair cut? why were Sikh boys called Singh and Sikh girls Kaur? and so on. Interestingly too a number of children picked up the connection between the Sikh naming ceremony and the Christian initiation ceremony of Baptism so on the following day a number brought into school photographs of their own or their younger siblings' christenings which led on to a discussion of baptism and other rites of initiation.

This example of work is rooted very firmly in the early learning goals principally in the area of learning, knowledge and understanding of the world. The children are beginning to know their own culture and beliefs and those of other people. They visited the parish church which was also a way of exploring their own environment. They listened to stories from a range of religious traditions and they had the opportunity to listen to and question a member of a major world faith. They handled artefacts and discussed their possible use. This example of work also relates closely to three other areas of learning: communication, language and literacy, creative development and personal, social and emotional development. Imaginative talk, response to experience, expressing and communicating ideas, listening with enjoyment to stories, extending their (religious) vocabulary, exploring new words, understanding that people have different views, beliefs and cultures which should be treated with respect and that their own views, beliefs and cultures should in turn be treated with respect, are all integral parts of the learning. In addition to all this the children through their digital camera used ICT in recording and developing the work on their visit to the parish church.

### EXAMPLE 2: LIVING TOGETHER

I teach the reception class of a one form entry primary school in a small town in southern England. I have found over the years that a very important part of my work with this age group is to foster such qualities as cooperation, care for each other and empathy. So, over a period of time, I have developed a theme which I call, 'Living Together'. I call it a theme because while it definitely contains specific planned teaching it also will keep appearing over the year in response to situations which arise in the classroom or the playground. My learning intentions are to help children to begin to:

- Explore appropriate religious stories.
- Reflect on their own feelings and experiences.
- See how people can show love and concern.
- See how people can help each other.
- Learn about the difference between right and wrong.
- Share in the experience of others.
- Understand the meaning of friendship.
- Develop empathy.

My strategy is to select four stories from the New Testament, two about Jesus and two told by him, to fulfil the learning intentions. In addition to this I will be presented with all sorts of situations from the life of the classroom which will form part of the work as well.

The four stories are:

Jesus and the children (Luke chapter 18 verses 15–17)
Zacchaeus, the tax collector (Luke chapter 19 verses 1–9)

The Lost Sheep (Luke chapter 15 verses 4–7)

The Lost (or Prodigal) Son (Luke chapter 15 verses 11–24)

*Jesus and the children* is a very brief story. Jesus' disciples tell a group of mothers to take their children away as they are being a nuisance. Jesus stops them, takes the children in his arms and blesses them. He tells those round about that the Kingdom of God belongs to them.

*Zacchaeus* is the account of a tax collector who was ostracised by his neighbours. Tax collectors then were in the habit of extracting from people more than they had to pay in tax and then keeping the excess for themselves. Zacchaeus heard that Jesus was visiting his village so, wanting to see Jesus, he went to the roadside but being a very small man he could not see over the heads of the crowd who lined the route. Being a resourceful man, Zacchaeus climbed a sycamore tree which stood by the road and hid in the branches so that he could look down on Jesus. To his amazement Jesus stopped immediately below the tree and looking up invited himself to dinner at Zacchaeus' house. The crowd showed its displeasure at Jesus dining with such a man but Zacchaeus welcomed Jesus into his house. No one knows what was said or done at that dinner but afterwards Zacchaeus came out a changed person promising to steal no more and offering generous restitution.

The *Lost Sheep* is a parable Jesus told of a shepherd who, when counting his one hundred sheep into the sheepfold in the evening, found that one was missing. He left the ninety-nine sheep in the fold unguarded and set off to look for the lost and presumably frightened sheep. When he found it he brought it back to the sheepfold on his shoulders rejoicing that he had rescued it from one of the many predators of the night.

The *Lost Son*, often called the Prodigal Son, tells the story of a farmer who had two sons one of whom wanted his share of his future inheritance now so he could enjoy it while he was still young rather than have to wait until after his father's death. His father agrees to this and gives him his half. The son goes a long way off to a far country while his older brother remains working on the farm. The younger brother lives a life of great extravagance but in a short time he spent all his money and is destitute. So reduced is he that, appalling for a Jew, he is forced to care for pigs. He reflects on his former life, how his father's servants and hired hands are much better off than he now is, so he resolves to return to his father's farm, not as a son but as a servant. However when he is still a long way off his father sees him coming and runs out to greet him. He hugs him and takes him home and organises a tremendous party to welcome his son home. 'Rejoice with me', he said, 'for this my son was dead but is alive again, he was lost and is found.' (NB the parable does not actually end here but goes on to consider the attitude of the older brother who remained at home. This second part is probably best left to a later age.)

I chose these stories because they are so full of issues related to love, concern, emotional warmth, caring, forgiveness, acceptance, regret for past actions. They also deal with less pleasant aspects of human life, the self-centredness of the lost son, the rudeness and bad temper of Jesus' disciples, and the rapaciousness of Zacchaeus. My approach in teaching essentially was through the telling of the stories, the fostering of discussion on them, a degree of role play, and the identification of similar situations which the children might have experienced. To give a taste of this we talked about the feelings of the father in the story of the lost son: how do you think the father felt when his son wanted to go away? Was his son a good son? Do you think he missed him? How do you think he felt when he saw him in the far distance coming back? How would you have felt? This produced a vast amount of discussion so each of those areas was followed up with further questions. Why was Zacchaeus disliked? Why were his actions wrong? Why do you think Zacchaeus changed? Do you think that the people who had been robbed by Zacchaeus would forgive him? Would you forgive him? We developed this through role play. Different children became

Zacchaeus or the father or the son and were questioned by the rest of the children and we also acted out the stories.

This example of RE's contribution to the early learning goals is rooted firmly in the area of learning personal, social and emotional development. It investigates with children important qualities in their relationships; it encourages children to reflect on their own feelings and the feelings of others; it fosters empathy; it gives children the opportunity to talk about similar situations which take place in their own lives and experiences; it looks at ways in which children can show love and concern in situations they encounter; it raises questions of right and wrong; it looks at the notion of forgiveness; it emphasises the need for treating others with respect.

## Summary

There are clearly many ways in which RE can contribute to the early learning goals. The two described above are examples of how two teachers, starting from different points, developed their RE teaching within the bounds of the Foundation Stage curriculum. Although very different in a number of ways, there were four features they had in common:

- Both encourage the children to be active learners fully involved in the work, especially through language.
- Both are very concerned to aid children to develop an understanding of feelings and values, both of themselves and of other people.
- Both foster empathy.
- Both are keen to promote respect for each other among the children.

# 8  Teaching RE in Key Stages 1 and 2

Clearly teaching children aged 5–6 and 10–11 years will be very different in many respects. The children aged 10 and 11 will have had a much wider range of life experiences, leading to a greater maturity. The younger children will be at a much earlier stage on the path. Whatever their age and stage RE will be seeking to ensure that it promotes

- Respect
- Understanding
- Tolerance

## Key skills

In addition to the development of these qualities, there are a number of key skills which are being developed across the whole curriculum and these are progressive. It is unclear whether any key skill is unique to RE. However there are a number which are of particular significance to RE and these will be utilised in RE teaching and through their use developed and enhanced further. In particular, the following skills play a very important role.

research: the ability to collect information from a range of sources and to deal with it with understanding

enquiry: the ability to identify and ask relevant questions

observation: the capacity to view intelligently so as to select the essential points

thinking: the ability to reflect upon their beliefs and those of others

empathy: the capacity to appreciate the thoughts, beliefs, feelings and attitudes of others

evaluation: the ability to consider different points of view thoughtfully

reflection: the ability to think about ultimate questions

communication: the ability to explain concepts, practices and so on using appropriate religious vocabulary

**Key Stage I**

*An overview of RE in Key Stage I*

Children in Key Stage 1 will learn about Christianity and one other principal religion, though they may have contact with another tradition through, for example, a festival observed in the school. They will hear stories from the sacred texts of the religions and talk about their meaning. Similarly they will be introduced to celebrations, especially festivals, worship and ritual. There they will note similarities – and, in some cases, differences. They will encounter artefacts and begin to understand their place in the religious tradition, using both information and imagination. Pupils will become aware of symbols and start to see their significance. Through their learning they will begin to recognise that beliefs come in a variety of forms and they will learn to respect these differences. They will learn the importance religion has in the lives of many people. As their learning develops, so their religious vocabulary will increase.

Arising from their learning about religion, pupils will look at ways in which this may affect them and their beliefs and attitudes. They will talk about what matters to them and how what is important to them affects their values and behaviour. They will be asked to consider difficult questions, especially ultimate questions. They will explore the importance of belonging.

Some of this might sound inappropriate to children of this age. Whether this is the case or not will depend on how it is treated. For example, the handling of difficult questions such as ultimate ones would be looking for a response of a 5- or 6-year-old child not that of a moral philosopher. It should be seen as the start of a process of asking questions, and the responses will become more sophisticated as the child's thinking matures and develops.

*What should RE in Key Stage I look like?*

Chapter 4 deals with the question of what is meant by the term 'religion'. There the work of Ninian Smart was used to demonstrate that religion is a living activity with broad overlapping and interlocking dimensions. This approach to religion will inevitably guide the planning of RE teaching, although different terms may be used. The categories recommended by the National Framework (p. 25) are:

| believing: | what people believe about God, humanity and the natural world |
|---|---|
| story: | how and why some stories are sacred and important in religion |
| celebrations: | how and why celebrations are important in religion |
| symbols: | how and why symbols express religious meaning |
| leaders and teachers: | figures who have an influence on others locally, nationally and globally in religion |
| belonging: | where and how people belong and why belonging is important |
| myself | who I am and my uniqueness as a person in a family and community |

### What sort of experiences should be provided at Key Stage 1?

- Visiting places of worship with a focus on symbols and feelings.
- Meeting and talking with visitors from local faith communities.
- The opportunity for children to use their senses and have times of quiet reflection.
- Sharing beliefs, ideas and values and talking about feelings and experiences.
- Beginning to use ICT to explore religions and beliefs as practised in the local and wider community.

## Key Stage 2

### An overview of RE at Key Stage 2

In Key Stage 2 pupils start to become increasingly aware that things are not quite as simple as they might have appeared in Key Stage 1. Their knowledge and understanding of religions is broadening. The focus on Christianity continues and they will probably carry on with some work on the other principal religious tradition which they met in Key Stage 1. Then in Key Stage 2 two new religious traditions will be introduced with their beliefs, teachings, sacred writings, practices and ways of life. This will all need to be assimilated and it will raise questions about diversity, similarity and difference which need to be discussed in class. Pupils too are becoming much more aware of the world beyond their own country and this in turn raises questions in their minds. It is in this key stage that many pupils start to raise the question of 'truth'. Can all these religions be 'true'? Pupils also have a growing awareness that not everyone believes in God or the supernatural and this raises the 'truth' question even more sharply. Many pupils will be examining the beliefs they have formed over their lives so far, and no doubt will be making adjustments to them. These questions will need to be handled through discussion and, where possible, through dialogue.

Pupils in Key Stage 2 are less willing to accept questions of right and wrong on authority than are pupils in Key Stage 1. They will want to question and discuss and to compare the ethical stances of the religious traditions they are studying. Teachers again have a very important role in guiding discussion through quite complex issues.

Over this key stage, through their work in school (and often outside school as well) pupils will be developing an increasingly sophisticated vocabulary which should help them in dealing with these questions which keep emerging.

Religious education at this stage is by no means all questions. Pupils need a very solid input of subject content, aimed at extending their understanding and empathy. This is for two main reasons. Questioning, discussion and dialogue do need to be based on a knowledge of the facts, otherwise they can easily become a mutual sharing of ignorance and prejudice. Secondly it is very important that pupils have a thorough understanding of the way that their fellow citizens from different religious traditions live their lives and have some awareness of the significance of these great religious traditions for their followers.

### What should RE in Key Stage 2 look like?

As with Key Stage 1, the work of Ninian Smart (see Chapter 4), which described religion as a living activity with broad overlapping and interlocking dimensions, will inevitably guide the planning of RE teaching in Key Stage 2, although different terms and headings might be used. The categories or themes recommended by the National Framework (p. 27) are:

- Beliefs and questions: how people's beliefs about God, the world and others impacts on their lives.
- Teachings and authority: what sacred texts and other sources say about God, the world and human life.
- Worship, pilgrimage and special places: where, how and why people worship, including particular sites.
- The journey of life and death: why some occasions are sacred to believers, and what people think about life after death.
- Symbols and religious expressions: how religious and spiritual ideas are expressed.
- Inspirational people: figures from whom believers find inspiration.
- Religion and the individual: what is expected of a person in following a religion or belief.
- Religion, family and community: how religious families and communities practise their faith, and the contribution this makes to local life.
- Beliefs in action in the world: how religions and beliefs respond to global issues of human rights, fairness, social justice and the importance of the environment.

### What sort of experiences should be provided at Key Stage 2?

- Encountering religion through visitors and visits to places of worship.
- Discussing religious and philosophical questions, giving reasons for their own beliefs and those of others.
- Considering a range of human experiences and feelings.
- Reflecting on their own and others' insights into life and its origin, purpose and meaning.
- Expressing their own and others' insights through art and design, music, dance, drama and ICT.
- Developing the use of ICT, particularly in enhancing pupils' awareness of religions and beliefs globally.

### A long-term plan for RE in Key Stages I and 2

What follows here is the long-term plan devised by a primary school to cover both key stages. The principles which underlay the planning were:

- The two religions in Key Stage 1 are Christianity and Judaism and the three in Key Stage 2 are Christianity, Hinduism and Islam.
- There is a preference in the teaching for focusing upon one religion at a time rather

than following a theme across more than one religion (although there are some themes in the plan).

- In Key Stage 2, Christianity appears in each year group but the other two religions are taught in blocks, Hinduism in Years 4 and 6 and Islam in Years 3 and 5.
- There is balance between the two attainment targets.
- Progression is planned for and this is most noticeable in the provisions for the annual celebration of both Easter and Christmas which are both progressive and varied.

## Reception

|  | Topics | Ideas, resources |
|---|---|---|
| Autumn | Celebration | Share in a form of celebration<br>Talk about birthdays |
|  | Harvest festival | Share in a harvest celebration<br>Help distribute goods<br>Talk about the beauties of nature and of the seasons |
| Christmas | A baby is born | Discuss preparations for the birth of a baby<br>Talk about Mary's long journey and the birth in the stable |
| Spring | Ourselves | Discuss how everyone is special and important<br>Bring in things which are special to them, e.g. toys, books<br>Discuss why these things are special<br>Special people who care for them at home and at school<br>Discuss why these people are special |
| Easter | Easter: new life | Brief account of the death and resurrection of Jesus<br>Focus on new life and hope: spring time, symbolism of Easter eggs |
| Summer | Our world | Explore and respond to the wonders of nature<br>Use seasons to explore changes in the natural world<br>Grow seeds<br>How to live in our world<br>Why do we need rules?<br>What sort of rules do we need? |

## Year 1

|  | Topics | Ideas, resources |
|---|---|---|
| Autumn | Caring and helping | 'The Good Shepherd'<br>Care of all living creatures<br>Attitude to each other<br>Attitude towards animals<br>Work of RSPCA |
|  | Well known stories | Enjoy hearing stories, e.g. Samson, King David, Joseph |
| Christmas | Jesus, a very special baby | Retell the birth story<br>Introduce the story of Gabriel's message to Mary and the visit of the shepherds |

*continued*

| Spring | Festivals (Judaism) | Hear stories behind the festival of Hanukkah |
|--------|---------------------|----------------------------------------------|
| Easter | Jesus: a loving person | Accounts of the Last Supper, the betrayal by Judas, the crucifixion and resurrection, with a focus on the love within the cruel events |
| Summer | Friendships | Discussion of what makes a good/bad friend<br>Identification of key qualities which make up friendship – help, trust, etc. Examples of people who have been good friends to others, e.g. Mother Teresa of Calcutta |

## Year 2

|  | Topics | Ideas, resources |
|--|--------|------------------|
| Autumn | Beginning and growing | Birth – baby photographs<br>Baptism – enact one<br>Visit a church<br>Barmitzvah/Batmitzvah |
|  | Living together | Discuss friendship and quarrels<br>Making up<br>Jesus' teaching on love and forgiveness<br>Stories of Good Samaritan and the Prodigal/Lost Son |
| Christmas | Jesus: love and hate | Retell the birth stories<br>Introduce the role of Herod and the family's flight into Egypt<br>Visit of the magi |
| Spring | The Bible | Special book for Christians<br>Opportunities to see various versions |
|  | Jewish festivals | The Sabbath – how it is kept<br>Its significance for Jews and for Judaism<br>Sabbath artefacts<br>Passover – the stories associated with the Passover Seder<br>Passover artefacts |
| Easter | Lent and Easter | Shrove Tuesday, Ash Wednesday, Mothering Sunday<br>Palm Sunday story with palm cross |
| Summer | Judaism | Importance of the Torah<br>Torah scroll<br>Visit synagogue<br>Introduction to Ten Commandments<br>Mezuzah, tefellin<br>Tallith<br>Importance of the Torah for Jews |

## Year 3

|  | Topics | Ideas, resources |
|---|---|---|
| Autumn | Myself – my family<br>my home | Belonging, self-worth<br>Living in the community |
|  | Friendship (sharing) | Jesus' friends, disciples |
|  | The story of Muhammad | Key facts of his life; five pillars of Islam |
|  | Precious things | Personal special things |
|  | Exploring artefacts | A look at a few key artefacts |
| Christmas | Advent | Retell both stories<br>Focus on waiting and expectation<br>Advent corona and Advent calendar<br>Story of Simeon in the temple |
| Spring | Rites of passage in<br>Christianity | Baptism – what happens?<br>Symbolism of water and candles/Paschal candle<br>Marriage – what happens?<br>Symbolism of vows and the rings<br>Death – funeral services |
| Easter | Easter: the first<br>witnesses | Focus on the reactions of the disciples to the Easter events<br>Peter, Mary Magdalene<br>The part played by Pontius Pilate |
| Summer | Symbols | Consider the function of symbols<br>Identify, e.g. the fish (ichthus) the crescent, the AUM<br>Special clothing, e.g. ihram at the Hajj<br>Special food, e.g. hot cross buns<br>Special features, e.g. water at baptism |
|  | Visit to mosque | Place of prayer in Islam – prayer mats and compass<br>Identify the component parts of a mosque (internal and external)<br>Discuss their meaning and purpose<br>Significance of wudu |

## Year 4

|  | Topics | Ideas, resources |
|---|---|---|
| Autumn | Who is Jesus? | A preacher, healer, teacher<br>Examples of these roles from Gospels<br>Son of God? |
|  | Christian worship | Well known prayers (e.g. Lord's Prayer)<br>Holy Communion – bread and wine<br>Hymns and music<br>Changing moods – thanksgiving at harvest, joy at Christmas, sadness<br>on Good Friday |
| Christmas | Christmas around the<br>world | Christingles<br>Stories of Baboushka, St Lucy and St Nicholas |

*continued*

| | | |
|---|---|---|
| Spring | Worship in Hinduism | Forms of Hindu worship<br>Individual devotion to your own murti<br>Puja corner in home<br>Puja tray<br>Visit to Hindu temple<br>Prashad<br>Arti |
| Easter | Symbols of Easter | Empty cross, the empty tomb<br>Paschal candle, the new fire |
| Summer | Rites of passage in Hinduism | Reference to:<br>    Birth and naming ceremonies<br>    The sacred thread ceremony<br>    Marriage<br>    Death<br>    The role of the householder, the monk and the sanyasi |
| | Hindu settlement in Britain | Patterns of settlement<br>The role of the temple/mandir |

## Year 5

| | Topics | Ideas, resources |
|---|---|---|
| Autumn | Festivals and pilgrimage in Islam | The Hajj and Id-ul-Adha<br>Ramadan and Id-ul-Fitr<br>What happens and why |
| | Pilgrimage in Christianity | The idea of the special/sacred place<br>The purpose of pilgrimages<br>Jerusalem and the Via Dolorosa<br>Lourdes – healing<br>Walsingham |
| Christmas | Christmas through art | Collect representations of the Nativity – postcards, slides, Christmas cards<br>Pupils to analyse themes and messages within them |
| Spring | Creation stories | Examples of Creation stories in Christianity, Islam and Hinduism<br>Distinguish between literal accounts and symbolic accounts<br>What do the Creation stories say about the world? |
| | Some issues in Muslim family life | Close relationships in the extended family. Arranged marriages<br>Second and third generation Muslims in Britain |
| Easter | Easter through art | Collect slides and postcards of crucifixion and resurrection of Jesus<br>Use analyses of these as a basis for discussion on the meaning of the events |
| Summer | Who is my neighbour? | Issues of interdependence and brotherhood. Zakah and Khums in Islam<br>Work of Christian Aid, CAFOD and/or TEAR Fund, Red Cross and Red Crescent |
| | Jesus – teaching | Concern for the outcast: the Good Samaritan<br>The Sermon on the Mount (Matthew chapters 5–8), especially:<br>The Beatitudes (Matthew chapter 5 verses 1–12)<br>Love your enemies (Matthew chapter 5 verses 43–48) |

## Year 6

|  | Topics | Ideas, resources |
|---|---|---|
| Autumn | How the Bible came to us | Early manuscripts/codices<br>Illuminated manuscripts – Lindisfarne Gospels<br>Printing – William Caxton<br>Authorised Version 1611<br>Recent translations |
|  | Diwali | Underlying story and practices<br>Detailed considerations of the story of Rama and Sita, looking at its meaning for Hindus |
| Christmas | Christmas: the two accounts | Read the birth stories in Matthew and Luke<br>Discuss and identify their similarities and differences<br>What is each saying about Jesus? |
| Spring | Some Hindu beliefs | One God yet many images<br>Ideas of Karma and Moksha<br>Artefacts – images of chief 'gods' |
|  | Death and beyond | Views of Christianity, Islam, Hinduism and Judaism on death and what follows it<br>Coping with grief |
| Easter | Easter: the Gospel accounts | Read the accounts of the trial, death and resurrection of Jesus in two Gospels<br>Discuss and identify similarities and differences<br>What is each saying about Jesus? |
| Summer | The church and the community | Visit a church<br>Identify various services<br>Check church newsletter and noticeboard<br>Interview priest/minister about the broader work of the church in the wider community |
|  | Faith and commitment | Faith into action<br>Biographies drawn from two of:<br>  St. Francis of Assisi<br>  Father Damien<br>  William Wilberforce<br>  Martin Luther King<br>  Helder Camara |

# 9 Approaching the teaching of Christianity

Christianity occupies the central place in RE in educational legislation. Described in the Education Reform Act (1988) as *the* principal tradition in Great Britain as opposed to the other principal traditions, it is taught across all four key stages and normally receives 50 per cent of the time allocated to RE.

Even in a multifaith society there do seem to be strong educational and social reasons for giving special attention to Christianity in RE. Western civilisations, including Britain, have been, and in many ways still are, very strongly influenced by Christianity. Art, music, drama, poetry, literature, customs, festivals, traditions, even many swear words, arise out of and are shaped by Christianity. It may well be that a majority of citizens have ceased to worship publicly in any serious way, but there can be no doubt that a large majority of the population identifies with Christianity as their religion. It can still be argued that, in a cultural sense at least, Britain is a Christian country.

From the point of view of most children, experience of religion in Britain tends to be of Christianity. We decorate our shop windows with, among other things, angels at Christmas, and many families have a crib at home, and we have pancakes on Shrove Tuesday, eat hot cross buns on Good Friday and receive and give Easter eggs on Easter Day. Children hear terms like God, Jesus, prayer and, while they may but dimly understand, use them. Christianity, whether realised or not, is part of their mental furniture.

If religious education, like the rest of the primary curriculum, is going to build on and extend existing experience and understanding, it seems inevitable that Christianity will have a central role to play. It is also very important that pupils from other religious traditions should gain a good understanding of Christianity as it is an important part of the culture of which they are now members.

## What is Christianity?

The obvious answer to this question is that Christianity is a universal religion, practised in every country of the world and numerically the largest. However the question can often be asked with some exasperation by teachers. They often complain that it is much easier to teach other faiths because they are perceived to be much more 'straightforward', while with Christianity they find it difficult to see the wood for the individual trees. Certainly it is true that Christianity can appear quite diffuse, probably because we are surrounded by it. On the other hand, this view oversimplifies the other traditions.

The Five Pillars of Islam – faith, prayer, pilgrimage, fasting and charity – are a very neat representation of Islam and very useful to teachers in Key Stages 1 and 2, but to a Muslim it would appear a narrowing down of Islam. Often teachers are led by textbooks directed at pupils in Key Stages 1 and 2 which tend to make bold simple statements. One often reads that Muslims pray five times a day, juxtaposed with a picture of a crowded mosque. Anyone who has heard the call to prayer in many Muslim cities will have noted that on the whole life carries on and that there is little evidence of prayer mats. It is more correct to say that Muslims are *called* to prayer five times a day.

This is not to criticise such primary RE textbooks. Learning needs to be along simple lines with younger children and their understanding becomes more sophisticated and differentiated as they meet and assimilate new information. The issue for Christianity is that many teachers find it difficult to discover a similar simple approach. We know too much about it. It is hard to make statements such as 'Christians go to church', as we know not all do, or 'In Christianity babies are baptised', because we know that in some churches they are not.

The most practical response here is to focus on what is normal across the practice of Christian churches, especially the traditional churches, the Roman Catholics, Orthodox and Anglican branches. So, for example, although Quakers and the Salvation Army do not practise baptism or celebrate the Eucharist, this does not prevent baptism and the Eucharist from being seen as normative across the vast range of Christianity now and over the past two millennia. The rule should be: Christianity is what most do and have done in most places in most centuries. What follows is a suggested subject content to form a basis for teaching about Christianity.

### Outline of proposed subject content

| | |
|---|---|
| Beliefs | God, Father, Son and Holy Spirit (the Trinity)<br>The creator and sustainer of the world<br>Just and loving |
| Worship | Different styles of worship, prayer and Bible reading, the Eucharist<br>Distinctive clothes<br>The role of the priest/minister |
| Festivals and seasons | Advent, Christmas, Lent, Mothering Sunday, Easter, Pentecost/Whit, Harvest, Remembrance Sunday |
| Rites of passage/ceremonies to mark stages in an individual life | Baptism, confirmation, marriage and death |
| Special places | Sacred places<br>Pilgrimage |
| The Bible | Structure and translation<br>Old and New Testaments<br>Different types of literature (prophecy, history, poetry, Gospels, etc.) |

|  | As a source of the knowledge of God<br>The use of the Bible in church |
|---|---|
| Key figures | Jesus, Martin Luther King, Mother Teresa, and many others over history<br>Any appropriate local figures |
| Ethics | The Ten Commandments, the two great Commandments (love God and your neighbour)<br>The Sermon on the Mount, forgiveness |
| The church | Both locally and internationally<br>The work of local churches (through contact)<br>The layout of and symbolism in church buildings |

### Questions which might be considered

As we saw in Chapter 8, there are many questions which will arise from pupils and there are others which the teacher may wish to raise for discussion. Some of the questions will focus upon encouraging pupils to look more deeply into their learning about Christianity, others will encourage them to reflect upon themselves and their responses. What follows next is a list of questions which might prove useful, but they are by no means the only ones. It is not suggested that these questions should dictate the teaching agenda but rather that they should be borne in mind and raised when relevant work is being done in class.

- How does belief, in particular Christian belief, affect a person's life?
- What does worship mean to believers?
- Why are some places and occasions sacred to Christians?
- What, for you, would be a special place to think, meditate or pray?
- What qualities do people have which inspire you?
- In what way can Christianity inspire people's lives?
- What makes the Bible a sacred text for Christians?
- In Christianity, what qualities would a 'good' person have?
- What symbols express Christianity?
- What does it mean to belong?

### Teaching Christianity

There are many examples of relevant teaching in the different chapters of this book. Some of the examples in Chapter 7 would be suitable for Key Stage 1. Chapter 10 looks at ways of teaching about Jesus, and Chapter 11 looks at the Bible. Chapter 13 contains material on teaching about Christian festivals and celebrations, and Chapter 14 considers pilgrimage in Christianity. The relationship between belief and action is explored in Chapter 15, and visits to churches are considered in Chapter 17. In Chapters 18 and 19 there is background material on Christianity as a whole and also a more detailed treatment of Christian festivals.

This chapter concludes with a focus upon the very popular topic of baptism. It begins by drawing together background information about baptism as a rite of initiation, and then shows how two teachers, one from Key Stage 1 and the other from Key Stage 2, drew from that source of material those parts which they felt were appropriate to the age and stage of the children they teach.

## *Baptism*

### Background information

Baptism, or christening as it is known popularly, is the Christian rite of initiation or admission to the church and the faith. In more traditional churches, the font in which people are baptised is often placed close to the church door as a symbol of entry. The Gospels record Jesus commanding his disciples to baptise all nations in the name of the Father and the Son and the Holy Spirit. Initially in the very early days of the church all candidates for baptism were adults, but as the church became more settled the babies of members were baptised and infant baptism became the established pattern, so now the large majority of those baptised are infants. Although Quakers and members of the Salvation Army do not practise baptism and Baptists and some other groups will only baptise adults, infant baptism is normative across Christianity.

Baptisms can either take place within a regular service or be held separately. Whatever the setting, it normally involves:

- A statement of belief in the teachings of the Christian faith.
- Promises made by the candidate or on his/her behalf.
- Water.
- Oil.
- A baptismal candle.
- The giving of a Christian name.
- The presence of godparents or sponsors.
- A welcome into membership of the church

The *statement of belief* is normally in the Trinity: God, the Father, God the Son and God the Holy Spirit. The words of the promises will vary but essentially the promise is to turn away from selfish and unkind ways and to follow the example of Jesus.

*Water* is placed in the font and blessed. The candidate is either sprinkled with the water or in some churches totally immersed. The water essentially symbolises both washing and cleaning and new life.

The candidate's head is anointed with *oil* which is a symbol that he/she is being set aside for God.

The *baptismal candle*, which is usually lit from the Easter or Paschal candle, indicates that the baptised person is now a light in the world, as Jesus himself was.

During the baptism, the priest or minister will use the child's *Christian name*: '[Name] I baptise you in the name of the Father and of the Son and of the Holy Spirit.'

Where an infant or a young child is baptised it is normal to have *godparents* or *sponsors* who make the baptismal promises on behalf of the child and also promise to help bring the child up so that he/she is aware of the teachings of the Christian faith.

The service also includes a *welcome* to the newly baptised person into membership of the church.

### Teaching about baptism

Here are two accounts by teachers of how they approached teaching about baptism, one in Key Stage 1 and the other in Key Stage 2.

#### EXAMPLE 1

I teach Year 2 children in a suburban primary school and each year I begin work on 'Beginning and Growing'. This starts with birth, moves into baptism and then on to the Jewish coming of age ceremony, Barmitzvah/Batmitzvah. Children are always happy to bring in photographs of themselves as babies and have an enjoyable time guessing whose each photograph is!

When it comes to looking at baptism I also invite children, if they had been baptised, to bring in photographs of the event. These are always forthcoming and I also receive christening robes, candles, certificates, etc., all of which I am able to use in the teaching. As the children are young and an understanding of baptism can be quite complex I usually focus on a small number of points:

- wearing special clothes for a very special occasion
- being given a Christian name
- the use of water/the font
- the promises (essentially the promise to lead a good life)
- the godparents
- parties afterwards

Year 2 children usually make a church visit in this term so I make a special point of focusing upon the font. I used to perform a pretend baptism with a doll in the classroom but the new Rector is very willing to do one himself: he performs it at the font in church with a doll and children as the parents and godparents. This is even more effective!

The second example of a unit on baptism describes how the subject was approached with Year 5 pupils. This is not from the same school as the first example but it still demonstrates progression in the understanding of the topic.

#### EXAMPLE 2

Early on, before I began this short topic in baptism, I ascertained that the children were quite aware of the main features of baptism: water, candles, promises, godparents and so on. I would therefore build on this existing base to dig a little deeper.

We began by downloading the service of baptism (the Common Worship version) from the Church of England website. The children read this through first and then picked out any items which they found interesting or important. Here they focused on the role played by the wider congregation of the church in the service, on the Decision, on the use of water and the emphasis upon light.

My plan therefore was to focus on three aspects:

- the Decision
- the symbolism of water
- the symbolism of light

The language of the Decision needed some 'unpacking'. We looked carefully at what could be meant by 'the devil and all rebellion against God', 'the deceit and corruption of evil' and considered what those sins might be which 'separate us from God and neighbour'. This proved a very fruitful discussion with evidence of considerable thought on the part of the children.

We explored the symbolism of water through looking at the part it plays in ordinary life: washing, cleansing, sustaining life and the creation of new life – watering a wilting plant, the transformation of a dry desert to living vegetation after a heavy rainstorm. The children began to sense the power of the water symbol in baptism – both cleaning and washing away previous wrongdoing and in nourishing the new Christian life in the individual.

Children were fascinated by the Easter candle used at baptisms as the source of light for all the individual candles of the baptismal candidates. We looked at the symbolism of light – to guide, to reveal or show up, to comfort – and began to see why candles were given at baptism – so that candidates should reflect in their attitudes, values and behaviour the light of Christ.

We ended the unit with a visit from the Rector who is one of our school governors. She gave a very interesting – and often amusing – talk about her role in baptisms and also dealt with some very searching questions from the pupils.

# 10  Teaching about Jesus

Any discussion with a group of teachers about work with young children on the life of Jesus shows that this is a controversial area. There is the clear problem for many teachers that the historical events of the life of Jesus are inseparable from a religious interpretation of them: that Jesus is the Son of God is assumed in the New Testament accounts. Some of the concepts too are difficult: teachers of very young children often have great difficulty in explaining what angels are to the more persistent of their young questioners. There are uncertainties about the helpfulness of telling miracle stories and parables. Very frequently these problems are resolved by a policy of ignoring – either the life of Jesus or the perceived problems!

## What do we know about Jesus?

What we know of the historical Jesus comes to us from the pages of the New Testament and principally from the four Gospels of Matthew, Mark, Luke and John. As far as we know, there are no contemporary references to Jesus in Greek, Roman or Jewish sources, though there are later (brief) references in Suetonius, Tacitus, Pliny and Josephus.

In the New Testament apart from the four Gospels there is very little interest shown in the life of Jesus, excluding his death and resurrection. St Paul, for example, is much more concerned with the significance of Jesus in the saving purpose of God than with what he said or did in Palestine. It is in the Gospels that we get the only detail.

Although there are only four Gospels in the New Testament, many others were written, often long after the events, which did not find their way into the New Testament. They form part of a great body of pious writing, including also lives of the Virgin Mary, which grew up in various parts of the Christian church. For school purposes it seems best to restrict our attention to the four authoritative Gospels.

If we are looking for an account of the life of Jesus, then we are bound to be disappointed. Gospels are not biographies. Gospel means literally 'good news' and so, for example, St Mark's Gospel is really 'The Good News of Jesus Christ according to St Mark'. Gospels therefore are proclamations. John, towards the end of his Gospel, makes this very clear: 'These [i.e. stories] are written that you might believe that Jesus is the Son of God; and that believing you might have life through his name' (John chapter 20 verse 31).

Gospels are therefore works with a confessional purpose and the material they include is selected for that end. Mark, for example, the earliest Gospel to be written, begins with Jesus at the age of 30, at the start of his mission. Matthew and Luke start the story much earlier with the birth of Jesus because they clearly feel this to be significant in their presentation of Jesus. Matthew, for instance, seems to be writing for a Jewish audience and so one of his purposes is to present Jesus as the expected one who fulfils the hopes of the Jewish people. His account of Jesus' birth is full of quotations from the Old Testament to show that Jesus is the one who fulfils the old prophecies. Luke dedicates his Gospel to one Theophilus, clearly a non-Jew, and the tone of his Gospel is very different, with material selected appropriate to his purpose. It is only in Luke that we get the parables of the Good Samaritan and the Prodigal Son and the story of Zacchaeus, selected presumably by Luke to reflect Jesus' concern for those outside the normative Judaism of his day – a theme which would be of particular relevance to Greek and Roman readers.

The Gospel writers therefore selected their material very carefully for a purpose and that purpose was to convince their readers that the person of whom they were reading was none other than the Son of God. The events, carefully selected, are therefore permeated by this conviction. It is very difficult to separate the Jesus of history from the Christ of faith.

It is clear too that underlying the events recorded in the Gospels are difficult and complicated themes. Jesus is not another prophet; anyone who sees Jesus has seen God. Jesus' death on the cross is not just another sad end to a noble man (like Socrates): it is the most significant event in the history of the world. Jesus is not just to be followed as a moral teacher who presented a compassionate and loving way of life; anyone who possesses him possesses eternal life.

These considerations tend to make the Gospels into books for adults rather than for children. This, of course, does not mean that all the stories of the life of Jesus are unsuitable for children. It does however place the onus upon teachers, when they select stories to tell to their children, to ask themselves whether the stories in question will be *stepping stones* or *stumbling blocks* to a *mature* understanding of the life and significance of Jesus.

**What about miracles?**

The Gospels are full of stories of miracles, be they stories of healing, raisings from the dead or nature miracles using miracle in the sense of an event for which there is no readily available natural explanation. That there are many miracles recorded in the Gospels is not surprising, because, to people of the time of Jesus, the working of miracles was a sign of special power or authority. It was not that miracles were unique to Jesus; miraculous workings are recorded of many other figures in the ancient world.

An unusual feature in the teaching of Jesus, however, is a definite attempt to cast a veil of secrecy over the miracles. Jesus did not want to attract followers merely because they were impressed by his miracles. His motive was not to impress but always invariably lay in his compassion: seeing a widowed mother burying her only son and so on. The miracles nevertheless are presented in the Gospels as signs, at least for those with eyes to see. 'If I with the finger of God cast out devils, then the Kingdom of God is come upon you' (Luke chapter 11 verse 20). The miracles were seen as evidence that Jesus, in his ministry, was driving back the powers of evil.

The miracle stories pose a number of problems to modern readers. There is the problem that many of the thought-forms of the world in which Jesus lived and in which the Gospels were written are different from those most people have today. This is particularly significant in two ways: in the notion of demon possession and in the general attitude towards the miraculous. A number of the healing miracle stories are tied up with the concept of demon possession. There was a pervasive view in the ancient world that there were personal evil powers (demons) who were in a constant state of warfare with God: evil versus good. When they could, these devils or demons entered into individuals and possessed them. The story of the Gadarene demoniac (Luke chapter 8 verses 26–40) is a good example of this. Most people today would be more inclined to interpret these stories as instances of various mental or physical illnesses rather than subscribe to the notion of demon possession. Older children can look at some of these miracle stories and discuss them. Younger children are not really able to do this.

Allied with this is the general attitude to the miraculous. Whereas to the first readers of the gospels the miracle stories would have provided a strong incentive to believe the claims about Jesus, to many readers today the miracle stories operate in the reverse way: they cast doubts in many minds about the truth of *all* the Gospel stories.

This can often be detected in the thinking of young children who have had a heavy exposure to the miracle stories of Jesus. The following extract from a conversation between 6/7-year-olds was overheard in their classroom as they were making up their own play of the story of Jesus feeding the 5,000 people which they had heard in collective worship that morning:

Jamie:　'Who's doing the magic?'
Emma:　'I will! I will!'
Danny:　'No you can't, you can't. You're a girl. I will, I will, I will. I'm doing the magic. I'm Jesus.'

Jesus the magic man! This characterisation of Jesus as a super-magician is very common among young children – and older ones too.

While it may be useful and interesting to discuss the whole idea of the miraculous with much older children, drawing on both the miracle stories in the Gospels and more modern (claimed) instances at, say, Lourdes, younger children are not really able to deal with it adequately and they file it away into the compartment of their minds labelled 'magic', where it tends to stay. When teachers of younger children consider telling a series of miracle stories to their classes – and the temptation can be very great – again the question which they should ask is whether the experience will be a *stepping stone* or a *stumbling block* to a mature understanding of the life and significance of Jesus.

**What about parables?**

Just as teachers often decide to tell a series of stories on the miracles of Jesus, so they often do the same with the parables of Jesus. After all, they are good lively stories, well loved and popular, and, of course, it is easy to choose one to tell each week in story time.

Because parables are stories about everyday life – or at least everyday life in the time of Jesus – and talk of vineyards, farmers sowing their seed, people travelling on donkeys and so on, it is often forgotten how difficult they are. On the one hand they tell a story of everyday life, but they really point to a meaning beyond that; and the problem is to move from the first level to the second. This is not a new problem: many in the crowds who heard Jesus tell the parables took them as fascinating stories. Not all, as Jesus himself put it, had eyes to see or ears to hear.

Immediately after the results of Goldman's research (see Chapter 2) were made available, many teachers claimed that all parables were beyond the reasonable comprehension of children under the age of 11 or so, when their thinking was beginning to cope with abstract ideas. This is certainly an overstatement but it does nevertheless make a serious point: if the parables are told so that the children can begin to understand something of the teaching of Jesus, then there is a problem because they are being asked to deal with the complex exercise of taking one story and then seeing its meaning in another completely different realm.

An example of this might be the parable of the ten maidens (Matthew chapter 25 verses 1–13). The story is about ten girls who take their lamps to go out to meet the bridegroom at a wedding. As the bridegroom is late in coming they all fall asleep. At midnight they are awoken by the shout that he is about to arrive and would they go out to meet him. At this point five of the girls realise that the oil in their lamps is used up and they ask the other five to lend them some. The other five whose lamps are full of oil decline to do so in case there is not enough to provide for all ten, and they send the foolish ones off to buy some more oil. While they are away at the shop, the bridegroom arrives and the five wise girls accompany him with their lamps into the marriage and the door is shut. When the foolish girls return with their fresh oil they find themselves excluded from the marriage.

In many ways this is a very attractive story for younger children. It involves looking at wedding customs at the time of Jesus; it has the excitement of the girls falling asleep and some being caught out; it has the satisfaction of the very simple justice of the unprepared girls being excluded from the marriage. 'It serves them right' is a common response from children! However, the parable is really dealing with other matters.

The parable centres around the notion of 'being ready' and is addressed to the hearers as a personal question. Underlying it is the idea of the Kingdom (or rule) of God which Jesus came to announce. At the centre of Jesus' teaching is the notion that God will break into human history and establish his reign. When that will be is unknown, so people should be in a state of readiness, both moral and spiritual. Those who are not, the parable seems to be saying, will be excluded. What seems at first sight to be an interesting story of ten girls at a wedding is really an awesome warning.

Few would dispute that this story as a parable is considerably beyond the level of understanding of young children. This one is not an isolated example and most of the parables are of similar difficulty to this, so great care is necessary in the selection of which ones to use.

Some of the parables are suitable for use with younger children. The Lost Coin (Luke chapter 15 verses 8–10) and the Lost Sheep (Luke chapter 15 verses 4–7) both have the same themes of the preciousness of the object lost, the great efforts made to find it and the great rejoicing when it is finally found, and so make the same point that every individual is immensely precious to God. The parable of the Lost (or Prodigal) Son (Luke chapter 15 verses 11–32) is similar in that it emphasises the complete forgiveness of the father for his son who has rejected him, but it also moves one step beyond to chide the pious and the good (in the figure of the elder brother) who do not share the same joy as the father. The Good Samaritan (Luke chapter 10 verses 25–37) too with its emphasis upon caring and compassion is also suitable, though it could well be looked at in more detail with 10-year-olds and older children to explore the idea of neighbourliness.

A serious problem with popular stories like the parables is one of *repetition*. The Good Samaritan and the Prodigal Son are told over and over again in class and it is quite possible to hear them fifteen to twenty times in school before the age of 11. Repetition of some stories (like the Birth stories) seems in most cases only to increase their appeal. In other cases it can lead to boredom. Teachers need to be sensitive to this and this may mean not using a particular story with younger children if that will spoil it for a later time when it may be more appropriate. The principle again is whether the use of a particular parable is likely to be a *stepping stone* or a *stumbling block* to a mature understanding of the teaching of Jesus.

## Possible approaches to the life of Jesus

### Festivals

Perhaps the commonest approach to the life of Jesus is through work on the two festivals of Christmas and Easter. Practically every school does some work in preparation for Christmas and a number of approaches are suggested in detail for different age groups in Chapter 13. Easter does not have quite the popularity of Christmas in schools but it is still a very common topic. An approach to Easter through the use of artefacts is described in Chapter 17. There are other lesser festivals celebrating events in the life of Jesus which many schools use either in classroom work or in collective worship, and these are included in Chapter 19.

Here is an example of a topic on Easter described by a teacher of Year 2 (6–7 years) children. She selected a number of relevant artefacts which served as concrete objects upon which the background stories of the festival could be hung.

When I was planning my work for the spring term I noticed in my diary that Easter was very early and that term did not end until the Wednesday of Holy Week. This seemed a good opportunity to make a proper attempt – one which I had often avoided – to tackle Easter and the events which led up to it. This involves a considerable number of stories and I feared that they might become all jumbled up in the children's minds. To try to avoid this I decided to select seven objects upon which I could focus or cluster the stories. The objects which I chose were:

> Palm Cross
> Maundy money
> Hot cross bun
> Picture of St Veronica
> A cross or crucifix
> Easter egg
> Picture of Mary Magdalene in the garden

I began the work by showing the children a Palm Cross which one of the class provided. I managed to 'undo' it without tearing it to show that it is in fact one leaf and we talked about palm trees. Nigel, who had brought the Palm Cross, told the class how he had acquired it the previous year which he remembered very clearly because a donkey had been brought into the church. A number of other children too remembered that they had been there as well. At story time the next day I told the story of Jesus' entry into Jerusalem in a dramatic and colourful way.

I had the good fortune to be able to borrow one of the Maundy coins which the Queen distributes on Maundy Thursday together with a picture I had of the occasion. The children had the opportunity to handle the coin and inspect it closely. I talked about the picture and encouraged the children to interpret what was happening. They were able to establish quite a lot of the story from the clues in the picture and I completed the rest. I then explained that originally the monarch used to wash the feet of poor people and I tried to find out from the children why that should be. On a subsequent occasion I told the story about Jesus washing his disciples' feet in the upper room.

It is amazing how early in Lent you can buy hot cross buns in the shops. I bought a few and we also made some in class. Most of the children knew the nursery rhyme *Hot Cross Buns* and from this I told them in a very simple way that on Good Friday Jesus had been put to death on a cross. The horrors of crucifixion was not an issue I wanted to raise or discuss with the children. I had a crucifix on the interest table and I felt that was enough.

I had a photograph of the Stations of the Cross from a modern local church which depicted St Veronica wiping Jesus' face. I told the children of Jesus' journey carrying his own cross from his trial to Calvary and described the crowd shouting abuse at him as he dragged himself along. Then out of the hostile crowd came a woman who wiped his brow with a cloth upon which his sweat made the impression of his features. The children found the story very moving but some, remembering the warm welcome given to Jesus on Palm Sunday, could not understand the change in the mood of the crowd. This provoked considerable discussion among the children as many had had similar experiences. 'Some days everybody likes you, other days the same people can be very nasty' was the way one child put it.

Although I realise that the Resurrection of Jesus is not accepted as a 'fact' by everyone I felt that I could not leave Jesus on the cross. Of the various Resurrection stories in the Bible I chose the one where Mary Magdalene, having found the tomb empty and thinking that Jesus' body has been stolen, begins to search first in the garden. She meets the man who she thinks is the gardener but finds it is Jesus.

We talked too about Easter eggs, both the type made out of chocolate and those which are hard boiled. We talked quite a bit about why we give eggs at Easter and the experience of seeing the hatchings gave a few of the children a glimmering. We made some Easter eggs ourselves by hard boiling them and then painting them. We also looked at the custom of egg rolling on Easter Day, rolling away the stone from the door of the tomb.

It is always difficult to evaluate work of this kind with young children – in the end you never quite know how they make sense of the stories. However, it seems that by selecting a few stories to tell and then relating them to a number of concrete objects the children seemed to be much more highly motivated in the work and to be able to talk about it with greater interest and understanding than I had noticed previously.

### Who is Jesus?

Over the age range from 4 to 11 years there is inevitably going to be a wide range of approaches, starting perhaps at 4 with the idea that Jesus was a very important man, to finding at 11 a number of pupils comparing Matthew's and Luke's accounts of the birth of Jesus and discussing their respective standpoints.

With children between 4 and 7, in addition to work on the life Jesus lived (home, school, games and so on) and the normal work on festivals, Jesus should be presented under such headings as 'The Friendly Man' or 'The Man who Cared'.

### 'The Friendly Man'

Suitable stories would include:

- Zacchaeus (Luke chapter 19 verses 1–9) – the Roman collaborator ostracised by his fellow citizens but accepted by Jesus.
- The Little Children (Luke chapter 18 verses 15–17) – Jesus receives the children his disciples had tried to send away.
- Parables such as the Lost Coin (Luke chapter 15 verses 8–10), the Lost Sheep (Luke chapter 15 verses 4–7) or the Prodigal Son (Luke chapter 15 verses 11–32) – all of which emphasise the openness of God to everyone.

With older children it is useful to begin to build up the more complex picture of Jesus being loved by many for his teaching and his compassion yet at the same time becoming an object of hatred to others. Two useful stories to use in this context would be:

- The Call of Levi (Luke chapter 5 verses 27–32).
- Jesus' feet are anointed in the house of Simon the Pharisee (Luke chapter 7 verses 36–40).

This can be further developed with 10-year-olds and older children by looking at the plots hatched by some of the religious leaders to have Jesus executed.

### Friends of Jesus

Another approach, particularly with young children, could be 'Friends of Jesus'. Suitable stories could include:

His disciples:
e.g. Simon Peter and Andrew        Mark chapter 1 verses 16–20
                                   Luke chapter 5 verses 1–11
Levi/Matthew                       Luke chapter 5 verses 27–32

Little children:                   Luke chapter 18 verses 15–17
Zacchaeus:                         Luke chapter 19 verses 1–9
Mary and Martha:                   Luke chapter 10 verses 38–41
Joseph of Arimathaea:              Luke chapter 23 verses 50–56
The man who lent his donkey:       Luke chapter 19 verses 28–40

With older children it is possible to develop this work by looking more closely at the implications of being a 'Friend of Jesus' with particular regard to the idea of 'discipleship'.

With older children, in addition to the two approaches already described which can be developed for children in the 9-plus age group, other approaches to 'who is Jesus' can be developed.

### Jesus the Messiah

One of the most startling features of the gospels is Jesus' reluctance to answer direct questions about the origin of his authority. A good starting point would be the highly symbolic story of the Temptations of Jesus (Luke chapter 4 verses 1–13) in which he is confronted with three different approaches to his ministry, all of which he rejects. This could be linked in with the expectations of messiahship which were current at that period.

### Jesus the miracle worker

With children able to deal with the issues, it would be sensible to consider miracles perhaps by exploring the following questions:

What do we understand by miracles?
Are there any contemporary examples heard by the pupils?
How do we distinguish between healing miracles and nature miracles?
What motives do the gospel writers attribute to Jesus in performing the miracles?
How do we respond to them?
What about the claimed miracles at shrines such as Lourdes?

### Jesus the teacher

With children aged 9–11 a valuable approach to exploring an aspect of the teaching of Jesus would be to study and discuss selections from the Sermon on the Mount (Matthew chapters 5–7):

The Beatitudes (Matthew chapter 5 verses 1–12)
Salt and Light (Matthew chapter 5 verses 13–16)
The New Law – good lies in the heart not just in outward action
'Thou shalt not kill' (Matthew chapter 5 verses 21–22)
'Love your enemies' (Matthew chapter 5 verses 43–48)
Real Religion: against being a hypocrite, almsgiving, praying and fasting (Matthew chapter 6 verses 1–18)
'Don't be anxious' (Matthew chapter 6 verses 24–34)
Parables of the rock and the sand (Matthew chapter 7 verses 24–29)

In this approach there is always the great danger of slipping over into sentimentality. This can easily be avoided but it is best to bear it in mind.

### Parables

It has already been noted how complex some of the parables are and that even those which are within the grasp of children of 10 years of age and older are often spoiled by frequent repetition. One teacher of a class of 11-year-olds who was confronted with this situation describes how she dealt with it:

> My class is not one that could be described as easy. In fact, I think that in my ten years of teaching it is the most difficult I have had. During the autumn term there was considerable concern among the school governors and the teaching staff about the instances of 'racist' behaviour in the school.

The staff agreed to adopt a number of strategies some of which might be described as direct and others indirect. One of my strategies was to focus some of my teaching upon the theme of neighbourliness, to link this with RE and as far as I could to try to involve as much discussion work as possible. I began with the Christian principle 'love your neighbour as yourself' and tried to explore with the class the meaning of the term 'love'. As I anticipated, this was difficult at first because of its immediate association with romance, boy friends/girl friends etc., but when we had worked through this and moved on to the way you treat and regard friends then things became much easier. Discussion, which was now much more relaxed because it was arising from first-hand experience, brought out a number of points – you must not split on your mates, you'd share things with them, you'd stand by them in a fight. They'd do the same for you. There was no shortage of examples, some of which I would have preferred not to have heard! So here we had, from the children themselves, the notion of loving your neighbour as yourself!

The next step could be more difficult. How do you define 'neighbour'? So we talked about perceptions of 'neighbours'. 'Next door neighbour' was seen to be too narrow a definition; in the end it seemed that the term 'neighbour' seemed to be synonymous with 'friend' and 'family'.

In order to move beyond this to develop a more inclusive notion of neighbour, I told the story of the Good Samaritan with some background on the Samaritans and the Jews preceding it. Unfortunately, but not unexpectedly, most of the children had heard the story *many*, *many*, times before and it had lost its freshness for them! I therefore asked them to write it in their own terms, not talking about Samaritans and Jews but telling it in the way Jesus might have done had he been a current resident in south London. This was a little more exciting but I must say that in general the results were rather disappointing but there was one exception. Alvin, who was generally very quiet and self-contained in class, wrote a story which did make the same point in answer to the question 'and who is my neighbour?' Technically the quality was poor so I have put it into acceptable English:

> There was a Front [National Front] rally in Tower Hamlets. A man who was speaking left. He put some leaflets in his pocket. They were sticking out so you could see them. He was walking down a street by some factories. He met some students who were anti-racists. They saw the leaflets in his pocket. They beat him up and tore up the leaflets. The man was lying on the ground. A bit later another man came along. He was a Front man too. He saw the beaten-up man and he saw the torn-up leaflets. He was frightened so he ran home. A bit later a black man called Alvin came along. He was driving a big car. He stopped. He saw the leaflets. He put the man who was still unconscious on his back seat. He drove him to the hospital. He rang the man's wife. Then he waited in the hospital till she came. Then he went home.

I read this out to the class and opened up discussion. The change was dramatic. 'He was mad! The Front hates blacks.' 'Should have left him there.' Only very gradually and only from a few children did ideas come that some human concerns are deeper than any ideology ('He might have died if he'd left him in the road') or that acts like this might in a gradual way begin to change attitudes ('That Front man couldn't be so anti-black after that').

I found the topic stimulating and challenging. I don't know how successful it was and I don't really know how you judge success in any area like this. I think that it made some of the children think about their attitudes. I think too that in areas like this, areas of attitude change, it is like water dripping on a stone. Any change will be very slow and very gradual.

# 11 Sacred books with special reference to the Bible

For many years up until the 1960s the content of RE was largely drawn from the Bible. This reflected the confessional nature of RE at that time. Modern approaches in RE emphasise much more a study of religions as living activities. The sacred books which underlie all the religions still remain very important because they provide much of the source information and the authority upon which the faiths are built. Hence it is important that teachers have some understanding of the nature of sacred books so that they can see their crucial role in a religious tradition.

In this chapter there is a general introduction to the sacred books of the principal faiths and then an increasing focus on the Bible, partly because it is the sacred book of Judaism as well as Christianity and has strong affinities with Islam, and partly because of its importance in the development of British culture. The chapter will consider how the Bible is used, the different types of literature within it and its transmission from papyrus scrolls to the books of today. The information is given at the teacher's level and it is hoped that teachers will be able to draw from it to plan work for their classes. The chapter ends with some classroom pointers.

**Sacred books**

All the major faiths have sacred texts which they draw upon for knowledge of God and the unseen world, for guidance upon how to live in the world and as a means of kindling devotion.

Buddhism:      several, e.g. Pali Canon, Diamond Sutra
Christianity:  Bible
Hinduism:      several, of which the Bhagavad Gita is the most popular
Islam:         Qur'an
Judaism:       Tenakh (Law, Prophets and Writings)
Sikhism:       Guru Granth Sahib

In all traditions the sacred texts are set apart from all other writing as being special. In some traditions this even extends to the physical treatment of the texts themselves. In Sikhism, for example, the Guru Granth Sahib is treated as though it is a living Guru and taken to a special bedchamber each night and brought back in the morning. In Judaism, when the sacred scrolls of the Torah are brought out of the Ark to be read with the synagogue service, no one is allowed to touch them; the reader has to follow the lines using a yad. In Islam, the Qur'an should not be touched with unwashed hands and when not in use should be wrapped in cloths and stored on a high shelf. More details of these traditions are given in Chapter 18.

## The Bible in Christianity, Judaism and Islam

The word 'Bible' originates from the Greek word *biblos* and means literally 'The Book'. Although seen by many as primarily the Christian sacred text it has close associations with Judaism and Islam; in fact the Qur'an refers to Jews and Christians as 'People of the Book'.

For the Christian faith, the Bible is regarded as a collection of books, sixty-six in all, which reached its final form, called the Canon, when it was accepted by the Council of Carthage in AD397. It consists of two Testaments, the Old and the New, of which the New Testament has always been seen as the more important because it contains the Gospels, which are the principal records of Christ, and the Acts of the Apostles and the many letters which present a growing picture of Christ's life and teaching in the Graeco-Roman world.

For all Christians, the Bible is a special book, but within the Christian community there are different ways of interpreting it.

The Jewish Bible has three divisions – the Torah (the Law), the Nevi'm (the Prophets) and the Ketuvim (the Writings) – and is often referred to as the Tenakh (TNK). Of these three divisions the Torah, the Law, is central. In fact the Tenakh is the same as the Old Testament as the greater number of books in the latter is caused by the splitting up of texts. Practically all of the Tenakh was written in Hebrew and in Orthodox synagogues only Hebrew is ever used in the readings. In Liberal or Reform synagogues the readings are usually a mixture of Hebrew and the vernacular language. An important part of the education of Jewish children is learning Hebrew so that they can read the scriptures in the original and, in particular, so that they can read a passage of scripture in Hebrew aloud.

In Islam, the sacred text is, of course, the Qur'an. This was revealed to Muhammad by the Angel Jibreel (Gabriel in the Judaeo-Christian tradition) early in the seventh century AD and is seen by Muslims as the revealed word of God. Because of its status as the revealed word of God and because even the most faithful translations inevitably make changes or shifts in meaning, Muslims study and read the Qur'an in Arabic. Again, because of its importance as the revealed word of God, many Muslims learn and can recite the whole Qur'an by heart.

The Bible is respected by Muslims because they acknowledge that in its original form it was revealed by God (Allah) and many of the key figures, from Adam to Jesus, appear in the Qur'an. However, they feel that the original revelation has become distorted and, in any case, it is incomplete. The final and full revelation of God came to Muhammad, so by definition the Bible only takes people part of the way in their understanding of God and his will.

### Interpreting the writings

Although all Christians and Jews would regard their sacred texts as authoritative, there is in both religions a variety of interpretations of the scriptures. Two examples, one from Judaism and one from Christianity, demonstrate a conservative approach and a liberal approach.

First, in the Torah there are prohibitions against the eating of certain foods which are described as unclean or non-kosher. These would include pork, animals which do not have cloven hooves or chew the cud, shellfish and fish without fins or scales. Orthodox Jews will be inclined to avoid all these foods on the grounds that God in the Torah has forbidden them and God ought always to be obeyed. Liberal Jews will be more inclined to ignore the injunctions on the grounds that they were appropriate at that point in history but now, with modern methods of food preservation, they are no longer relevant.

Within Christianity a similar situation arises over the place of women within the church. Some passages in the New Testament would seem to suggest that it is inappropriate for women to be leaders in the church. Some Christians see this as a truth for all time and that God intended it; others see it as representative of views on the role of women in the first century and no longer relevant to considerations of women's roles in the church today.

### How is the Bible used?

Within the Christian tradition, the Bible occupies a crucial and central place. In one sense it is perhaps the one and only possession that the varying Christian churches and denominations hold in common. It is interesting to note that in the Chapel of Unity in Coventry Cathedral, a chapel devoted to prayer for Christian unity, there is only one object – a Bible, the one thing that all Christians share.

Essentially the Bible is the chief vehicle for knowledge and learning of the Christian faith, so it is used for teaching about God, about his activity in the world and about Jesus Christ. It provides guidance for those who seek it about how to live out a Christian life in the world. Many people claim that reading it has provided support for them in difficult circumstances.

In the public arena, the Bible is very prominent in church worship. It usually stands on a reading desk or lectern which in England is often shaped like an eagle or pelican, with the Bible placed on the outstretched wings. These two birds are symbolic: the eagle conveying strength and the pelican self-giving love (it was believed that when a pelican plucked its breast feathers to line its nest, it was in fact plucking out its own flesh to feed its young). Within the Eucharist, normally three passages are read out to the congregation, the first from the Old Testament, the second from the New Testament and the third and final one from one of the four Gospels. The three are usually held together by a common theme. All are important but the final reading from the Gospels is especially significant because it will contain the words of Jesus himself. To emphasise this significance the congregation will stand for the Gospel reading, and at a main service the Bible will be carried in procession to a central point in the church where all can see it and hear the reading. The address or sermon in the service is usually based on one of the Bible readings. In some churches, a Bible study group meets during the week to study passages more deeply.

Many individuals also read the Bible privately at home. There are agencies such as the Scripture Union and the Bible Reading Fellowship which provide explanatory notes for each daily reading. Others claim to find great comfort in times of need from certain passages. Particularly significant passages valued by many are Psalms 23 and 27, Matthew chapter 6 verses 25–26 and John chapter 3 verse 16.

Although the Bible plays this supreme role within Christianity, there are other works which many Christians also turn to for inspiration, comfort and support. Here might be mentioned great Christian classics such as *The Cloud of Unknowing*, the poems of St John of the Cross and John Bunyan's *The Pilgrim's Progress*.

Because of the value that Christians place upon the Bible, great efforts are made by various Christian organisations to ensure that it is readily and easily available. There are many different versions to choose from, it comes in all shapes and sizes and, of course, languages too. The Bible Society is active around the world and is especially concerned to ensure that the Bible is translated into every known language. The Gideon Society ensures that every hotel bedroom in the United Kingdom possesses one and there are an increasing number of Bible storybooks suitable for children on the market.

**Understanding the Bible**

The Bible as a collection of sixty-six books, thirty-nine in the Old Testament and twenty-seven in the New Testament, was composed over a very long period and written by a wide range of authors. Many scholars would judge that the earliest piece in the Old Testament dates from the twelfth century BC and the most recent part of the New Testament from the second century AD. Within that sweep of material there is a range of different types of literature which have different purposes.

Take the case of the 8-year-old boy who was browsing in an encyclopaedia on the origins of life and asked his teacher which was true, the Bible's account of creation or Darwin's – in other words, which was true, what the encyclopaedia said or what he was taught in his Sunday school. The only criterion on which he was able to judge the truth of a thing was 'did it really happen?' Was the universe created in six days? If the answer is yes then the story is true, if not then the story is false. Now the large majority of Christians would not see these early chapters of the Book of Genesis as in any way a scientific account yet they would want to say they are true in another sense: that what they say about the world and people is profoundly true.

This example highlights the fact that the Bible is made up of different types of literature which have different purposes – myths, legends, stories, prophecy, history, law, poetry, letters. It is important that children as their understanding develops should be introduced to this so as to help them to escape the trap of literalism (as instanced above) into which they will almost certainly wander. This will enable them to move into a more mature understanding of biblical literature. The aim is not that they will accept the truth of the Bible but that they can appreciate it in a much fuller, richer and more complex way and not dismiss it for inadequate reasons.

### Myths

In this context myth is not used in the everyday way of describing an untrue story but in the sense of a story which intends to convey a truth. There are many stories of this kind – why the robin has a red breast, how the leopard got its spots, why the giraffe has a long neck and so on. These are all stories to explain some phenomenon in the world around us.

More developed myths can be found among the Greeks. The story of Persephone gives an account of why there are seasons, seed time and harvest. A particularly interesting Greek myth is that of Pandora and the whispering box. This can be found in most collections of Greek myths. Briefly told, the story is about a young woman, Pandora, who lives in the newly made world, a world of joy and happiness, without pain, sorrow or disease. In this paradise she lives a carefree life of bliss with her husband and their friends. This is interrupted by the arrival of the messenger of the gods, Hermes, carrying a heavy box. He asks Pandora and her husband if he might leave it with them for a few days until he can collect it. The only condition is that it must not be opened. Pandora is obsessed by the thought of the contents of the box. She sits by it, she pores over it, she speculates about its contents and she becomes convinced that whatever is inside is alive and is begging her to let it out. She is reminded of the god's prohibition but in the end can resist no longer. She opens the box. Instantly out pour unpleasant fly-like creatures which sting Pandora and her companions. Their laughter turns to shouts of pain and they turn on each other in anger. In panic Pandora slams the box shut but it is too late – the bearers of pain, disease and unhappiness are already released into the world. Only one creature remains in the box and this Pandora also sets free. This is gentle and moth-like and flies from one to another healing their stings. This last creature is Hope.

At a superficial level this is a pleasant story, but a closer look suggests that it is offering an analysis of why there is pain, discord and disharmony in the world. Why is it that there is warfare and conflict? This analysis places the cause firmly *within* people, in their disobedience to the divine command, in their pride and self-centredness. The myth of Pandora is the means of communicating this analysis.

The Creation stories in Genesis chapters 1, 2 and 3 operate in the same sort of way. Chapter 1 with its magnificent account of creation in six days is concerned with three main issues: that there is *purpose* in creation ('and God said "let there be light" etc.') – it did not just happen by chance; that there is *order* in creation; and that the creation, the physical world, is *good* ('and God saw that it was good'). Chapter 2, which is in fact a second account of creation, differing in some respects of order from the first account, emphasises the creation of man and woman and their relationship to the created order. It introduces too the picture of the Garden of Eden, an earthly paradise of harmony and peace. This paves the way for the story of the Fall in Chapter 3. The writer wants to account for the difference between the human situation we all experience, which encompasses suffering, disease, death and disharmony, and that which must have been the intention of a loving Creator (as symbolised by Eden). The writer frames this analysis in the story of the eating of the forbidden fruit from the tree of the knowledge of good and evil. The serpent tempts the woman to eat the fruit with the words 'you shall not surely die: for God doth know that in the day you ate thereof, then your eyes shall be opened, and you shall be as gods, knowing good and evil' (Genesis chapter 3 verse 5). In other words, the analysis places the cause firmly within people: the cause is human pride, man's desire to be always at the centre. This, the story suggests, is at the root of human problems.

When we want to ask questions about the truth of these stories we are not therefore asking whether there was a Garden of Eden, a first man and woman or a tree of the knowledge of good and evil, but whether the analysis of why things are as they are is true or helpful.

### Legends

A legend is usually defined as a story which has a basis in history but which has become exaggerated. Examples of this are the stories of such figures as Robin Hood and Davy Crockett ('killed him a bear when he was only three').

Given the ancient literature in parts of the Bible, and allowing for a period of oral transmission, it would be surprising if the Bible did not contain examples. Samson is perhaps the outstanding example. An Israelite folk hero, Samson was renowned for his courage and for his considerable strength. He is best known for his battles against the Philistines, his relationship with Delilah and the connection between his strength and his uncut hair. Among the stories which are recorded about him in the Book of Judges chapters 13 to 16 are two which seem to have the touch of legend about them:

- Judges chapter 15 verses 14–17. Samson is bound by his fellow countrymen and handed over to the Philistines who are ruling over the country. When he is delivered to the Philistines he breaks his bonds and seeing a new jawbone of an ass lying on the ground, he picks it up to use as a weapon. And with the weapon he slew *one thousand* men.
- Judges chapter 16 verses 1–3. Samson's overnight presence in Gaza is noticed by the inhabitants, who plot to kill him at dawn. Samson rises from bed at midnight and, finding the city gates locked, picks up the doors of the gates of the city with the two posts and with the bar as well and, hoisting them on to his shoulders, carries them to the top of the hill by Hebron.

There is nothing surprising about the fact that there are legends: it is just something to bear in mind.

### Stories

There are in the Bible a number of books which were written for a special purpose and were not intended to be historical accounts. Notable among these are the books of Jonah, Ruth and Daniel. All are firmly embedded in the historical situations in which they were written and, as these are largely unfamiliar to most modern readers, it is not surprising that their purpose is misunderstood.

#### Jonah and Ruth

Jonah and Ruth both appear to arise out of the same series of events in the history of Israel. Briefly told, in 587 BC the Kingdom of Judah was overcome by Nebuchadnezzar, Jerusalem was captured and the people taken into exile in Babylon hundreds of miles from their native land. It was a time of great bitterness for the Jewish people and also a time of much religious questioning. Why had God allowed this to happen to His chosen people? Was he less powerful than the gods of Babylon? With the help of their prophets the Jewish people came to see purpose in their exile. It was not a sign of God's weakness, rather of his power and uniqueness. Rather it was a punishment on them for their complacency and their unwillingness to share their knowledge of God among the nations. The prophet who above all fostered this is unknown to us by name and is referred to as Second Isaiah or Isaiah of Babylon, as his writings appear in the prophecy of Isaiah chapters 40 to 55. He speaks towards the end of the sixty years of exile. The Jewish people, he says, have learnt their lesson and God has forgiven them (Isaiah chapter 40 verse 1). He speaks of God working through the events of history. Just as he caused the Jews to go into exile so he is now arranging the events for their return. He is raising up a young king, Cyrus, who will overthrow the Babylonian empire and replace it with his own, the Persian empire. He will permit the Jews to return to their land to rebuild Jerusalem and fulfil their vocation as the chosen people to bring the knowledge of God to the whole world.

In 537 Cyrus allowed the Jews to return. Not all did, as many had put down deep roots in Babylon and after sixty years of exile few were alive who had clear memories of home. Those who did return went with high hopes to live out their vocation. However, the high hopes faded. Jerusalem was a ruin; they were not welcomed either by those who lived among the ruins or by those who ruled the province from their seat in Samaria; there was a succession of poor harvests. Life became a battle for survival and for safety's sake this meant that top priority must be given to the rebuilding of the walls of Jerusalem. The rebuilding of the walls became symbolic of what was happening to the restored community. It turned increasingly inward and the vision of the spreading of the knowledge of God among the nations faded. Maintaining the *purity* of the faith became pre-eminent; the Law was rigorously enforced and there were purges of people who did not meet the necessary criteria. This religious exclusiveness culminated in the requirement that all Jewish males who had married foreign wives must divorce them and these women must leave the community. So the wheel had come full circle. The only difference between the Jews at this point and those before the exile was that the current ones were even more exclusive.

These developments did not meet with the approval of all and there were some who stood in the universalist tradition of Second Isaiah. The Book of Ruth serves in particular as a strong protest against the compulsory divorcing of foreign wives. It is the story of a Moabite woman (therefore a foreigner) of singular grace, beauty, gentleness, faith and compassion who was also the great-grandmother of the great King David. She would have been put away too.

The Book of Jonah is a more complex allegory. It is the story of a Jew whom God told to go and preach at Nineveh (a symbol of pagan power). Rather than do this he fled to Joppa and took ship for Tarshish. But a great storm arose which threatened to sink the ship, so the sailors cast lots to see who was the cause of this. The lot fell on Jonah who confessed that he was fleeing from God's will and asked them to throw him into the sea. They did so and the storm ceased. Meanwhile the Lord had prepared a big fish to swallow up Jonah. This it duly did and Jonah spent three days in its belly during which time he repented of his actions. The big fish then vomited up Jonah on the shore and he proceeded straight to Nineveh where he preached so successfully that they repented in sackcloth and ashes – so much so that the Lord forgave their extreme wickedness. This angered Jonah who went away and sulked. The Lord chided him for his lack of pity.

This in allegorical form is the history and direction of the Jewish people. The refusal to spread the knowledge of God (Jonah's flight), the terrible conquest by the Babylonians (the fearful storm at sea), the exile and the change of heart (the three days and nights inside the fish), the return to Jerusalem (Jonah vomited up by the fish). Then comes the parting of the ways. Jonah does preach but is angry and sulks and God chides him. Here is the message to the readers of the day – the plea to keep fast to their universalistic principles. Seen in this context, discussions about whether a person can survive for seventy-two hours inside a fish miss the point!

### The Book of Daniel

The Book of Daniel, which contains the well known stories of Daniel in the lions' den and of Shadrach, Meshach and Abed-nego in the burning fiery furnace, arose in a very different historical setting. It was written during the reign of the Seleucid emperor, Antiochus Epiphanes (175–163 BC), by an unknown writer who wrote to his contemporaries through the mouth of one Daniel, whom he placed in the court of Babylon during the Jewish exile.

The immediate crisis was one of intense persecution. Antiochus ruled a large empire of which Israel was only a small part. In an attempt to create a greater sense of unity throughout his diverse empire, Antiochus actively encouraged the spread of Hellenism (the Greek way of life). Most of his subjugated people took to this quite readily. They renamed their gods by Greek names; they began to use the newly built gymnasia. A number of Jews cheerfully adopted such a way of life but pious Jews were horrified and would not cooperate. Antiochus reacted by forbidding the practice of the Jewish religion and by taking the temple in Jerusalem in 167 BC where he erected a pagan altar in the Holy of Holies and sacrificed pigs' flesh which to Jews was unclean meat. This desecration was seen by faithful Jews as the 'abomination of desolation'. Jews who refused to comply were treated very savagely. The first book of the Maccabees in the Apocrypha (those books between the Old and New Testaments) describes the period in great detail. The faithful Jews did not remain passive. Under Judas Maccabeus many revolted and resisted Antiochus Epiphanes with great courage (mainly through guerrilla warfare).

It was to this situation, of faithful Jews in a tiny minority against a large and powerful empire bent upon their destruction, that the Book of Daniel was addressed. Through their courage, fortitude and skill they won through and in December 164 BC the temple was cleansed and restored to the worship of God. (It is this event which the Jewish festival of Hanukkah celebrates.) The message is clear: that God will not let the persecution last for long. Israel is the chosen people of God and He will not allow them to be destroyed. The secret is to remain faithful and God will protect and save. Hence in the story of Shadrach, Meshach and Abed-nego (Daniel chapter 3), King Nebuchadnezzar erects a golden statue to which all are commanded to bow down and worship whenever they hear the sound of certain musical instruments. The three Jews, who are all officials of the king, refuse to do so because the Jewish religion forbids it. In his anger, the king orders that the penalty for disobedience to the command be implemented and the three Jews are thrown into the burning fiery furnace which has been heated to seven times its usual heat. Yet in the furnace, God is with them and nothing of them is burned. The king issues a proclamation that no one must speak amiss of the God of Shadrach, Meshach and Abed-nego. So faithfulness to God and to his commands is vindicated.

In a similar way, Daniel himself disobeys the command (Daniel chapter 6) that for thirty days no one should ask a petition of any God or man except for the king on pain of being thrown into a den of lions. Daniel continues his normal practice of praying in his window and his enemies report him to the king, to the king's great distress. The king has no choice because the law of the Medes and the Persians cannot be altered. So Daniel is cast into the lions' den. During the night the lions do not touch Daniel and he comes out unharmed. And so the God of Daniel is honoured. Again it is the same message of faithfulness and vindication. Daniel was faithful to God and God protected him. These were powerful messages to the Jews who were resisting Antiochus.

### Prophecy

A particular mark of the Old Testament is prophecy. Contrary to the current notion that a prophet is one who can see into the future and tell what is to be, the Old Testament prophet was much more a spokesman to his own people and generation about the present time. To oversimplify, the Old Testament prophet was a forthteller rather than a foreteller.

Now it is certainly true that there were prophets in Israel who could be consulted as fortune tellers but this style of prophecy was rejected by the great prophets. When the prophet Amos is called a prophet by Amaziah, the priest of Bethel, he reacts speedily: 'I was no prophet neither was a prophet's son' (Amos chapter 7 verse 14). The prophet believed that he was supremely the instrument of God in speaking to his own generation. When speaking an oracle to the people the prophet usually prefaced it with the words, 'Thus saith the Lord', emphasising therefore his or her role as a mouthpiece of God.

Amos is perhaps the most straightforward of the prophets to understand. From Tekoa, he was by occupation a herdsman and a tender of sycamore trees. He believed that God had called him to go and speak His word to Israel. The situation was that the people of Israel had largely forgotten their distinctive way of life as the chosen people. There was a great disparity of wealth between the rich and the poor and, although all were brother Israelites, there was very little concern about it. Moreover there was bribery in the courts, so that the poor had little opportunity of getting justice there. There was slavery in the land – it was possible to buy a slave for the price of a pair of shoes. Amos paints a picture of the wealthy citizens lying on their ivory beds, eating the best lambs and calves, anointing themselves with the best ointments and drinking bowls of wine. The harshest words came for the women of the capital city, Samaria: 'Hear this word, ye cows of Bashan, that are in the mountains of Samaria, which oppress the poor, which crush the needy, which say to their masters "Bring, and let us drink"' (Amos chapter 4 verse 1). 'The word of the Lord' which Amos brings is one of judgement but with the appeal, 'Seek me and ye shall live' (Amos chapter 5 verse 4). Unless this happens there will be the 'Day of the Lord', a day of judgement which will be mediated through outside military forces. The country will be overrun and the people taken captive. This is a note of hope in Amos. In his final chapter (if it is not a later addition) he points to a time when an Israel, chastened and purified by her punishment, might rebuild her life on the right lines.

Prophets were speakers rather than writers and it seems that their followers wrote down their oracles, the memory aided by the tradition of prophets speaking in poetic form. Often their oracles are not written down in a logical sequence and this can be confusing to readers. Prophets inevitably were unpopular figures in their own day and it is possible that one, Jeremiah, might have been murdered. But such is the fate of prophets in all ages including our own.

Old Testament prophets include Hosea, Isaiah of Jerusalem (Isaiah chapters 1–39 inclusive), Isaiah of Babylon (Isaiah chapters 40–55) (see earlier section on stories), Ezekiel, Jeremiah and Micah. The message of each one is tied very closely to the historical and social situation of the day.

### History

Although the point was made earlier that the Bible is not all history, this does not mean that some of it is not history. In fact, the biblical drama is set in the context of history, beginning with the Patriarchs, Abraham, Isaac and Jacob, through Moses, the monarchy and right through to the life of Jesus and the activity of St Paul. This historical story is acted out against the background of the history of the great world empires – the Sumerian, Assyrian, Babylonian, Persian, Greek and Roman – always there and often appearing directly on the stage.

Generally speaking, the history in the Bible is corroborated by other contemporary accounts unearthed by archaeologists. For example, in the reign of Hezekiah, King of Judah (715–687/6 BC), the Assyrian emperor, Sennacherib, came up against Judah so overwhelmingly that Hezekiah sued for peace, offering a much larger annual tribute (2 Kings, chapter 18 verses 13 onwards). This was accepted by Sennacherib. Reference to this is found in the Assyrian annals:

> As for Hezekiah the Jew, who did not submit to my yoke, forty-six of his strong walled cities in their neighbourhood . . . I besieged and took . . . Himself, like a caged bird, I shut up in Jerusalem, his royal city . . . As for Hezekiah, the terrifying splendour of my majesty overcame him . . . and his mercenary troops . . . deserted him.

This was but a breathing space while Hezekiah set about strengthening the defensive position of Jerusalem. 2 Kings chapter 20 verse 20 talks about the acts of Hezekiah and about 'how he made a pool and a conduit and brought water into the city'. This conduit was uncovered in 1880 and from this discovery it is possible to describe the tunnel very clearly and to walk along it.

This is quoted in some detail to show that historical writing in the Bible tends to find corroboration from other sources. This, of course, does not prove the truth of the faith of the Bible but it does show that where it is intending to write history the biblical text is reasonably accurate.

There is one further point to make about the history in the Bible. It is *interpreted* history or *theological* history. The biblical faith is that God is constantly active in the world. History is the arena of his operation. Hence when something happens it is because God causes it to happen. Hence, to refer back to the earlier material on the Exile, under 'Stories', the modern historian might note that the Jewish people were taken into exile in Babylon by Nebuchadnezzar and account for it in terms of the strength of Babylon, the comparative weakness of Egypt and so on. The biblical writers were much more concerned to account for why God had caused it to happen, in other words to interpret it to discover his purposes.

### Law

Within the Old Testament there is a considerable concern for Law, that is, for the requirements which God makes of humans. At the heart of the Old Testament faith is the notion of Covenant. This means an agreement freely entered into by God and Israel with requirements on both sides. The divine undertaking is contained in the words 'I will be their God'. The human side involves an undertaking to obey the divine commands. These are expressed centrally in the Ten Commandments (Exodus chapter 20) and form the core of the *moral* law. There is also the *ritual* law which lays down regulations about the worship of the community.

### Poetry

The best-known poems in the Bible are the Psalms, 150 in number, which figure prominently in worship. They come from many sources: some are songs of praise, others of dereliction; some arise out of specific historical situations. Psalm 148 for example is a song of praise. Psalm 24 is thought by many scholars to arise out of a particular situation. The second part of the Psalm (verses 7–8) reads:

> Lift up your heads, O ye gates;
> And be ye lift up ye everlasting doors;
> And the king of glory shall come in.
> Who is this king of glory?
> The Lord strong and mighty,
> The Lord mighty in battle.

It has been suggested that this Psalm relates to the entry of the Ark into Jerusalem. The 'question and answer' style suggests too an antiphonal versicle and response between the priests and the people.

Psalm 137 clearly arises from the period of the Exile in Babylon. It expresses the deep sadness of exile, the deep devotion to Jerusalem and the deep bitterness towards their captors.

Another book of poetry, known as the Song of Solomon or the Song of Songs, is a collection of love poetry. It has often been interpreted, perhaps rather piously, as an allegory of the love between Christ and the church, but it does have a rather more carnal flavour about it.

### Letters

Much of the New Testament consists of letters (or epistles) written by leaders in the church. Notable among these are St Paul, St Peter and St John. The letters were normally written to one or other of the small churches scattered around the Mediterranean and dealt with problems which had arisen and were causing disagreements. Should Christians eat meat which had been first sacrificed to idols? How should Christians behave in a hostile environment? Sometimes they were written to admonish. The Corinthian church was remarkably quarrelsome and this worried Paul and so he wrote to chide its members.

Our only way of knowing this, though, is by a careful reading of the letters, as this is our only source of information.

The shortest epistle in the New Testament is that of Paul to Philemon about one Onesimus, a runaway slave.

## The transmission of the Bible

The two principal writing materials for the Bible for many centuries were papyrus and vellum. *Papyrus* is made from the stems of the papyrus plant which grows on the banks of the River Nile in Egypt. It is cut into strips about 40 cm long which are laid side by side. Then similar strips are laid across them at right angles making a second layer, and the two layers are then fused together to make a strong sheet. Sheets like this can then be glued together so as to form a scroll. Many of the early papyrus scrolls perished with time but there is a very early fragment of papyrus in existence: it contains part of the Greek text of St John's Gospel chapter 18 verses 31–33 and 37 and it dates from about AD 130.

A *Codex* is written on parchment which is made of leather – usually from the skins of sheep and goats as they were more readily available. The skins were dried and polished so as to be suitable for writing on. The individual sheets were then sewn together to make a book.

Perhaps the most famous Codex is Codex Sinaiticus. This is the earliest complete New Testament manuscript in existence and dates from the fourth century. It was found in the ancient monastery of St Catherine in the Sinai region of Egypt.

All ancient manuscripts, including all the books of the Old and New Testaments, therefore both the Jewish Bible and the Christian Bible, had to be written out by hand. This made them both expensive and comparatively rare. This was the situation until the invention of the printing press in the fifteenth century.

### *The Dead Sea Scrolls and Qumran*

A very powerful insight into the making and use of papyri scrolls is afforded by the remarkable discovery in 1947 of the Dead Sea Scrolls.

#### The finding of the scrolls

In the spring of 1947, a Bedouin boy, Mohammad the Wolf, was tending his father's goats in the remote and little visited area to the west of the Dead Sea. The limestone cliff face which rises from the plain of the Dead Sea is honeycombed with caves and it was into one of these that Mohammad the Wolf accidentally threw a stone while he was searching for a wandering goat. The noise the stone made when it fell to the ground was that of breaking pottery. Afraid, the boy did not enter the cave alone but returned with a friend and together they explored the cave.

Inside, the two Bedouin boys found several tall, thin clay jars, about four feet high, topped with bowl-like lids. Around these were the fragments of other broken jars. Inside the jars they found black objects which on investigation turned out to be long rolls of manuscript wrapped in lengths of linen and covered over with a pitch-like substance. When unrolled the scrolls were long manuscripts, inscribed in parallel columns on sheets which were sewn together. The boys did not recognise the lettering: in fact it was Hebrew. The boys belonged to a party of contrabanders who were smuggling goods into Palestine to sell on the black market in Bethlehem and it was here that they first tried to sell the scrolls.

The story of how the existence of the scrolls became known both in archaeological circles and to the general public is long and involved and considerably hampered by the hostility between Jews and Arabs at the time. The cave which had contained the scrolls was identified and in 1948 searched. Early in 1952 a five-mile stretch of the cliffs around it was scrutinised and twenty-seven caves were identified, of which two contained further manuscript material and twenty-five showed signs of use or habitation from that period. In the next four years, further caves were found which yielded documents. Other caves further away were also discovered containing manuscripts but the most important came from the caves around Qumran.

## The community

On a low plateau above the western shore of the Dead Sea and just over half a mile from the cave where the first scrolls were found by Mohammad the Wolf stand the ruins of Khirbet Qumran. Because of its proximity to the cave where the first scrolls were discovered it was fully excavated over five seasons of digging.

As our focus here is upon the recording and transmission of the biblical text, it is not our purpose here to look in detail at the community. However it seems clear from both the archaeological evidence and the contents of the scrolls that Qumran housed a Jewish religious community which had a large library. The community clearly flourished and lived out its separate life until the buildings were destroyed by the Romans in AD 68.

In the view of Roland de Vaux, the principal archaeologist of the scrolls, Vespasian's Tenth Legion marched from Caesarea, took Jericho and established a garrison there. From there Vespasian pushed on down towards the Dead Sea. Josephus, the Jewish historian, adds the information that Vespasian was curious to see the Dead Sea and to test whether its waters were as buoyant as reports described. Accordingly he took a number of his men who were non-swimmers and, with hands tied behind their backs, had them thrown into the sea. Fortunately they all floated. It seems that Qumran was taken at this time, and that the inhabitants either fled or were killed. Signs of burning and Roman arrow heads were uncovered. De Vaux is of the opinion that the Dead Sea Scrolls were the library of the Qumran community and that it was hidden or left in the caves by members of the community as the Roman army advanced upon them. Thereafter the scrolls were left and forgotten until Mohammad the Wolf's chance stone brought them to light after almost 1,900 years.

Three discoveries from the Qumran excavations are significant for work on the early versions of the Bible.

First, in the ruins of the Qumran monastery there is evidence of a scriptorium, the place where the scrolls were both copied and written. A large table made out of brick, which had fallen through from an upper storey, contained three ink wells each containing evidence of dried ink. It is highly likely that this formed the centre of a scriptorium where at least some of the manuscripts had been copied.

Second, from the storage of the scrolls in their jars we gain some picture of how papyrus and leather scrolls were produced, used and preserved.

Third, the scrolls, well over 600 in number, range from fragments to almost complete documents. Only one, the Isaiah Scroll, found in the first cave, is complete. Of the manuscripts found roughly one-quarter are biblical and contain all the books of the Hebrew Bible and the Christian Old Testament with the exception of the Book of Esther.

Fourth, what is truly remarkable is that these books of the Hebrew Bible, except for Esther, all date from the first century AD and are written in Hebrew. Prior to these discoveries, the earliest Hebrew texts of the Hebrew Bible date from the eleventh century AD – a thousand years later. The older texts raised a number of points for scholars but only of a minor nature. The changes in the transmission of the biblical text had been minimal. This finding is especially important as it was usually assumed that many errors would inevitably have crept in through the human frailty of scribes, who might, for example, doze off and on waking jump a few lines, or who might consciously try to 'improve' upon the text they were copying.

### From manuscripts to the printed version

Over the centuries, until the invention of the printing press in the fifteenth century, the normal means of transmitting the sacred text was through the copying work of innumerable monks, for whom it was their life's work. Many examples survive and demonstrate that many of these Bibles were works of art, with the monks developing both the script and the illumination of the manuscripts. Particularly famous examples are the Book of Kells and the Lindisfarne Gospels.

Here is a verse found in the margin of a biblical manuscript in Ireland in the seventh century. It was obviously written by a monk sitting with his cat. It sheds a human light on the work.

> Side by side our tasks we ply
> Pandurban my cat and I
> In our own work we find our bliss
> I in mine and he in his

The language in which these manuscripts were written was Latin because that was the language of the church. Although the Bible was originally written in Hebrew and Greek, St Jerome (345–420) made a translation based on the Greek versions of both the Old and New Testaments which became known as the Vulgate, which was the principal version of the Bible for over one thousand years.

The development of the printing press enabled books to be available readily and much more cheaply. It also had the effect of spreading ideas so it is perhaps not surprising that the Reformation followed in its tracks. The reformers wanted the Bible to be widely available to all and this naturally meant in the vernacular. In the sixteenth century complete versions in English began to appear:

> Miles Coverdale's (1537)
> The Matthew Bible (1537)
> The Great Bible (1539)
> The Geneva Bible (1560)
> The Authorised Version (1611)

Since then many new translations have appeared, often more accurate than the older ones. These include the Revised Standard Version, the New English Bible and the Good News Bible.

## The Bible in the classroom

### *Story*

A danger of teaching from the Bible in the primary school is always the response 'It's boring'. Of course, it can be. Much depends on the selection of material, its appropriateness to the children and the style of teaching. It can be very boring or it can be interesting and exciting. Here a teacher, looking back at his own experience of RE in the 1950s, reflects on two different styles of teaching:

> RE (or RI as it was then) in school was appalling. It is hard to credit it but every morning straight after assembly, Bibles were handed out from the cupboard, one per pupil, and we each read out a verse round the class beginning where we had left off the previous day. When we had all read one verse, the Bibles were collected in and replaced in the cupboard until the next morning when the same regime would be practised. No explanation, no help with the meaning of unfamiliar words, no sense of meaning. What a contrast this was with Sunday School. My teacher here was Mrs Pilling, an elderly widow. She was just wonderful. She knew how to tell stories and she knew her material. She made all those Old Testament figures come alive: Abraham, the vindictive Sarah, the rather sad Isaac, the deceitful but rather amazing Jacob and so many others. We saw them in dazzling colours. When she told us the story of Jacob's dream of the ladder between earth and heaven and quoted Jacob's words 'This is none other than the house of God, this is the gate of heaven' we all sensed the awe and other-worldliness of the experience. She kept faithful to her stories too except in one case: she was clearly unhappy about God's command to Abraham to sacrifice Isaac so from the beginning she kept emphasising how upset Abraham was ('tears rolling down his cheeks') and how God had no intention of allowing Abraham to go through with it!
>
> Mrs Pilling was not a trained teacher – she was not one for discussion and never asked what we would call an 'open question' – but she was brilliant at making the stories live for us so vividly. No one in that class could ever find the Bible boring! Mrs Pilling's setting was Sunday School and not teaching RE in a primary school but much can be gained from her approach. Tell the stories at the pupils' level with vigour, colour and life. More does need to be included for classroom RE – some discussion on the stories needs to be added to give the children the opportunity to ask questions and to reflect. This can add an exciting dimension for both teacher and pupil.

One great strength of Mrs Pilling's approach was that God was always there in her storytelling. This was rightly so as God is the central actor and mover throughout the whole Bible story. There has been a tendency in some schools (perhaps unconsciously) to remove God from the scene and to turn some of the stories into moral tales. A popular story with many children is the account of David's victory over the giant Goliath. The young shepherd boy comes to meet in single combat the great champion of the Philistines and destroys him with a well aimed pebble from his sling. Now underlying this story is the old Hebrew belief that when the people were in danger God's spirit would rush on to an individual and give him (or her in some cases) the power to ward off the danger. This is what is happening here: the Philistines are the enemy threatening the chosen people and so God intervenes through the young David who becomes his instrument – and remains so for the rest of his life. This story can easily have all its religious significance removed and become a story about bullying – the little guy victorious over the big bully. The parable of the Good Samaritan and the story of Noah are also always in danger of a similar fate.

### Using a Bible

Pupils will need to handle Bibles so that they can begin to know how to use them. It is helpful when arranging this to ask pupils to bring in as many different versions of the Bible as possible. Such a display will demonstrate differences in translations, in printing and in layout. Many people find the printing of the Bible as separate verses and in columns off-putting, and there is no reason for Bibles to be like this: verses were only invented for convenience, the original being continuous prose. Although many educated adults would have a preference for the beauty and dignity of the language of the Authorised Version of 1611, it is much less suitable for young children who can find that they almost have to learn a new language to access it.

One teacher used some passages from the Bible as part of her literacy teaching and, instead of photocopying the passages, gave the children Bibles from the RE resource cupboard and showed them how to find the passages in the Bible. This can even be done as a game: 'Who can find . . .?'

### Learning the diversity of the Bible

It is very important that children should have the opportunity to become aware of the different types of literature there are in the Bible and to appreciate that 'truth' is not just concerned with the question 'Did it happen?' It is important that even young children should become aware gradually that truth is more complex than this.

It is helpful in the primary school if pupils can, for example, be introduced to the notion of 'myth', and explore it in different cultures (Norse, Greek) and begin to look at some of the biblical narratives in this light. Material earlier in this chapter should provide enough information for teachers to devise an appropriate unit of work.

Similarly, understanding of a popular story such as 'Daniel in the Lions' Den' can be enhanced considerably with older Key Stage 2 pupils if it is seen against the background of the Jewish people suffering persecution under the conquering emperor, Antiochus Epiphenes, and in danger of abandoning both their faith and their destiny. Stories of a hero figure such as Daniel who remained faithful and was vindicated by God must have buoyed up the failing spirits of the Jewish guerrilla fighters as they resisted the emperor's armies. Again there is material earlier in this chapter to provide a unit of work on this topic.

The teacher mentioned earlier in this section who trained her pupils to find their way around the Bible used passages from the Bible as part of her literacy work. She chose two passages, both poems, which she read with the class and discussed with the children as she would any poem, with special reference to the imagery. The two poems were Psalm 23, 'The Lord is my Shepherd', and 1 Corinthians chapter 13 in which St Paul writes about love. This again helped pupils to see much more into the richness of much beloved literature.

# 12 Approaching the teaching of other world faiths

Attitudes to the teaching of world religions other than Christianity vary considerably. Here are a few representative ones:

- 'They [i.e. the children] have enough difficulty understanding their own so I don't see how they are going to understand very different ones.'
- 'I think that as they live in a multicultural society the sooner they begin to understand that people have different beliefs the better.'
- 'I'm not happy about it. There is so little time, not enough to get into Christianity.'
- 'I think religious education is about religion and religion is broader than Christianity.'
- 'I think that it's good for children to see that people all over the world are committed to religion – and not just that funny lot at the church down the road.'
- 'I don't know enough about them!'

Within these views it is easy to detect a number of underlying attitudes. There is the lingering notion that the real aim of religious education is still confessional and that we should, therefore, be using all our energy in commending Christianity. In such a view, a study of other religions is something of a distraction and a waste of time. There is also the fear of confusing children – religious ideas from others are too difficult for young children.

There is also the recognition that children need this broader understanding and experience. Teachers who lack confidence in their own knowledge will have to do a bit of research.

Contrary to much received wisdom, children do enjoy RE, providing it has colour, challenge and bite. The old 'tell a story and draw a picture' approach certainly can discourage interest unless the story is exceptionally exciting. However, most people are interested in knowing how other groups of people make sense of their world and find satisfaction and meaning in their daily lives. At root it is these questions which religions attempt to address. Many teachers of older Key Stage 2 children will have been involved in lively discussions on arranged marriages which have moved from the horror of living in the same house as one's mother-in-law to a growing realisation that beneath the practice of arranged marriages is a complex of beliefs about the nature and the role of the family which includes relationships between spouses, between grandparents/parents and children and between siblings. From this realisation has come a new thoughtfulness and reflectiveness about their own previously unexamined concepts of family, relationships and marriage, with their strengths and weaknesses.

One teacher, twenty-five years ago, now enthusiastic but then suspicious about the introduction of teaching about other religions to young children, records his conversion:

> It was on a cold Monday morning, when I was gathering my 8 and 9-year-olds into the classroom, that our one and only Muslim pronounced that she wasn't going to have any school lunches for a month. This information was greeted with cries of horror and disbelief from those gathered around my desk. 'What not for a whole month. You'll die of starvation' and so on. Fortunately it occurred to me that Ramadan was due to start about that time so I got Karim to explain. Very quietly she told to what was now the whole class listening that, for one month in the year, Muslims were supposed not to eat or drink anything in the hours of daylight and that the month had begun the day before. Although, because it was cold and she was quite young, she could have been exempted from the fast, she had wanted to join in with her family and her father had agreed.
>
> This revelation proved the day's topic of absorbing interest. It kept bubbling up at what seemed every other minute with questions addressed to me like 'We don't do things like that, do we?' and various comments made sotto voce 'It's mad.'
>
> It was the combination of these two comments that made me feel that the class ought to be doing some work on other religions. And so we began – on a topic on 'How people worship'. What amazed me was how well it went. There was none of the boredom that some colleagues predicted. Rather the interest in and the quality of the work – research in the library, written work, art work – was exceptionally high – much higher for this work than for any other unit of work done over the year.
>
> The school was situated in what is often called a 'deprived' area.

As already discussed in Chapter 6, over the last quarter of the twentieth century, RE was broadening its subject base considerably. All these developments which we have seen were confirmed in the National Framework for Religious Education which identified two prime focuses:

- Widening inclusion, understanding diversity and promoting tolerance.
- Providing pupils with a wide range of experiences that enable them to develop a realistic and positive sense of their own beliefs and ideas.

At one time world religions were taught so that white British pupils could gain an understanding of the main faiths which had settled and were growing in Britain. Now it is more so that all can understand each other. Hindu pupils, for example can begin to understand the Christian base of British society and also develop an awareness of Buddhism, Islam, Judaism and Sikhism, as well as looking afresh at their own tradition, Hinduism. The hoped for outcome of this is that all pupils will feel that they belong in British society and that, through the awareness and understanding of this diversity, there will be greater tolerance of difference. This in turn should lead pupils, through knowledge and understanding, to be confident in what they believe and value.

**The selection of content**

Although six religions are to be taught, educational considerations are brought into play when it comes to planning how this might happen. Given the usual timetable allowance of one hour per week, and with Christianity normally occupying half of that, it would be completely unfair to the great religious traditions to allocate them four hours per year each, as well as creating that phenomenon, *mishmash* – a mess of many undifferentiated stories, facts and beliefs in pupils' minds. To avoid these pitfalls, there has been a strong national steer on agreed syllabuses to require that in Key Stage 1 pupils should study Christianity and one other faith and in Key Stage 2 Christianity and two other faiths. As each agreed syllabus determines which religions those should be, often from their own local situation, it means that there is considerable diversify across the country. Many, however, appear to nominate Judaism for Key Stage 1 and Hinduism and Islam for Key Stage 2. In an agreed syllabus which has this pattern there is no embargo on doing some further work in Judaism in Key Stage 2, nor for that matter on making reference to Buddhism and Sikhism, perhaps in connection with a festival, but Christianity, Hinduism and Islam would be the principal focuses.

If pupils are to learn about different faiths, subject content is vitally important, but so also are all those qualities that RE is expected to foster: empathy, interest in other people's situations and cultures, understanding, tolerance and respect. Content alone is not enough as religions can be taught in a negative way which can create and reinforce prejudice. On the other hand, understanding, empathy, tolerance and respect cannot be fostered unless there is knowledge about the different faiths and that knowledge is taught in such a way that the adherents of those faiths are satisfied with the teaching.

If the teaching is to be successful, teachers have to think very carefully about the age and stage of their pupils. The selection of the material to be taught is crucial. What they are teaching must relate or attach in some way to pupils' current experience and this to some extent will depend on the situation. It is, for example, much easier to teach about other faiths if the school is multifaith in composition, as the pupils naturally have first-hand experience of other faiths which sparks off their curiosity. It is also misguided to teach 5-year-olds the Christian doctrine of the Trinity or to talk to them about the Buddha's diagnosis of the human condition in the Four Noble Truths, as there is as yet little in their experience which is likely to foster understanding. They may use the right words but these are likely to be hollow. On the other hand, young children experience birthday parties and Christmas and these are excellent ways to move into an understanding of festivals and special occasions. The selection of teaching material should be designed to act as stepping stones to a positive and developing understanding of religions, and not stumbling blocks. It became popular in recent years to develop a topic in Key Stage 1 called 'Festivals of Light'. This topic included the three autumn and winter festivals in which light is a powerful feature, Diwali (Hindu), Hanukkah (Jewish) and Christmas (Christian). Stories were told, lamps were made and a good time was had by all. However, from an RE point of view the topic often proved to be less than satisfactory. Pupils often became very confused about the boundaries between the festivals and the faiths from which they were drawn and were left with a welter of misconceptions. Despite excellent intentions the topic often proved to be not a stepping stone but a stumbling block.

**Tackling religions**

What follows is a consideration of the key content of which pupils in the primary school should have some knowledge. This is a personal judgement and others may wish to make some additions and subtractions. This is undertaken for Buddhism, Hinduism, Islam, Judaism and Sikhism. In the case of Judaism and Islam, units of work are also developed from this key content. These two traditions have been chosen because they are the most frequently taught in primary schools. The approach adopted can easily be applied to the other religious traditions as well.

It is important to note that not all the key content and key questions are appropriate to all age groups within Key Stages 1 and 2. Teachers will, of course, use their professional skills to develop appropriate work for the children in their care.

## Islam

### *Key content*

Allah, the Arabic word for God
The Shadanah – 'There is no God but Allah and Muhammad is his prophet'
The significance of Muhammad – stories from his life
The Qur'an – the revelation of God to Muhammad
The People of the Book along with Jews and Christians
The role of the mosque
The madrasah – teaching the children
The role of the imam
Salah (prayer) five times a day
Sawm (fasting) during Ramadan
Zakah (almsgiving)
Hajj (pilgrimage)
Festivals: Id-ul-Fitr, Id-ul-Adra
Strong sense of brotherhood among Muslims

### *Possible approaches*

Unit of work 1: The role of the mosque within Islam

Possible content to be drawn from:

- The place of prostration; beliefs about the nature of Allah
- The parts of the mosque; the mihrab indicating the qiblah, the direction of Makkah
- The preparation for prayer, especially wudu (washing)
- The call to prayer; minaret, muezzin
- Public prayer (salah) five times each day
- The midday Friday prayers (Jumu'ah)
- The mosque school (madrasah)
- The role of the imam
- The role of the mosque and the madrasah among Muslims in Britain

It is assumed that a visit to a mosque will be a part of this topic. This is partly because of the importance of first-hand experience to make the subject come alive but also because it can provide lots of information about the role of the mosque within the Muslim community.

How this unit of work is developed will depend upon the age and previous experience of the pupils. Pupils should be encouraged to develop an informed and sympathetic understanding of the material and, progressively, to look at and ask questions such as:

- What do we mean by a 'sacred' place?
- What do we mean by 'worship'?
- Why do people wash in preparation for prayer?
- Why do many mosques have schools for children?
- What role does the mosque play in sustaining the Muslim community?
- What roles might the mosque have with reference to the wider community in Britain?

Teachers will know how to select from these ideas to develop the unit of work most appropriately for their own pupils. Throughout, pupils should be encouraged to relate their learning and discussion to themselves and their own thinking, asking themselves questions such as:

- What does it mean to belong to a community with strongly held, shared beliefs?
- What beliefs about right and wrong are emerging?
- What makes things right or wrong?
- What is the benefit of prayer?

### Unit of work 2: The Qur'an

Possible content to be drawn from:

- Muhammad, the messenger of Allah
- Allah's final and complete revelation of Himself to humanity
- The implications of the Qur'an being regarded by Muslims as the complete and unchanging Word of God
- The story of the first revelation to Muhammad on the Night of Power
- It is recited in the original Arabic as translations inevitably change meaning
- Children taught Arabic so as to read the Qur'an
- The respect shown to the book – handled with washed hands, wrapped in protecting cloths and kept on a high shelf
- Great respect for hafiz, those who know the whole Qur'an by heart
- In it are descriptions of God's nature: the ninety-nine beautiful names of God, e.g. the Lord, the High, the Great, the Creator, the Lifegiver, the Sustainer, the Compassionate, the Merciful, the Judge
- The Qur'an gives direction and guidance on how people ought to live in this world: human relationships, dress, good acts, bad acts, punishment

It is assumed that a copy of the Qur'an will be available with a translation so that pupils not conversant with Arabic can read sections of it so as to form their own impressions. Although the copy of the Qur'an is likely to be one produced for schools' artefact collections, it is still important to encourage the children to treat it with the respect which Muslims show towards the Qur'an: only touch it with recently washed hands, keep it wrapped when not in use and store it high up overnight.

Pupils should be encouraged to appreciate the absolutely central place of the Qur'an and its teaching in Islam, and to understand that most Muslims regard it as the direct and true teaching of God and that the role of Muhammad was essentially as a mouthpiece for the Word of God.

As with the first unit of work, teachers will know best how to develop this material with their own classes, based on their age and previous experience. The following questions seem important for pupils to ask:

- What do we mean by a 'holy book'?
- Why do Muslim children spend so many hours learning Arabic and reading the Qur'an?
- In what ways does the Qur'an influence the lives of believers?
- Should the Qur'an influence the lives of non-Muslims?

In addition to these questions pupils ought to be encouraged to ask:

- Do Christians understand the Bible or Sikhs the Guru Granth Sahib in the same way as Muslims understand the Qur'an?
- What other sources of moral guidance are there?

## Judaism

### Key content

The Shema: 'Hear, O Israel, the Lord our God is one'
God the Creator and Sustainer
God the Father
Moses, the Law Giver
The Torah, especially the Ten Commandments, the mezuzah
The food laws
The significance of Jerusalem
Shabbat (Sabbath)
Festivals, e.g. Pesach (Passover)
   Yom Kippur (Day of Atonement)
   Hanukkah
Synagogue, Ark, Sefer Torah (Torah scroll)
Tallit, yamulka/kippah, tefellin

### Possible approaches

Unit of work: The importance of the Torah (the Law) in Judaism

Possible content to be drawn from:

- Moses and the giving of the Torah on Mount Sinai
- The Shema
- The Ten Commandments
- The food laws
- The place of the Torah in the synagogue
- The Sefer Torah – how it is made, treatment, jewelled cases, the yodh
- The tefellin and the mezuzah
- The Barmitzvah/Batmitzvah

It would be very helpful if a visit to a synagogue could be made as part of this unit of work. The focus for the visit could be on the features of the synagogue which are particularly relevant to the Torah, especially the Ark, with its contents of elaborately encased Sefer Torahs, the bimah from which it is read and the tefellin (in Orthodox synagogues). Normally when a school party visits a synagogue, the rabbi or a senior member of the congregation is present. Ask them to show the children both the inside of the Ark and a copy of the Torah and explain the special (and expensive) way in which it is made. It is also helpful if there can be a demonstration of the Torah being read and the use of the yad in the process.

This unit can be developed for children in both Key Stage 1 and Key Stage 2, and teachers will focus on the subject content which they wish to use. Questions for the children to consider are:

- Why is so much effort made to beautify the Sefer scroll and its containers?
- What difference might a mezuzah on a house door make?
- What are the benefits and possible disadvantages of having clearly laid down laws or rules?
- To what extent is the age of 12 (girls) or 13 (boys) a good age to take on adult responsibilities?
- What part does the Torah play in sustaining the Jewish community?

### Other approaches

Other approaches to Judaism can be made from many angles including 'The Jewish Home', 'The Sabbath', 'The Synagogue', 'Festivals', e.g. Pesach (Passover). (See also Chapter 13 'Teaching festivals and celebrations', which develops a unit of work on Barmitzvah/Batmitzvah.)

## Buddhism

### Key content for Key Stages 1 and 2

- Karma, Dharma, rebirth
- The life of Buddha
- Nirvana – Enlightenment
- The teaching of the Buddha
    The Five Precepts
    The Four Noble Truths
    The Noble Eightfold Path
- The Sangha: monks, nuns and lay people
- Temples
- Meditation
- Pilgrimage
- Respect for all living things

## Hinduism

### Key content for Key Stages 1 and 2

- Brahman – the ultimate all-pervading reality from which all derive. One with many names and images
- Murti – an image of God used as a focus for worship
- Trimurti (Brahma, Shiva and Vishnu)
- Karma, Samsara, Moksha
- Caste
- Puja (worship), arti
- Mandir
- Stories of Rama and Krishna
- Mahatma Gandhi
- Festivals: Diwali, Holi
- The four stages of life
- The sacred books, especially the Ramayana and the Bhagavad Gita
- Pilgrimage – Banares
- Ahimsa (respect for life)

## Sikhism

### Key content for Key Stages 1 and 2

- One God, the creator
- All humans equal before God
- Stories of Guru Nanak
- Stories of Guru Gobind Singh
- The Sacred Book – the Guru Granth Sahib

- Khalsa (Brotherhood)
- Amrit ceremony
- Panj Kakke – the Five Ks
    - Kesh (long uncut hair)
    - Kangha (comb)
    - Kirpan (sword)
    - Kara (steel wrist band)
    - Kachera (shorts)
- Gurdwara
- The langar
- Karah parshad
- Festivals: Gurpurbs, Baisakhi, turban tying

# 13  Teaching festivals and celebrations

Festivals are important features of religion and, because of their obvious appeal to both teachers and pupils, they have assumed a considerable share of the time allocated to RE in many schools. Some critics have claimed that RE is really only festivals! This is an exaggeration but it does point to the fact that festivals are only one element in religion and that pupils need to undertake work in other dimensions too. Nevertheless festivals will always remain very significant, especially with younger pupils, as they give an insight into the beliefs, practices and stories within the religious traditions.

Festivals are celebrations but not all celebrations are festivals. Later in the chapter the Jewish rite of passage Barmitzvah/Batmitzvah, a tremendous celebration both for the individual and for the community, is considered in some detail.

Festivals are a feature of all religions and appeal to worshippers of all ages. By their very nature they are community affairs (social dimension) and they re-enact in a familiar way (ritual dimension) aspects of the religion which are significant to believers. In addition to this they inevitably both reflect and point to central beliefs of the religion, though the understanding possessed by worshippers may be at different levels. A case in point is Christmas. Christians celebrate Christmas together, performing certain rituals including the singing of special hymns or carols. Christmas for Christians reflects and points to the centre of Christian belief, the Incarnation, but the festival can be understood by different believers at different levels, ranging from a thanksgiving for a special baby to a thanksgiving for the Incarnation of God in humanity. Festivals are an important means of enabling believers to work their way both emotionally and intellectually into the heart of their religion. They are also a real mark of belonging.

In this section there will be a consideration of some approaches to teaching about a number of festivals, but before this there are some important foundations to lay in the infant years.

## Foundation work on festivals

Before a teacher does specific work on any one festival with children, it is important to examine the underlying notion of *special days*. Children can learn facts about different festivals but if they are to understand what believers feel about them then they must see them in the same way as they see festivals (special days) in their own lives – such as birthdays. Children can study birthday customs of children in other parts of the world and this can be both interesting and informative. When they realise that involved with these customs are the same feelings of anticipation, excitement and joy which they feel on their own birthday then the whole exercise takes on a new depth of meaning. So it is with festivals. Festivals can be very interesting things to study but they can be amazingly impersonal (for example, 'On Palm Sunday, people in church carry palm crosses . . .'). They take on a new depth of meaning when the person studying festivals suddenly realises that participants feel about these occasions as they feel about their own special days.

It is therefore very important that young children should be encouraged to focus on 'celebrating'.

### A possible approach

Learning intentions: to encourage children:

- to think about their special or happy days;
- to acknowledge the rituals which happen on these days;
- to recognise and to begin to articulate the emotions associated with these occasions.

Focus upon 'my birthday' because it:

- is highly significant in the lives of most individuals;
- has widespread and time-hallowed rituals associated with it;
- is one of the closest experiences to a religious festival.

### Possible development

Teachers will wish to develop the idea in a variety of ways, through talk, pictures, stories, simple writing, drama, music and so on. The following are points of focus arising from a consideration of a fairly common pattern of a child's birthday in Britain:

waking up and being given the first cards and presents
waiting (impatiently) at the window for the post to come
opening cards and presents, special wrapping paper, difficult string
preparing for the party:

the smell of cakes being baked, sandwiches being made
preparing for party games – wrapping up the parcel for pass the parcel
laying the table; putting out the names by each place; who is going to sit by me?
getting washed and dressed in party clothes

The party:

waiting for the doorbell to ring
opening the door; the bustle; the presents; not enough time to open them
being the centre of attention
playing the party games – pass the parcel, musical chairs, musical statues, sticking the tail on the donkey

being entertained by the conjurer
having tea; special cake; candles, one for each year of age
the singing of Happy Birthday
blowing out the candles
packing up the cake in napkins to take home
goodbye, tiredness and bed

## Christmas

### *Preliminary considerations*

1   This is the most popular Christian festival of the year, at least in Western Christendom. It will therefore be celebrated in each of the seven or eight years during which the child is in primary school. Great care is needed not to evoke the reaction 'Not again' with the 11-year-olds.
2   It is possible to understand the significance of Christmas at different levels and it is important not to rush children's understanding. It is better to get them *pointed in the right direction*.
3   Like most festivals Christmas has many themes within it (for example, babies, gifts, light in darkness). It is often best to focus on just one of these on a given occasion, and some are, of course, more suited to different age groups.
4   It is possible to 'understand' Christmas on an emotional as well as an intellectual level.

Below are some possible approaches to teaching about Christmas, directed towards different age groups.

### *With Foundation Stage and Key Stage 1*

The adult understanding of Christmas as the Feast of the Incarnation is clearly beyond most young children. It is obviously best to concentrate upon the *emotional feel* of Christmas rather than the intellectual understanding.

#### The 'feel' of Christmas

Aims: (a) To examine the different elements of Christmas.
       (b) To enrich and enhance the associated feelings of joy, excitement and wonder.

Most people know the feeling of Christmas. The excitement which gradually builds up: only ten shopping days to Christmas! Children share this too and can be helped to see more of the significance of Christmas.
   Children will find in the celebration of Christmas a number of elements: holly, ivy, mistletoe, Christmas trees, paper decorations, candles, yule logs, Father Christmas, cards, presents, nativity scenes, carols in the frosty air, cribs, roast turkey, plum pudding, cake and so on. These elements are from different sources, by no means all Christian, but together they make up the emotional feel of Christmas. To enrich the child's existing joy,

excitement and wonder is both a very important foundation for a developing appreciation of Christmas and also a realistic and reasonable approach at the level of the child.

### Birthdays

Aims: (a) To tell the story of the birth of Jesus in the stable.
  (b) To focus upon the sort of birthday Jesus as a child might have enjoyed.

Christmas celebrates the birthday of Jesus and a birthday is a point of contact with young children.

- Introduce the birth of Jesus in the stable, bringing out the themes of absence from home, the inns being full, and the warm welcoming straw.
- What sort of things happened at birthdays in the time of Jesus? What sort of games did children play? A number of teachers have looked at the birthday of Jesus when he was 5 or 6 years old.

### Babies

Aims (a) To discuss the sorts of things involved in preparing for the coming of a baby today.
  (b) Against that background to tell the story of Mary's journey and the birth of Jesus in the stable.

A popular approach with many infants teachers is 'Babies', especially if any of the class is expecting a brother or sister. One particular teacher with a Reception class did a very successful strand of work over a six-week period in which the children followed the preparations of one of the mothers for her expected child: refurbishing the pram, repainting the cot, scrubbing the car seat and so on. All this made the story of Mary's preparation seem much more like real life and her unexpected trip to Bethlehem at such a late stage quite horrifying.

### With Key Stage 2

### Giving

Aims: (a) To study the Nativity stories with a special focus upon those concerned with gifts.
  (b) To discuss the reasons why people make gifts.
  (c) To look at examples of people who have given a lot.
  (d) To consider different ways in which all of us can give of ourselves.

A deep-rooted theme within the Nativity stories is that of 'giving'. The whole event is about the gift of Jesus to the world and within the stories there are two particular examples:

1   The magi with their gifts of gold, frankincense and myrrh.
2   The visit of the shepherds to the manger bringing (at least according to tradition) a lamb.

These stories can be told and a discussion can take place about gifts given and received.

- Focus upon the reasons for giving gifts: love, affection, thanks, concern, respect, regard and so on.
- What sort of gifts have we to offer? Health, strength, hands, feet, time, talents. . . .
- Do some work on people who have been or are outstanding in their giving of themselves:

  - Jesus himself – stories of Jesus teaching, healing, helping and finally being executed.
  - Father Damien, the priest in the nineteenth century who volunteered to serve as priest on the leper island of Molokai in the Hawaian Islands. He worked tirelessly for the welfare of his lepers and eventually contracted the disease himself.
  - Mother Teresa who worked among the sick and dying in Calcutta.

- Consider ways in which all can give. For example, the work of Oxfam, Christian Aid, Shelter, the Red Crescent.

Effective ways of working within this theme, in addition to discussions and the use of various types of writing, are through music, drama and art.

### The human family

Aims: (a) To discuss the significance of the Feast of the Epiphany.
      (b) To consider the notion of the Family of God.
      (c) To investigate the implications within the idea of the Brotherhood of Man.

- Tell the story of the magi following the star. Make the point strongly that they were *non-Jews* and that the story was included to emphasise the fact that the gift of Jesus was for all people irrespective of race or creed. Refer to the Feast of the Epiphany (see Chapter 19) and to Candlemas (see Chapter 19) which makes a similar point.
- Introduce the idea of the Family of God – that all people are children of God. Reference can be made to people like Martin Luther King and Gandhi who were motivated by such ideas. Begin to examine the notion of the Family of God. What are its implications? How does a family operate?

#### Concept of sharing, caring, protection, concern

- Begin to examine the kindred concept of the 'Human Brotherhood'. What implications has this for treatment of fellow humans?
- Look at the role of agencies which work for the elimination of poverty.
- Tell the story of the Good Samaritan. (To whom am I neighbour?)
- Examine the strong notion of brotherhood in religions: in Christianity the notion of people being sons and daughters of God and the church his family; in Islam the strong notion of brotherhood which underlies the Hajj and Zakah.

Christmas: the festival of light

An important theme of Christmas is the entry of Christ as a light in the darkness. It can be very illuminating to explore with older juniors the symbolism of light. It can be linked with the Jewish festival of light, Hanukkah which falls in December. For further details see Chapter 6.

## Diwali

Diwali is a very popular festival among Hindus and is often called the Hindu festival of light. There are many traditions underlying it but for most Hindus it celebrates among other things the story of Rama and Sita. This is recorded in the Ramayana, a very popular religious book among Hindus. There are different versions of the story but, in outline, Vishnu, one of the trimurti, takes human form in the person of Rama in order to destroy Ravana, the ten-headed demon king of Lanka (Sri Lanka). Rama is heir to the throne of his kingdom but is tricked out of it by his stepmother in favour of her son. Rama is sent into exile by his father for fourteen years and being an obedient son he goes. He is accompanied by his wife, Sita, who insists on accepting exile with him, and also by his half-brother, Lakshman. By trickery, Ravana kidnaps Sita and takes her to his island of Lanka where she resists his wooing. Rama and Lakshman, informed of this by the birds, journey towards Lanka to rescue her. Although Rama is Vishnu in human form he still is not strong enough to overcome Ravana and his hosts of demons alone, so he needs the help of the monkeys and the bears. They build a causeway across the sea to Lanka and a terrible battle ensues. Both Rama and Lakshman are mortally wounded but are saved by the bravery of Hanuman, the monkey general and hero of the battle, who has become a very popular figure in Hindu devotion.

The battle ends with single-handed combat between Rama and Ravana. Rama takes a single arrow which he blesses and fires it straight into the heart of Ravana. With Ravana's death the demon kingdom is overthrown, Sita is rescued from her demon jailers and Rama is restored to his kingdom. The people are delighted at his return and light hundreds of lamps to welcome him back.

This in essence is the story which underlies the festival of Diwali. Over the four-day festival, participants light lamps, families meet up, special meals are enjoyed and many hands and feet are decorated with rangoli patterns.

With *younger children* it is likely that teachers will remain with the story and look at diva lights and rangoli patterns. One Reception class was taken to a temple at Diwali time and were thrilled and excited by the wonderful atmosphere created by the lights. There may not have been much cognitive understanding but the children did pick up on the beauty and the joy and the excitement of the festival.

However there are deeper themes in the story which can be considered by *older pupils*. The story reflects the great battle between good and evil – which all religions deal with. This underlies too the story of the life, death and resurrection of Jesus in Christianity (and is reflected in the children's novel, *The Lion, the Witch and the Wardrobe*). The story of Rama and Sita also brings out the duties of relationships, what people owe to each other. So Rama is presented as the ideal king or ruler and ideal son, Sita as the ideal wife, Lakshman as the ideal brother, Hanuman as the ideal friend. These figures are models which have strongly influenced Hindus over many centuries.

With older pupils some of these themes can be explored:

* What do we mean by good and evil?
* How do they respond to the idealised relationships?
* How do they perceive relationships? What makes a good son/daughter, parent?
* Are there role models today?

## Barmitzvah/Batmitzvah

Barmitzvah/Batmitzvah is not a festival but a religious celebration within Judaism, often called a 'rite of passage'. Barmitzvah means literally son of the commandment, and Batmitzvah daughter of the commandment, and it is a celebration and ceremony which marks the coming of age of Jewish boys and girls. This normally takes place when a boy is 13 and a girl 12.

It needs to be noted that in Orthodox Judaism, only boys normally have such a ceremony but in the Liberal and Reform movements both boys and girls are treated equally in this respect. At the ceremony the boys or girls take on the responsibility of keeping the Torah and so take their places as Jewish adults.

### Learning intentions

Children should:

* be taught the significance of the Torah in Judaism;
* learn about the preparation for the Barmitzvah/Batmitzvah and the ceremony itself;
* consider issues of responsibility and maturity for themselves.

### Content

* Significance of the Torah across the whole of life
* Different interpretations within Judaism, especially over the food laws
* Centrality of the Ark containing the Torah scroll in the synagogue
* Preparation for Barmitzvah/Batmitzvah with the rabbi
* Learning to read from the Torah in Hebrew
* Reading out the appropriate passage at the ceremony
* Promising to keep the Torah – and so becoming an adult and full member of the Jewish community
* Large celebration party with presents
* General reflection with the class about:

    what it means to be adult
    what responsibilities adults should have
    what moral standards should be shared by all

# 14 An extended topic: pilgrimage

The aim of this chapter is to develop a topic on pilgrimage. Pilgrimage is a widespread phenomenon across all religions, and across the world hundreds of millions of people undertake one at least once in their lifetime. Even Sikhs make pilgrimages to the Golden Temple, although the founder, Guru Nanak, argued against pilgrimage on the grounds that, as all places are equally sacred and special, pilgrimage is pointless. It is important to recognise that there are two aspects to a pilgrimage. There is the actual physical journey to a place, but this journey is also symbolic of an individual's internal or spiritual journey towards arriving at a sense of meaning, a fulfilment of selfhood. That fulfilment can well be in God or Nirvana, as in the case of the troubled pilgrim to Lourdes who came home feeling that he had been made whole. It could also be a self-knowledge, self-awareness and acceptance, as in the case of those who went on the 'hippy trail' to India in previous decades and often discovered through their pilgrimage what was truly important to them. In fact an individual's pilgrimage does not even have to be a journey – it can be entirely in the mind, a mental journey. When the topic is being taught it is important that both aspects are included and provided for. Pupils will need to gain knowledge and understanding of important pilgrimages drawn from some religious traditions (AT 1), but they should also have the opportunity to consider their own growth in understanding of the great issues involved in discovering meaning (AT 2).

This chapter, developing an understanding of pilgrimage and the journey of life, begins with material for the teacher: information about places of pilgrimage, Lourdes and Walsingham for Christians and the Hajj for Muslims. Included also, so as to give a flavour of what a pilgrimage can be like in human terms, is an account written by a young teenage girl about her pilgrimage to Walsingham. In order to develop the affective dimension, reference is made to three novels appropriate to Key Stage 2 which feature children making journeys to discover who they are. In order to help bring the topic alive to pupils, various approaches are suggested, especially for use with younger children.

## Teachers' material

Underlying most religions is the notion that life is a pilgrimage – an interior movement from what one is to what one ought to be and can become. John Bunyan in *The Pilgrim's Progress* tells the allegory of Christian's journey from his home in the City of Destruction to the Celestial City and relates what he encountered on the way. Pilgrimage as a physical journey is also a widespread phenomenon in most religions. Islam has the Hajj, the pilgrimage to Makkah which is one of its Five Pillars. Each year at Passover, Jews use the phrase 'next year in Jerusalem'. Hindus travel great distances to Banares to bathe in the Ganges. Christians make pilgrimage to Jerusalem to retrace the steps of Christ. Sikhism has a strong tradition which is against pilgrimages, though this does not prevent many Sikhs making pilgrimage, especially to the Golden Temple at Amritsar.

Behind the notion of pilgrimage is the idea that certain places are special or, to use a religious term, holy (literally: set apart). That certain places have special significance is part of everyday experience. The couple who return each year on their wedding anniversary to a forest to locate a particular tree under which they agreed to marry are making a sort of pilgrimage. Devotees of Shakespeare who visit the sites associated with him in and around Stratford-upon-Avon are demonstrating the same phenomenon. So too were the Russians who queued all day in order to file silently past the embalmed body of Lenin in his mausoleum by the Kremlin walls.

In religious practice certain places are made sacred by history and by prayer and so they are marked off from the territory round about. In Judaism, for example, the land of Israel is sacred. In Jewish theology it is the promised land, given by God. In that sense it is marked off from every other piece of land. Within the promised land there are also different degrees of specialness. Jerusalem occupies a special place in people's loyalty and affection. It housed the temple and the Ark of the Covenant. In particular the Western Wall (usually known as the Wailing Wall), all that remains of Herod's great temple and of ancient Jerusalem, is now of special significance. This is special and sacred.

Sacred places are often associated with the 'Founders' of religions. For Christians, for example, Jerusalem is pre-eminent because it was the scene of the most significant events in the life of Jesus. Here God walked! In Islam Makkah is intimately associated with Muhammad. In Hinduism Banares is associated with both Shiva and Rama. In Sikhism, the Golden Temple at Amritsar, built by the Fifth Guru, Arjan, is a place of special pilgrimage to many.

### Lourdes

Many holy places are associated with special holy people or saints. In the Christian religion, for example, places associated with appearances of Mary, mother of Jesus, are very popular. Especially well known are the shrines at Fatima in Portugal, Guadalupe in Mexico, Knock in Ireland, Walsingham in England and, of course, most famous of all, Lourdes, in south-west France. A brief look at Lourdes will indicate another aspect of pilgrimage – the notion of being made whole.

Lourdes is a small town in the foothills of the Pyrenees. In 1858 a 14-year-old girl, Bernadette Soubirous, witnessed eighteen appearances of Mary at the Grotto of Massabiele. At first she was teased by her friends and her mother forbade her to go again to the grotto for no one else saw the 'lady, young and beautiful, exceedingly beautiful, the like of whom I have not seen before'. However, her simplicity and quiet persistence led them all to change their minds and, after the visions ceased, she was able to convince the suspicious church authorities that she had indeed seen the Virgin. Mary did not appear again at Lourdes, nor indeed again to Bernadette, but she left a spring of water which continues to flow. Bernadette herself became a nun; she died in 1879 and was canonised in 1933. Long before Bernadette was canonised, Lourdes had become a great centre of pilgrimage. Many sick people came to bathe in the waters of the spring and there were many reported cures. The sick come in their hundreds of thousands each year to Lourdes and one of the most impressive sights for the visitor to Lourdes, whether as tourist or pilgrim, is to see the sick wheeled out on beds or in chairs to attend either a mass at the grotto or the Blessed Sacrament Procession. Naturally most of the sick hope deep down for a cure from their disease but the official view is that healing may take other forms and is, at root, about reconciliation with God. Lourdes is now the largest centre of Christian pilgrimage.

### Why go on pilgrimage?

It is clear that pilgrimage is therefore a large-scale activity within a number of religions and that many believers will put themselves to considerable expense, trouble and inconvenience to make pilgrimages. In Chaucer's *Canterbury Tales*, which is itself set within the context of a pilgrimage from London to the shrine of the martyred archbishop, Thomas à Becket, at Canterbury, it is revealed that one of the pilgrims, the Wife of Bath, has also been on pilgrimage to the shrine of St James at Compostello in northern Spain and also to the Holy Land itself.

What makes a pilgrimage different from a sightseeing holiday? The answer seems to be in the attitude of the individual. Those who go to the holy place to stare are the tourists, those who go to worship are the pilgrims. The pilgrim's motive may be an expression of devotion; it may be an offering of thanks; it may be to seek the healing of body, mind and spirit. It may be to seek a bridge between the present and the past. Above all, though, it will be a desire to draw nearer to God, if only for a short time. That is the central motive of the pilgrim.

### Walsingham

There is a common impression around, and certainly among many children, that pilgrimages are odd and exotic, and this view is reinforced by stories of extravagancies such as climbing steps upon the knees. Those who have been on pilgrimage are usually more impressed by the normality and ordinariness of it all. This point is made in the account below written by a very articulate teenage girl of a pilgrimage she made to the English shrine of Our Lady of Walsingham from her suburban Church of England parish. This conveys, one suspects, the atmosphere of a fairly typical modern pilgrimage.

Walsingham is a small village in the county of Norfolk which houses the restored shrine of Our Lady. In 1061 Richeldis, Lady of the Manor of Walsingham, received three visions of Mary in which she was shown the Holy House in Nazareth where Jesus had grown up. She was particularly told to note the dimensions so that she could build a replica. Richeldis did this and also built a church to cover the Holy House. So Walsingham, England's Nazareth, became a shrine of international patronage until the Reformation when it was destroyed and the Virgin's image burnt at Smithfield. In 1931 the vicar of the parish began the process of restoring the shrine. The Roman Catholic Church acquired the Slipper Chapel in 1934, the place where pilgrims remove their shoes to walk the last mile. About half a million pilgrims now visit Walsingham each year.

The coach was due outside the church on Saturday morning at 8 a.m. to take us to Walsingham. At five to eight all but two of us were there because Father Alan said that the coach was going to leave on time and anybody who missed it would be left behind and not get a refund. In the end the only person late was Father Alan and we couldn't go without him because he was leading the pilgrimage. I went with my mum. My dad didn't want to go so he stayed at home to look after Andrew and Paul. On the coach I sat with my friend, Carol, who is thirteen. We stopped at Newmarket at a hotel with a nice garden. We sat in the sunshine and had sandwiches and a drink. Carol and I had cokes and lots of others had beer. Father Alan had gin. When we left the hotel the coach driver said that the next stop was Walsingham.

I had not been to Walsingham before but my mum had and she thought it was nice. Father Alan had told us about the story of the Virgin Mary appearing to a lady called Richeldis in 1061 and telling her to build a copy of Jesus' home in Nazareth. My friend Carol asked Father Alan if it was true. He said he didn't know but whether it was or not Walsingham was a very special place because so many people had been there to pray.

As we got near to Walsingham some people began to sing a long song which told the story of Walsingham right from the start. About a mile from Walsingham we stopped at a place called the Slipper Chapel which was where in olden days pilgrims used to take off their shoes and walk the last mile with bare feet. Some from our church wanted to walk the last mile. Carol and I were a bit stiff from sitting so we decided to walk too but we kept our shoes on.

Walsingham was really lovely. It was very pretty but it wasn't just that. It was sort of still and deep as well. We all met up with Father Alan and the coach outside the church. Father Alan was a bit cross because he thought the walkers had taken their time. We all went into the shrine and said some prayers by an altar near the door. Father Alan said we could have five minutes in the shrine church before we had to go to find out where we were to sleep. The shrine was lovely. It was quite dark and there were golden altars everywhere. Inside the church was a much smaller building and my mum said this was a copy of Mary's house at Nazareth. We went inside this. It was quite small and would have been very dark except that hundreds of candles were burning in it. They made it very hot. At the other end was an altar and above it was a statue of Mary wearing a golden robe holding the baby Jesus in her left arm and a large lily in her right arm. It made me feel quite excited.

Then we had to go to find out where we were to sleep. Carol and I were lucky as we were sharing a room in the convent. Mr. and Mrs. Pink had to sleep out in the village and weren't very pleased. We had supper and in the evening there was a procession outside round the shrine grounds. Four men, all from our parish, carried a statue of Our Lady of Walsingham and the rest of us – and there were lots of people – carried candles and sang the hymn we had sung in the coach. A man took photographs of us as we walked. After this Carol and I had to go to bed. All the grown ups seemed to go out. In the morning my mum told me that they had all gone down to the pub for a drink and played snooker. Father Alan surprised them all by being really good at snooker.

Early Sunday morning each parish had its own Eucharist in different parts of the shrine church. We were lucky because we were given the Holy House for our service. After breakfast Father Alan was doing Stations of the Cross. All round the gardens there were pictures of Jesus on his way to his crucifixion. On the way he stopped fourteen times and there was a picture for each one. Father Alan took us from one to the next and stopped to say a prayer before each one.

After that we were free and Carol and I went for a walk round Walsingham. It was really lovely. We found a funny old railway station with the door open. We went inside and it was a church but different. We asked Father Alan and he told us that it was Russian Orthodox.

In the afternoon, Carol and I were walking with our mums down the main street going to look at the photographs the man had taken the night before when a fleet of coaches, full of

Afro-Caribbean pilgrims arrived. They all climbed out and began to process to the Slipper Chapel. They were led by a steel band and everyone was singing and dancing and clapping. It was really happy and you couldn't help joining in. Father Alan told us that they were Roman Catholics and that they kept the Slipper Chapel as their shrine.

Before we left, there was another procession – of Christ in His Blessed Sacrament. Some boys from our parish helped with this. This made Carol ever so cross because she felt it wasn't fair that boys could do all these things but girls never had the chance. It didn't worry me because I was happy just to watch. Just before the coach went I had the chance to go by myself into the Holy House. This was the loveliest bit and I said a prayer for my Grandad who was ill.

At five o'clock prompt the coach left and we were on our way home. I liked Walsingham. It is a very special place. I want to go again soon.

This account conveys something of the pilgrim's feelings – of atmosphere, of 'specialness', of awe and devotion. It also portrays pilgrimages as a group activity – pilgrimages are rarely solitary – with all that that entails in terms of togetherness and *bonhomie*. It presents too the idea of pilgrimage as an interweaving of religious feeling with the rest of life: the pilgrimage weekend to Walsingham contained both moments of deep and tender devotion and also playing snooker in the pub and grumbling about lodgings! This is a long way from many people's idea of pilgrimages as humourless and unsmiling affairs.

### The Hajj

The Hajj, one of the Pillars of Islam, is the annual pilgrimage to Makkah. Makkah is the most holy place on earth for Muslims (Medina and Jerusalem are second and third) because it was the home of Muhammad and it was also the place, so Muslims believe, in which he received the revelations of Allah (God) through the Archangel Gabriel. All Muslims are expected, providing their circumstances permit it, to make the pilgrimage at least once in their lifetime. Muslims can visit Makkah at any time in the year and make an umrah, but to undertake the Hajj requires pilgrims to gather at the set time during the year when Muslims from all over the globe gather. With the easy availability of air travel now, many more Muslims have the opportunity to make the Hajj and about two million come to Makkah each year. All who have made the Hajj can add the title to their name: Hajji for a male and Hajjah for a female.

For both the Hajj and the umrah all pilgrims remove their normal clothing and put on the ihram, a simple outfit consisting of two pieces of unsewn cloth, one to put around the waist and the other over the shoulders. All dress alike to emphasise that, whatever class distinctions or nationalities there might be, all are equal brothers and sisters before God during the pilgrimage. The ihram is like a burial shroud and this symbolises the death of self which enables the pilgrims to focus all their attention upon God. After the Hajj pilgrims pack away their ihrams so that they can become, when the time comes, their actual burial shrouds.

During the Hajj, pilgrims undertake a number of activities together. It is probably counter-productive to go through all the elements in the pilgrimage with pupils. The following might be regarded as especially significant. All are symbolic acts.

The Hajj begins and ends at the Ka'bah, a large black stone, possibly a meteorite, of very special significance, housed in a splendid cube-shaped structure in the centre of Makkah. Pilgrims process around the Ka'bah seven times in a vast crowd, kissing and touching the black stone each time and repeating the shanadah (the confession that there is no God but Allah and Muhammad is his prophet) continuously.

Among other activities undertaken on the Hajj are the following:

- At the field of Arafat, said to be the place where Adam and Eve were taught that people were created to worship God, pilgrims pray for forgiveness from noon until sunset for all the sins committed which have separated them from God.
- At Mina, a village close to Makkah, pilgrims throw stones at three pillars which represent the devil who tempted their ancestor, Ishmael.
- Pilgrims sacrifice an animal in remembrance of Abraham who was willing to sacrifice his longed-for son, even though at the crucial moment God provided a ram to sacrifice in Isaac's place. The meat from these sacrifices is largely shared among the poor and needy (and has incidentally presented Saudi Arabia with significant problems of refrigeration and storage). Again, this is an act symbolising a willingness, like Abraham, to sacrifice oneself and all that one has to the service of God. This act of sacrifice, although a part of the pilgrimage, is celebrated at the same time throughout the Muslim world, as the festival of Id-ul-Adha.

For Muslims, taking part in the Hajj is a tremendous spiritual experience. It increases devotion to God, it enhances loyalty to the Prophet and his teaching, and it renews faith. It binds Muslims together and it inspires. In a way, Ramadan, the month of fasting, has similarities with Hajj. It is a pilgrimage of faith although people stay at home. Like Hajj it increases devotion to God, helps people to give more time and reflection to the teaching of the Prophet, renews faith and binds people together.

The pilgrimage ends with a final visit to and procession around the Ka'bah. Then comes the journey back to the huge King Abdullah Aziz International Airport at Jeddah for the journey home to Britain, Russia, the USA, Canada, Pakistan or wherever. This reflects the international composition of Islam.

**Pilgrimage in the classroom**

Any work on pilgrimage in the classroom should attempt to move beyond the level of information: pupils do need to know the facts of the Hajj just described but they also need to develop some understanding of its significance for Muslims, as well seeing some relevance for their own lives.

The following aims should point the work in the right direction. Pupils should be helped to:

- know about pilgrimages made in different religions;
- develop some awareness of why people go on pilgrimage;
- begin to see life as a pilgrimage/journey in search of meaning.

On approaching the work it is likely that there will be a stronger focus on *explicit* work on pilgrimage with pupils in Key Stage 2. Before that, foundation work is likely to be provided by a general topic on 'Journeys', though this should also include explicit religious material.

### Journeys

'Journeys' is a popular topic with younger children because it arises so naturally from their own experiences and can be developed in so many different ways:

> How we came to school this morning
> > What roads did we go down?
> > How did we come – on foot, by car?
> > Did we come on our own, with friends?
> Journeys on holiday – by car, coach, train, aeroplane, boat
> Difficult journeys – being stuck in the snow, breaking down in the car
> Frightening journeys – crossing a rough sea, driving over a high bridge or viaduct
> > ('I kept my yes shut tight!')
> Exciting journeys – into space, climbing up hills and mountains
> Boring journeys
> Imaginary journeys – journeys I would like to make
> Good places to arrive at – grandparents' house, holiday centre, a funfair

It is very easy to see how this can extend language work and develop mathematics, early map work and a host of other things. It can also extend into other areas of study such as transport and into related areas such as the journey of a letter.

As far as religious education is concerned, there may be explicit material. For example, if this topic was being followed close to Christmas, then it might be appropriate to include the terrible journey that Mary had to make, according to the Nativity stories in St Luke's Gospel, from Nazareth to Bethlehem. Certainly the children's work on difficult journeys and frightening journeys would give them a much more human understanding of it. Seen as preliminary work on pilgrimages the content of 'Journeys' is much more likely to be implicit. It would be concerned to focus upon encouraging the children to reflect upon their *experiences* of journeys: of the excitement of anticipation, of the pleasure of arrival and of some of the hazards which occur on the way.

### Approaches to pilgrimage

With children in Key Stage 2 the teacher can plan work much more specifically geared to pilgrimage and reflecting the aims which have been identified.

Because the teacher is concerned to develop the children's *affective* understanding of the activities as well as a cognitive understanding, an approach through literature can be very helpful. This would be an example of *implicit* religious education, but RE none the less.

An approach which many teachers have found successful is that of studying books which deal with the notion of an individual's or a group's search or quest for something which is of great importance to them. This in itself will not meet the first aim of providing knowledge about pilgrimages such as that to Lourdes. It is more concerned to deal with the third aim of helping children to begin to see life as a pilgrimage in search of meaning.

The following section contains detailed discussions of two useful books and a brief description of a third.

*Ninny's Boat* by Clive King

*Ninny's Boat* is set in Europe in the fifth century AD. Ninny, a slave boy in the land of the Angles (modern Denmark), is the property of an unpleasant owner, Sprott, who works him hard. So distrustful is he of people – they laugh at his name and at his small dark appearance – that he opts for the company of his animals, his true friends. He knows nothing of his true friends. He knows nothing of his origins or his age with the exception of a recurring bad dream – a dream in which there is darkness and the sound of women screaming and he, a tiny child, is wrapped in a blanket in the dark and the rain – and then there is the heaving of waves. . . .

One morning Ninny awakes in his hay loft in Anglia to find himself isolated in the middle of a great flood. The others have fled, forgetting him, so he sets about rescuing himself and his animals from drowning. He finds safety on a larger island in the flood waters and, after initially an unpleasant reception by the people there, he begins to find friendship and respect and to be regarded as an equal. When the elders ponder how they might escape, it is Ninny who suggests that they build a boat. When the boat is being built, Ninny plays an important part in the process. When the boat sets sail for the Isle of the Ocean, Ninny also travels in it, taking his precious animals. After a terrifying journey across the sea, it is Ninny who steers the boat in a storm over the sand bar which brings the people safely to Britannia, the Isle of the Ocean.

Here Ninny finds that people do not laugh at his name and that there are others who resemble him physically. He begins his search in a long journey up the centre of Britannia, through the mountains and moors, to the Great Wall and then to the sea. He is caught up innocently in a great and terrible battle and, in ferrying the dying king in a boat with two black-clad women, he reaches a white building in a rocky bay – all of which he has dreamed before.

It is in this building, a Christian monastery, that Ninny learns who he is. He is no longer Ninny, but Ninian, named in honour of the great Celtic saint, and the kidnapped son of King Urr, a prince but without a kingdom.

The story is full of symbolism of pilgrimage and journey. The flight from the flood and the building of the boat evoke the story of Noah and his Ark. There are also very clear allusions to the Arthurian legends. It is not especially for this reason that a teacher may want to use the book in the context of a study of pilgrimage. Above all, the story is of a physical journey, which both parallels and facilitates Ninny's own journey of self-discovery.


*I am David* by Anne Holm

*I am David*, perhaps because it was written some years before, is much better known in schools than *Ninny's Boat*. *I am David* also uses the device of a physical journey to mirror a spiritual journey.

*I am David*, set in the last century but without any clear location, is the story of a boy who escapes from the concentration camp in which he has been reared, with the instruction to travel north until he comes to Denmark. He knows nothing of his parents or of his origin: only that he is David. In the camp he had one friend, a man called Johannes, who was like a father to him but who died. It was Johannes who taught him all he knew. For all other humans, David felt suspicion and hatred. His journey to Denmark is full of adventure and hazard but out of these experiences David begins to make discoveries for himself, slowly and suspiciously. He begins to discover an appreciation of beauty, of laughter, of love and affection and of freedom. The story is of David's journey to Denmark but embedded in it are the experiences which help him to see who he, David, really is. It ends in Denmark where David finds his mother and so also his roots and the place where he belongs.

This is the real value of the book to the theme of pilgrimage: presenting life as a search for meaning, as a continuous journey. There are specific incidents in the book which could be seen as either directly religious or close parallels. David prays to 'the God of the green pastures and still waters'; one of his earliest actions after escape is to wash his clothes and his body until they are thoroughly clean; a sheepdog which attaches itself to David is shot so that he can escape. There is a natural tendency for a teacher, especially one looking at the book from a specifically religious angle, to develop these: the meaning of faith, the parallels with baptism and with crucifixion. These temptations should be resisted, unless the connections arise naturally. In this context, the reason for using the book is to encourage the children to reflect upon David's personal journey of discovery.

### The Silver Sword by Ian Seraillier

Like *I am David* this book is well known to children. Set in wartime Poland, it tells of three children who are separated from their parents. After surviving the war they set out with a friend on the seemingly impossible task of finding their parents in the haystack of Europe.

### Pilgrimages in world religions

The aims here would be the same as those listed at the beginning of the section:

- To help children to know something of pilgrimages made in different religions.
- To help children to develop some awareness of why people go on pilgrimage.
- To help children to begin to see life as a pilgrimage/journey in search of meaning.

In this approach the religious material will be explicit. Possible alternative approaches would be:

- A discussion of secular parallels to religious pilgrimage, emphasising sharing enthusiasm, fellow feeling and common purpose, e.g. pop concerts and festivals, political marches, special sports games.
- An introduction to a medieval pilgrimage such as the one to Canterbury described by Chaucer, emphasising the mixed nature of many of the pilgrims, but also the religious nature of the journey for many of the pilgrims.
- The idea of special places, sacred to different religions, e.g. Jerusalem for Jews, Christians and Muslims, Makkah for Muslims, Lourdes and Walsingham for Christians, and so on.
- Case study I: Jerusalem

  (a) Western ('Wailing') Wall of the temple for Jews
  (b) Via Dolorosa (Christ's final journey) for Christians
  (c) Dome of the Rock for Moslems

- Finding out why these places are sacred.
- Case Study II: The Hajj
  What happens on the Hajj? Why is it so special?
- Case study III: Lourdes or Walsingham
  What made Lourdes/Walsingham into a special place of pilgrimage? What happens there today?

# 15  Beliefs in action

In Chapter 4 religion was presented as a six-dimensional activity in which all the six dimensions – doctrinal, mythological, ethical, ritual, experiential, social – represent essential aspects of religion, all of which are interrelated. In helping younger children to understand religion teachers naturally concentrate heavily upon the mythological and ritual dimensions because these are most appropriate to the age and stage of the children. Two of the dimensions, the ethical and the social, together present an important area of religious understanding, often neglected in schools, which is the relationship of the religious adherent to the world at large. Religion does not just take place in the place of worship; believers live in the world, in some places a hostile world, and live out their religion there.

There are two different aspects to this. First, all religions lay upon their followers certain ethical rules or principles which should govern their conduct or behaviour. Examples of these are the Ten Commandments in Judaism and the Law of Love in Christianity. It is everyday experience that believers fail to live up to these ethical requirements. Many of the rules or principles regulate one individual's behaviour towards another. In the Ten Commandments, for example, there are injunctions against stealing, bearing false witness, committing adultery, and so on. The ethical dimension of religions stresses such matters as caring for the poor or helping those in need. In Judaism, for example, there is great concern for the 'stranger within the gate'; in Islam there is the tradition of hospitality to strangers, and also zakah, the tax for the poor.

Second, religions have within themselves a vision of how the world ought to be and convictions about the relationship of human being with human being and human being with the world at large. Islam, for example, has the noble vision of the 'Brotherhood of Man'. The Judaeo-Christian tradition has a great vision of the human race made in the image of God and all men and women as brothers and sisters and children of the same God. During some periods of history these visions are ignored or forgotten; at other times, they assert themselves. William Wilberforce's work in the eighteenth century towards ending slavery in the British Empire is an example of this religious vision: Wilberforce believed that the Christian view of the human race as all children of God precluded some from owning others. This same vision has spurred others on to work for the relief of poverty, hunger and suffering and for the creation of just and free societies. In very recent times it has led to great concern for matters of conservation: if this is God's world which he has entrusted to us, it is argued, then we should be good stewards and not exploit it for short-term gain.

This is an area of controversy. There are many, both within religious communities and without, who draw a clear line between the *sacred* and the *secular*, and argue that the only proper sphere of activity for religions is the sacred. This usually means that religions should concern themselves solely with what is often called the 'spiritual' (worship, prayer, teaching about God, etc.) and with personal morality. Many others would reject this as too narrow a view. It seems likely to remain an area of permanent debate and disagreement.

If it is the teacher's concern to help children to understand religions as *living* activities, then as well as looking at, say, festivals it is very important to consider both the ethical demands laid upon believers and the relationship of religions to the societies in which they are set.

Much of this work will be suited to the older children in the age group because the younger ones may have insufficient experience to understand the issues at stake. There are also stories which are suitable for younger children, but in general the focus of the work will be directed to the older children.

Two approaches will be considered: individual case studies and a project on planning the ideal community.

## Individual case studies

A significant aspect of religious education has always been the individual case study or biography. Rather than, say, talking in general terms about Christian principles of loving your neighbour as yourself and about the concern for the poor and the unwanted rooted deep in the Christian tradition, why not tell the story of Mother Teresa?

Concrete examples are so much clearer than abstract ideas and certainly far more vivid, and they pinpoint the principles in real life. This is the theory behind the use of individual case studies.

All religions have within their traditions people who might be described as 'saints', that is, people who have exemplified in their lives or their actions some qualities which have set them above the general level of adherents and made them to some extent examples or models. They are also seen as inspirational figures, enthusing others.

### *Preliminary considerations*

As there are very many case studies from which to select, a number of factors should be borne in mind:

- Be careful of *overusing* individual examples. Mother Teresa, for example, is in danger of this fate. The nature of her commitment, the nature of her work and the award to her of the Nobel Peace Prize account for her extreme popularity as a case study, but she is in danger of overexposure. 'Not Mother Teresa again!'
- Select carefully. Dr Schweitzer figured on most teachers' lists of case studies for many years because he gave up a dazzling career in order to devote his medical talents to the relief of leprosy in Africa at his hospital at Lambarene. Since then he has fallen from favour because of his alleged racist views and attitudes.
- It is important that case studies are drawn from different religious traditions, and

this should happen in schools without any children from ethnic minorities as well as in those which are ethnically mixed. When we are considering the teaching of children up to the age of 11, it may well be that a majority of the examples are drawn from the Christian tradition but it would be very sad if there was no mention of the tolerance and understanding of Guru Nanak, the courage of Guru Gobind Singh or the non-violent tradition of Mahatma Gandhi.

- Make sure that the children have some understanding of the situation in which the chosen case study took place. If, for example, Desmond Tutu is taken as a case study then it is essential that children have *some* understanding of apartheid.
- If it is at all possible, try to use people in the local community. One teacher discovered that a church in a socially deprived area quite close to her school ran a sheltered workshop for disabled people. A visit there did much more to assist pupils to see religion in action than lots of case studies from distant places. The same was true of a Gurdwara in west London.

## Examples

### Young children

The most suitable approach at this stage would be to select a particular quality, for example courage or caring, and to choose an example which illustrates that quality. To take 'courage', the old favourite example of Grace Darling who risked her own life in rowing out in stormy seas to rescue shipwrecked sailors is as good as any.

To take 'caring for animals', the old story of St Francis is a good example, though it should be remembered that there is much more to St Francis than that.

In general, with younger children it is useful to take examples within the children's own experience. To take 'caring', for example, it is often more appropriate to look at people within the children's experience – the school nurse, the school crossing officer, the community police officer, the school secretary, and so on – and to look at ways in which they demonstrate caring qualities.

### Older children

The use of case studies with the older children can be a very rewarding approach, adding both interest and excitement. The stories tend to be heroic in that they represent the subjects making a stand for what they believe to be right, often against a background of great resistance and at great personal cost. Some are comparatively straightforward, others are more complex because of the situation in which they are set.

One type of case study would concentrate on the *possible cost of discipleship*. An excellent example of this is the wartime story of Maximilian Kolbe, a Roman Catholic monk who was imprisoned in a concentration camp because of his religious allegiance. While in there he substituted himself for a Jewish prisoner on the way to the gas chambers because this prisoner had a wife and family. Stories of this sort should speak for themselves as impressive human actions. They will almost certainly provoke discussion and the teacher may well use this opportunity to consider the strength of religious belief.

Another type of case study would focus on the activity of individuals who felt driven by their religious beliefs *to concentrate upon a particular task*, often at personal cost. A popular example of this is Father Damien, the nineteenth-century Belgian mission priest who while working in Hawaii heard of the plight of the lepers in the leper colony on Molokai. He sought permission to go as their priest and despite initial hostility from the lepers and indifference from the authorities managed to create a self-respecting community – before he himself contracted leprosy and died.

A third type of case study would concentrate on the activity of individuals who felt compelled by their convictions to resist laws and systems which they felt to be unjust. One example here would be Trevor Huddleston, the Anglican monk sent by his community to work in the large black parish of Sophiatown in South Africa. Here he found that many of the regulations and laws with regard to blacks so offended his conscience that he was compelled to protest on both a national and international scale. Similar case studies would be those of Martin Luther King and Helder Camara. In all these three examples the pupils need to have some understanding of the political and social background.

There are, of course, numerous case studies which could be selected: Mother Teresa, Elizabeth Fry, Lord Shaftesbury, Dr Barnardo, Mahatma Gandhi, to name but a few. The great problem is always one of relevance and very often a local person, perhaps far less heroic, can seem more real.

## Planning an ideal community

A useful way of encouraging children to think about and discuss the practical implications of beliefs for living is to set them the task of planning an ideal community. A teacher of 10- to 11-year-olds describes how such an activity worked:

> In my RE work with my class I had been looking at the implications of religious faith for the way life is lived. My method had been the time-hallowed one of telling stories of remarkable men and women. In some senses it has all gone very well. I know I tell stories well and the children have enjoyed them, have been prepared to talk about and seemed to have remembered them. On the other hand, I was not convinced that it has had much personal impact upon the children! I was very puzzled about what to do until I overheard a heated argument between two children. The news had just been leaked to the press of a proposal to close the local cottage hospital on the grounds of cost. One girl was shocked by this while a boy thought it a sensible idea. I joined in the argument and asked the question 'why'. The girl was not very articulate but it became clear that she was worried that if the physiotherapy section closed, it would make life very difficult for many old people. The boy thought that money should focus on the big hospitals. It struck me that this was really an argument about values, about what was really important. That was where the idea began.
>
> The following week I talked to all the children as a class and explained to them that I was going to split them into groups of five and that each group had to plan the ideal town/village. The end product was to be a model of the community showing roads, houses and other buildings. In order to reach that goal, each group would have to sort out (a) what buildings and services ought to be there and (b) where these ought to be placed. I thought the task might daunt the children but it didn't seem to. In fact the groups settled down to it very quickly.
>
> The quality of the discussion, in terms of ideas, in interactive argument and in language use, was very impressive indeed. There were many discussions on the need for facilities like hospitals, fire-stations, dentists, hairdressers, supermarkets, parking, family housing, housing for old people, places of worship, community centres and many, many other things. The next stage was where to place them. Should the community centre be at the centre, or perhaps the church or mosque or the supermarket?

In the end seven different village models were produced – in some ways very similar, in others very different. What of course was important was the decision-making process that went on during the work with a free discussion of values. I felt that this was a much more constructive approach. Nothing was imposed but the children had been challenged to think and to make decisions on questions of values?

# 16 Assessment, recording, reporting and accountability

The process of assessment, recording and reporting has become an increasingly important area of development in schools since the Education Reform Act of 1988. This does not mean that teachers before this date did not assess the work their pupils were doing or keep records or report back to parents either orally at a parents' consultation evening or through the written school report. Since 1988, however, there has been a statutory requirement that in the core subjects assessments will be made (and published) at 7, 11, 14 and 16 and that each child's progress in all the foundation subjects must be reported annually to parents.

## The purpose of assessment

In broad terms, assessment is usually perceived to have four main interlocking purposes:

1 *Informative* – assessment finds out what progress has been made and this information can be conveyed to pupils and their parents.
2 *Formative* – in this way pupils can be helped to be involved in the assessment process.
3 *Diagnostic* – assessing pupils' progress identifies strengths and weaknesses and enables teachers to act accordingly.
4 *Summative* – assessment makes it possible to present a record of attainment at a particular stage.

In practical terms, for most teachers, assessing RE enables them to *measure* the progress of pupils in the subject. This in turn enables them to know with some precision the level of attainment of individual pupils so that they can provide additional support for those who require it. Similarly pupils themselves can become more clearly aware of areas which need development. Only with this knowledge are teachers able to report securely to parents on the progress of their children; a general impression unsupported by any firm evidence is a poor basis for such reporting. Assessment is also part of the monitoring and evaluation process. There is an educational jingle which goes 'plan, do, review' and assessment provides teachers with an opportunity to evaluate their own effectiveness in planning and doing and can therefore lead to a review both of the teaching content and of the delivery.

**Assessing in RE**

Talk of assessing RE can cause an instant concern in some teachers because of fear that such an assessment will intrude upon a pupil's proper privacy. However, there should be no intention of assessing pupils' orthodoxy or whether they have or do not have a religious commitment, or whether they have 'right' or 'wrong' values. These would be quite inappropriate areas to assess given the aims and intended outcomes of RE in schools. Rather it is pupils' knowledge and understanding which is the subject of assessment. Pupils are taught, for example, a considerable amount of information about religions and part of the assessment will be the ability to recall significant facts, to see them within a context and to communicate them clearly either in speech or in writing. Beyond this, pupils are helped to see the implications of religious belief for ways of living and for moral issues. These, for example, would be entirely appropriate areas to assess and this would not intrude in any way into a pupil's privacy.

*Criteria for effective assessment*

- Assessment is an essential part of the learning process and not something bolted on.
- Assessment tasks are related to the learning intentions.
- Teachers' judgements are based on an informed knowledge and understanding of religions.
- Planned assessment tasks are realistic both in the demands of the activity and the frequency of implementation.

It is important to emphasise two of these points. First, all teachers when delivering RE should have identified clear learning intentions in their planning. Assessment should seek to discover to what extent these have been achieved. On a larger scale, too, most agreed syllabuses identify end of key stage indicators of attainment. Assessment at the end of a key stage will be related to these indicators. Second, assessment must be manageable otherwise it will not be successful. If, for example, there are three RE topics a year, one assessment task for each is likely to be both achievable and adequate.

In this way, evidence starts to accumulate from formative assessment which is an integral part of teaching and the means whereby teachers begin to build up a picture of their pupils' needs, achievements and abilities. This leads on in turn to summative assessment, which is reached by using the information gleaned from formative assessment to form a judgement about pupils' overall levels of achievement. Identifying summative achievement may also be supplemented by specific assessment tasks related to attainment targets for RE, as described in the example below.

This is an account by a Year 6 teacher of approaches in his junior school to the summative assessment of RE:

> Assessment in RE has caused some ruffled feathers among one or two colleagues because, basically, they are still working their way into a non-confessional approach to RE. However, we did agree in Year 6 that we would undertake a formal assessment on the children's understanding of festivals. Some colleagues thought the best approach to it would be through observation and discussion but I felt that we needed to collect some hard evidence which I could keep in preparation for any inspection which might come our way.

Our agreed syllabus expects that at the end of Key Stage 2 pupils should be able to show an understanding and knowledge of religious festivals and ceremonies and this understanding and knowledge should involve both being able to describe how two different festivals or ceremonies are celebrated and give reasons why they are celebrated.

The children had studied examples of both festivals and what we call 'rites of passage' so they had covered major festivals such as Christmas, Easter, Passover, Diwali and Id-ul-Fitr and also, as examples of rites of passage, baptism, weddings, Barmitzvahs and the sacred thread ceremony.

We therefore set the pupils a task which was designed to elicit their general knowledge of the structure of an identified festival or ceremony and their awareness of the reasons behind the festival. We 'brainstormed' for a few minutes about the assessment task: write a guide for tourists about a festival to be held, produce a booklet on baptism for parents, produce a tape explaining the significance of a festival, give a group presentation on. . . . In the end we opted to offer a choice, either the guide for tourists or the book for parents.

The actual tasks were enjoyed by the pupils and I also had my evidence!

Although this task was used for summative assessment, it could equally be used as a piece of formative assessment in an RE topic in Key Stage 2.

## Approaches to assessing RE

Unlike the subjects of the National Curriculum there is no legal requirement that pupils' understanding of RE should be assessed and it is left up to every agreed syllabus to determine whether or not this should happen. Initially there were those who thought it should not be assessed, usually for fear of stepping over into that area which is private and personal to the individual, as we noted earlier. However, most felt or have come to feel that RE should not be excluded, either from the benefits to the teacher, pupil and parents which assessment provides, or from general accountability to stakeholders.

### *Statements of attainment*

Some agreed syllabuses make provision for assessment by identifying *end of key stage statements of attainment*. Such statements do provide a focus for assessment but there are problems about levels of knowledge and understanding.

In one agreed syllabus an end of key stage statement of attainment for Key Stage 2 is: 'Explain the significance of a specified rite of passage.' This is a broad question and rites of passage could include among others baptism, Barmitzvah, marriages in different traditions, and death rites in various religions. If we take baptism as the focus, some children may just get it wrong: 'It's when you die.' This is quite straightforward: these pupils clearly do not meet this statement of attainment. Others may say: 'It's blessing a baby' or 'It's giving a baby its name' or 'Christians believe that in baptism a person becomes a child of God and a member of the church.' Now the first two responses are very weak definitions. It would be hard to say that neither has any truth in it but they both represent a much lower level of understanding than the third account. Yet all three could be seen as meeting this statement of attainment. This demonstrates the weakness of this method: it does not discriminate sufficiently between responses and so is a blunt instrument.

### Level descriptors

Other agreed syllabuses preferred to work with *models of assessment involving levels*. One which received considerable support was developed in 2000 by the Qualifications and Curriculum Authority (QCA). This was later taken up by and forms part of the Non-Statutory Framework for Religious Education (2004). It identifies eight levels of attainment with an additional level which recognises exceptional performance. Each level contains two sets of level descriptors, one for attainment target 1 and one for attainment target 2. It is expected that pupils at the end of Key Stage 1 will be placed on levels 1–3, with the bulk at level 2. For pupils at the end of Key Stage 2 it is expected that their range would be levels 2–5, with the bulk at level 4.

### National Framework level descriptors

The first five attainment levels are set below – the ones which are relevant to pupils in the Foundation Stage and Key Stages 1 and 2.

### Level descriptors for attainment target 1

**Learning about religion** refers to how pupils develop their knowledge, skills and understanding with reference to:

- Beliefs, teachings and sources
- Practices and ways of life
- Forms of expression

### Level descriptors for attainment target 2

**Learning from religion** refers to how pupils, in the light of their learning about religion, express their responses and insights with regard to questions and issues about:

- Identity and belonging
- Meaning and purpose and truth
- Values and commitments

### Attainment targets for religious education

### Level 1

Attainment target 1

Pupils use some religious words and phrases to recognise and name features of religious life and practice. They can recall religious stories and recognise symbols, and other verbal and visual forms of religious expression.

Attainment target 2

Pupils talk about their own experiences and feelings, what they find interesting or puzzling and what is of value and concern to themselves and to others.

### Level 2

Attainment target 1

Pupils use religious words and phrases to identify some features of religion and its importance for some people. They begin to show awareness of similarities in religions. Pupils retell religious stories and suggest meanings for religious actions and symbols. They identify how religion is expressed in different ways.

Attainment target 2

Pupils ask, and respond sensitively to, questions about their own and others' experiences and feelings. They recognise that some questions cause people to wonder and are difficult to answer. In relation to matters of right and wrong, they recognise their own values and those of others.

### Level 3

Attainment target 1

Pupils use a developing religious vocabulary to describe some key features of religions, recognising similarities and differences. They make links between beliefs and sources, including religious stories and sacred texts. They begin to identify the impact religion has on believers' lives. They describe some forms of religious expression.

Attainment target 2

Pupils identify what influences them, making links between aspects of their own and others' experiences, They ask important questions about religion and beliefs, making links between their own and others' responses, They make links between values and commitments, and their own attitudes and behaviour.

### Level 4

Attainment target 1

Pupils use a developing religious vocabulary to describe and show understanding of sources, practices, beliefs, ideas, feelings and experiences. They make links between them, and describe some similarities and differences both within and between religions. They describe the impact of religion on people's lives. They suggest meanings for a range of forms of religious expression.

Attainment target 2

Pupils raise, and suggest answers to, questions of identity, belonging, meaning, purpose, truth, values and commitments. They apply their ideas to their own and other people's lives. They describe what inspires and influences them and others.

### Level 5

Attainment target 1

Pupils use an increasingly wide religious vocabulary to explain the impact of beliefs on individuals and communities. They describe why people belong to religions. They understand that similarities and differences illustrate distinctive beliefs within and between religions and suggest possible reasons for this. They explain how religious sources are used to provide answers to ultimate questions and ethical issues, recognising diversity in forms of religious, spiritual and moral expression, within and between religions.

Attainment target 2

Pupils ask, and suggest answers to, questions of identity, belonging, meaning, purpose and truth, values and commitments, relating them to their own and others' lives. They explain what inspires and influences them, expressing their own and others' views on the challenges of belonging to a religion.

When using this approach to assess the performance of a pupil it is important to look at the statements and to see which level best reflects a child's achievements. It is essentially a 'best fit' approach. When undertaking this task teachers need to look very carefully at each descriptor, and also look at it in relation to the descriptors in both the level below and the level above. Considering the descriptors in the adjacent levels assists both in interpreting the statements and also in adding greater precision to the judgement made.

It is important to note that such an assessment instrument is useful not only for making more precise assessments of pupils' progress and achievement but also for providing important guidance on identifying *progression* in RE. In a very simple way a teacher can look at level 1 and identify its marks. How do we move on? We can look at the descriptors in level 2 and so on up the levels. If we take, for example, religious story, which plays a very significant part in RE work with young children, we can note the progression through the levels. In level 1 pupils *recall* religious stories; in level 2 pupils *retell* religious stories; in level 3 they *use* religious stories (now linked with sacred texts) to make links between beliefs and sources. Thereafter religious stories are not referred to explicitly.

### An example from Key Stage 1

Here is an account written by a 7-year-old child towards the end of Key Stage 1 on the subject of 'Our Class Visit to the Church'. The work was set by the teacher to provide a piece of hard evidence for identifying the level the pupils had reached. It has been tidied up a little for presentation but the content is completely original.

> The visit to the church was very nice and I liked the stained glass windows best. I liked the colours and I knew some of the stories in them. We were very busy and noisy doing sketches and taking photographs of the windows, the altar, the pulpit and the big Bible.
>
> When we were in Reception we went to a Hindu temple. It was Diwali and there were lots and lots of lights and people everywhere. It was very noisy. We had to ring a bell to tell the gods we were there. At the end I was given an apple and Ben got some nuts.
>
> Once I went into the church on my own and sat on a pew. I liked it. It was so quiet I heard the clock ticking. Ben says that God lives in the church and it's scary but I don't think he does. He is too big.

Clearly in making a judgement on which is the appropriate level for this child we would need other evidence, such as other pieces of work and, very importantly, the class teacher's observations over a period of time, to be fed into making the decision. From this piece of writing we can deduce that there is a developing religious vocabulary (altar, pulpit, Bible, Diwali, church, temple); there is knowledge of some religious stories (some of those represented in the church windows); certain features of both a church and a Hindu temple are described and to a degree contrasted (the busy noise and movement of the temple and the peace of the church); and there is a description of some forms of religious expression (especially of the temple and of Diwali). All these would relate to attainment target 1. With reference to attainment target 2, the pupil in question is thinking about and reflecting on religion and trying to make sense of beliefs (can God really live in the church?) and contrasting his viewpoint with that of Ben. He is also identifying an approach to the religious quest which suits him (the calm and quiet of the church).

Providing that the rest of the evidence is of a similar standard, the level for this pupil would seem to be level 3. He does not meet all level descriptors in level 3 but he has certainly moved beyond level 2 and is not yet up to level 4. The levels do have to be seen as 'best fit' and they are to a degree a rough and ready guide, but they are none the less very helpful in many ways. This pupil would then be judged to be above average for his age and stage and progressing well.

### Examples from Key Stage 2

A teacher of any class is bound to find that there is a range of levels among the children. With 11-year-old pupils at the end of Key Stage 2, the bulk will probably be operating at level 4 while some will reach level 5 and others will be placed at level 3 or in certain cases perhaps lower. Here are two examples from the same Year 6 class. The class, after a unit of work on Islam, was asked to write a piece on the following subject: 'You have a Muslim friend living in Britain. Placing yourself in that position, write a letter explaining why prayer is so important to Muslims, drawing on any similarities or differences with Christian practice in Britain.' Both pieces of work have been tidied up but the content remains as it was.

EXAMPLE 1

We pray five times a day and have to get up early in the morning for the first one. In a Muslim country a man calls out the times from the mosque tower. This doesn't happen in Britain. Lots of people join in but not everyone. It can be in the mosque but it can be anywhere. We face Makkah and have a prayer mat and some prayer mats have compasses in them to point to Makkah. We do it because we are taught to. Christians in Britain don't seem to pray much.

EXAMPLE 2

Prayer is very important for us Muslims. We pray five times a day as the Qur'an says. We also have the subhah (prayer beads) for other times. These have 99 beads on them and as we feel one of them we think of one of the 99 beautiful names of God. We believe that Allah is the creator of everything. He is Lord of all people and things. Because he is so great he expects our worship. He has a plan for everyone and we accept this. We praise him for his power and majesty. We don't really ask for things. We pray five times a day (not everybody does and some of my friends don't) so that the whole day from dawn to night is filled with his praise. Each time of prayer is like bathing in cool water on a hot day, very refreshing. We lose ourselves in his greatness. It is important that in a Muslim country the muezzin calls out from the minaret of the mosque so that everybody in the city knows to stop and pray where they are or to go to a mosque. It is important for both men and women to pray but women are allowed to stay and pray at home.

Christian prayers are very different. People go to the church on Sunday but not usually on other days. They may pray on their own but I don't know. People don't talk so much about prayer. I think it is hard for Muslims to pray five times a day in Britain especially for people who work or go to school.

This is quite a difficult assignment but it did come at the end of a unit of work on Islam so relevant knowledge should have been to hand. The teacher also commented that she recognised echoes of what she had taught in both pieces. At what levels then should they be placed?

Example 1 uses some appropriate vocabulary: the pupil uses the terms Muslim, mosque, Makkah, but he does not appear to know the terms muezzin (the man who calls to prayer) and minaret ('the mosque tower'). He has some very basic knowledge of the prayer customs (the call to prayer five times each day, facing towards Makkah – he remembered clearly the detail about the compass in the prayer mat). But he does not answer the question asked. It is clear from what he says that prayer must be important because, for instance, of its frequency, but there is no hint of any reasons *why*. On the basis of this alone he would seem to fit best into level 2. However other pieces of evidence may suggest that overall a higher level might be more appropriate and it is, of course, possible that there might be issues of written articulacy so if his teacher talked to him about the reasons for the importance of prayer in Islam he might be able to display more knowledge and understanding than he has in his written piece.

Example 2, like the first example, uses appropriate vocabulary, though rather more words (Muslim, Qur'an, subhah, Allah, muezzin, minaret, mosque). The pupil is well aware of the traditions around the daily prayer but also includes the devotional private prayer using the subhah. What is impressive is her understanding of the importance of prayer in Islam. The teacher could recognise particular phrases and clauses (e.g. losing ourselves in his greatness) but the pupil has absorbed what was being taught and made it her own. She shows a very good understanding of Muslim belief about Allah – the creator, the sustainer, the protector, the ultimate Lord who is both powerful and majestic – which underlies the attitude to prayer. Prayer is essentially praise rather than intercession. She understands that the frequency of praise over the whole day has the effect of sanctifying it. Prayer is seen as a joy and a refreshment rather than a burden (like bathing in cool water on a hot day). The pupil also puts in some less welcome realities: not all do pray five times a day, and it can be quite hard for those Muslims in work or school to keep this up, presumably because society in Britain does not revolve around these five spots in the day as it does in Muslim countries. There are also a few comparisons with Christian practice in Britain.

The contrast between the two pieces of writing is considerable. A close look at the descriptors would indicate that the level achieved here should certainly be level 4, but if other pieces of evidence displayed an equally high level of insight and awareness it might be possible to place this pupil at level 5, as this is the level at which the question *why* (which she has been dealing with in her writing) rather than *what* and *how* comes more strongly into play. Whichever level is finally agreed upon, as a piece of work it is far above the average for her age group.

## Recording

Recording is a highly important activity in the assessment process because teachers' memories are fallible. First and foremost, recording acts as an *aide-mémoire* for teachers. Recording the results of assessments made, whether ongoing or at the end of the key stage, acts as a powerful and tangible source of information for future planning in the subject – for future teachers who will want to build on firm evidence and for reporting to parents on the achievement of their children. Recording should focus upon what pupils can do, and so it can be a celebration of achievement, though at the same time noting areas which should be developed.

There are different types of recording. There is the more informal approach which operates on a day to day basis, and the more formal approach using systems which operate across a whole school. Whatever system is in use it must be simple, manageable and easy to handle. If it is not, it will cease to be used sufficiently because it will prove too time-consuming. If it does not provide the evidence to help teachers to plan the next stage of learning, or the evidence for reporting to parents, then it will be seen as an expensive luxury and cease to be undertaken other than in a perfunctory way.

There is a variety of ways of recording achievement which are worth considering:

- *A school portfolio*
  This would be a portfolio of work in RE undertaken over a period of time. This can be very useful in that it can provide a visual standard of reasonably achievable work which can be very helpful both for teachers less confident in the subject and also for parents and governors.
- *Individual portfolio*
  A number of teachers find it very useful to keep a small collection of the work of individual pupils, suitably annotated. This can be a useful source of evidence in discussions with parents and in the task of drawing up a profile at the end of a key stage.
- *A record book*
  Many teachers keep an ongoing record book, with a page for each child on which they

note down significant information about the pupil. Significant observation about RE should also be recorded in this book.

- *An individual pupil record sheet*
  It is possible to devise a record sheet for RE which can be carried forward by the pupil over a school career. To create one of these it is important to identify what information needs to be recorded, for example, understanding the programmes of study, pupil's attitude and commitment to the work.

- *Pupil self-assessments*
  Pupils can be encouraged to be involved in assessment of their own work and performance. This involves teachers discussing progress with pupils, explaining the learning outcomes of the work and the approaches to assessment. In this way pupils can begin to identify their strengths and those areas which they will need to develop. Older pupils can keep an ongoing record of their progress.

Many schools will have whole school assessment and recording approaches, such as records of achievement, into which RE will fit. Some of the above approaches, however, do produce the sort of firm evidence which is needed for reporting.

## Reporting

Reporting to parents should be based firmly upon the evidence of a pupil's performance, based upon assessment activities which have been recorded accurately. The statement should, therefore, be an accurate reflection of the pupil's performance based upon the teacher's assessment. It should explain clearly the pupil's achievement across the range of programmes of study and should also focus upon the positive achievements of the pupil, along with areas for improvement. The report will therefore be summative and individual achievement will be placed in the context of what the pupils have undertaken in RE and what the school is trying to achieve.

## Accountability

It should be clear from this account that assessment, recording and reporting are all intimately related to each other and jointly they represent the school's accountability to parents and the wider community. Schools plan learning experiences for pupils based on learning intentions which they develop from syllabuses, whether National Curriculum or, in the case of RE, local agreed syllabuses provided by the wider community. These learning experiences are then carefully assessed and these assessments recorded so that schools can know much more accurately how groups and individuals have benefited from the teaching. This in turn enables schools to assess the needs of individuals and of whole classes and to respond to these in subsequent planning. This collection of evidence and the formal reporting of it to parents, either orally or in writing, is highly symbolic of the accountability of schools to those who maintain them.

# 17  Four powerful resources: ICT, artefacts, places of worship, visitors

**Information and communication technology (ICT)**

One of the great changes in education and schooling over the past few years has been the increasing importance of ICT. Videotapes have been a good way of introducing young children to faiths not on their doorstep but now, with careful use, the richness of material to be accessed from the internet can be a very powerful tool for learning, especially in the primary school – for the teacher as well as for the pupil. It is important to pause a moment on the use of the term 'careful use'. Websites do need to be vetted before use with pupils as, in the rather fraught relationships within and between some religious traditions, some websites are highly partisan. Websites too are subject to the same old problem which affected the use of reference books – pupils printing out information in quantity which they never truly make their own. Having noted this it must also be said that in careful hands the internet is an invaluable resource.

An initial step is to search for 'religious education websites' and 'religious education resources'. Always type in the full title 'religious education' rather than just RE and then a wide range of possibilities present themselves. As a start, teachers would benefit from exploring thoroughly two websites:

re-xs.ucm.ac.uk
reonline.org.uk

The former is based at the University College of St Martin, Lancaster and the latter at the Culham Institute. These are both excellent starting points as they also point to other websites as well. They are so rich in valuable material for the teacher and the pupil that many teachers will feel that they have been given as much support material as they need. If you want illustrated material on religious texts, art, pilgrimage, buildings, rites of passage, community, ultimate questions across all the major religions, then it can be easily accessed from re-xs.ucsm.ac.uk – and it also includes virtual reality tours of the religious buildings of the different faiths.

So for teachers who are seeking information, textbooks, reference books, posters and other visual aids a search through these sites will provide many of the answers.

**Artefacts**

Over a period of time artefacts have become an established element in religious education. It may not be possible to arrange a visit to a place of worship for all sorts of reasons but it should always be possible to provide pupils with first-hand experience of some of the artefacts associated with different religions. If these can be backed up with video material showing them in use, so much the better, but on their own they still provide a very valuable resource. They do have the strengths of being first-hand experience, tangible and also physically there.

An artefact is essentially an object which is used in worship, such as a prayer mat in Islam or a chalice in Christianity. In the classroom they can be used as a stimulus for work or as a reinforcement of work done. They can also be set out on an interest table for children to handle and perhaps speculate upon both their significance and their usage.

A teacher who was developing a topic on Islam wanted to focus upon the practice of prayer. Using a wall chart depicting a prayer mat, he asked the pupils to design their own mats. The work came to life when he produced a real Muslim prayer mat which the children could handle and sit upon. It also had a compass incorporated into it which enables the worshippers to face Makkah with ease. This was the real thing!

There is a concern among some teachers that they might be causing offence unwittingly by an insensitive use of artefacts. If artefacts are handled and treated with respect, there is unlikely to be any affront caused, but there are some specific points which are worth noting: for example, only handle a copy of the Qur'an with clean hands, keep it from contact with dirty floors and when it is not in use keep it wrapped in a clean cloth, again away from the floor; tell pupils not to touch the Torah scrolls on a synagogue visit, and display tefellin in a box and do not handle; in a Hindu mandir, pupils should be told not to attempt to touch the murti. By emphasising this with children teachers not only avoid causing affront but also help them to develop feelings of reverence and respect.

Artefacts can be expensive so they will need to be chosen with care and this is one of the advantages of having a clear scheme of work in a school – it is then possible to acquire those which support the areas being taught. Artefacts can probably be purchased most cheaply in shops which serve members of different religious traditions and this can be an option for those who have access to these. There are also a number of agencies which supply artefacts for educational purposes. Notable among these are:

| | |
|---|---|
| Articles of Faith | History in Evidence |
| Bury Business Centre | Unit 4, Park Road |
| Kay Street | Holmewood |
| Bury BL9 6BU | Chesterfield S42 5UY |

If funding is a serious issue then a good 'second best' is to make some artefacts. One school, actually as part of a design and technology task, arranged for its Year 5 pupils to make Buddhist prayer wheels; another school had children making a Torah scroll and mezuzahs.

### Religion box

A number of schools build up a number of artefact boxes – their Christianity box, Hinduism box and so on. These are (usually small) collections of artefacts significant to the religion in question.

Here is an account by a teacher of her rationale in choosing five artefacts.

> When I came to choose five objects for my Christianity Box I began to find difficulties immediately – difficulties, that is, of restricting my choice to five: it seemed obvious that a copy of the Bible should be in the box because of its importance in Christian life and worship and because it is the source of many of the stories about religion. Next I chose a crucifix because this representation of Christ on the cross is so widespread in Christian art and worship and such a focus for prayer and devotion. Then I chose a book of prayers because worship of God is tremendously important in Christianity. Candles are highly symbolic of light and prayer – they burn on altars and they twinkle before statues in churches so I included one of those. Lastly I chose a rosary because its use is widespread, because it is pleasant and attractive to handle and because it emphasises prayer and worship. Inevitably this is a personal selection but it does represent what I see as highly significant in Christianity.

This clearly is a personal selection. It could have included an icon or statue of the Virgin Mary with the infant Christ, a chalice or a wafer representing the Eucharist, or a palm cross, but the selection was made to support her teaching about Christianity.

This teacher described a 'Christianity Box' but Jewish boxes, Muslim boxes, Sikh boxes and so on are equally important. As with the Christianity box the artefacts need to be chosen carefully, both to reflect their significance in the tradition and also to support the focus of the teaching.

### Festivals box

Because of the importance of festivals in religions and consequently in RE, especially with younger children, it is important to be able to use artefacts to support the teaching. With the appearance of Christmas and Easter each year in the life of the school, it is especially important to have artefacts to assist here, but all the festivals taught in the school over the year need the same level of support.

### Basic artefact collections

A full collection of artefacts for a religious tradition would be almost endless; below are listed some of the key artefacts which are most appropriate to the areas of work normally covered in primary schools.

#### Christianity

| | | | |
|---|---|---|---|
| cross | crucifix | Bible (various versions) | stole |
| small statues | candles (votive, | chalice, paten and wafers | |
| (e.g. Virgin and Child) | baptismal, Paschal) | Advent candle | |
| palm cross | rosary | icon(s) | |

Buddhism

statue of the Buddha        prayer wheel

Hinduism

murtis (i.e. images of Rama and Sita, Krishna, Vishnu, Shiva, Lakshmi, Ganesh, etc.)
puja tray          arti lamp          Diwali cards          Divas          garlands

Islam

Qur'an and cover   Qur'an stand          prayer mat                 compass
prayer beads       calligraphy plaques

Judaism

tallith (prayer shawl)    yamulka (prayer hat)    Torah scroll (small)
yad (pointer)             mezuzah                 Sabbath candlesticks   Seder plate
Menorah/Hanukkiah        Havdalah candle          matzos                 festival cards

Sikhism

kara (bangle)       kangha (comb)   kirpan (dagger)    turban
turban length       chauri          rumala (covering cloth for the Guru Granth Sahib)

## Visiting places of worship

All religions express themselves in buildings and it is in these buildings that the faithful believe that in some special way they meet with the divine. Here, too, various significant rituals take place, festivals are celebrated and special objects or artefacts are housed, for example, the altar in a church, the murti in a mandir, the Ark in a synagogue, and so on. To try to understand any religion without experiencing its place of worship is very difficult if not impossible. To try to experience it additionally as a *living* centre is infinitely preferable though not always possible in the working week.

There can be few schools which are not within walking distance of a church, whether it be the village church, a town church or a cathedral. Many, too, will also have access to synagogues, mosques and temples/mandirs. A place of worship is an extremely important resource in RE – children find their visits very memorable – yet it is one which is often neglected.

Visiting places of worship is time-consuming both in the teacher's time in making the arrangements and in the pupils' time out of school so it is therefore important that visits are planned carefully and are integral to the effective teaching of a unit of RE. Generally, visits to places of worship can have two main purposes, cognitive and affective:

- *Cognitive*: pupils will be able to see the objects of worship and identify them and also to understand something of their significance in the practice of the religion.
- *Affective*: the atmosphere of a place of worship can 'speak' to the feelings. Many people

who visit churches say that in some they feel a sense of peace or tranquillity, in others they have feelings of timelessness or eternity.

Visitors to Durham Cathedral often claim that it speaks to them of majesty and power, Chartres Cathedral of mystery and depth. Some buildings do speak to people at a level deeper than that of conscious thought and it is this experience which can be very important for children. This is equally true of places of worship in other religious traditions.

There can be no doubt that for most children in the primary age range, visits to places of worship are both an enjoyable experience and a powerful source of learning.

It is very important when arranging a visit to a church, say, to ensure that the focuses of the learning are to do with religion. It is amazing how many children make such a visit and do everything but religion. Here is an account of such a visit:

> Year 5 went to the parish church last week but as far as I can tell, nothing they did was really relevant to RE! They sketched the shape of the windows and their tracery, they rubbed gravestones, wall memorial tablets and pew ends, they calculated the height of the tower and they counted the different varieties of wild flowers in the churchyard – nothing about religion at all.

Here are two further responses from teachers:

> I swear by visits to places of worship. The children love them and they remember so much about them – even the details of stained glass windows seen two years ago! I make sure that each age group makes a visit to a place of worship every year – each one with its own purpose and these are progressive.

> I took the Year 1 children to the Hindu temple at Diwali time. It was full of blazing candles. The temple looked so beautiful with the images all around and the masses of candles. The children were absolutely thrilled, so excited that they were bubbling over. Their stories and their pictures afterwards were a joy to see. When I described the visit at an RE meeting at the Teachers' Centre, I received a very poor reception: what a waste of time, the children couldn't possibly understand Hinduism! What they couldn't seem to understand was that I was concerned to foster religious feeling and experience not cognitive knowledge.

### A visit to a church at Key Stage 2

Here is the plan of a visit to a parish church by Year 3 children as part of their work on places of worship.

#### OUTSIDE THE CHURCH

Look at the architecture. How do we know it is a church?
Look for clues. How old is the building? Are there any special features, signs and symbols? Is there a graveyard? Why do you think older churches often have graveyards? What can we learn from inscriptions on gravestones?

INSIDE THE CHURCH

First let the children 'get the feel' of the church. Sit them down quietly and get them to close their eyes.

What do they feel? smell? hear?

What can they see? Look at the colours, the light, the shape, the textures.

What do they like/dislike about a church?

Look at the architecture. How do you know it is a church?

Look for clues. Look at the furniture – the font, pulpit, lectern, altar, pews, organ – mark them on the worksheet.

Are there any artefacts or special objects – statues, pictures, crucifixes, crosses, candles? Why do you think they are there? What do you think they mean to people?

Look at the windows. What stories do the stained glass windows represent?

Find the church noticeboard. What activities does it have? Look for clues? Are there any Brownies, Guides, Cubs or Scouts?

It is important to note that on such a visit the worksheet, so important both for focusing and recording, should be a servant rather than a master. On entering the church the children are settled down, 'stilled' and invited to appreciate the atmosphere before being allowed to move around so as to begin to understand their tasks.

### Visits to places of worship in other traditions

Schools which are close to synagogues, mosques, gurdwaras or mandirs will want to arrange for their pupils to make visits there. Arranging a visit to one of these places of worship should not differ significantly from planning one to a church. Some things do need to be borne in mind.

1 Sikhs, Jews, Muslims and Hindus feel at least as strongly as Christians and probably more so about appropriate behaviour in places of worship.
2 Different religious traditions have different ways of showing respect. Jewish, Sikh and Muslim worshippers would normally cover the head when entering a place of worship. Sikhs, Muslims and Hindus take off their shoes at the entrance. Sikhs would expect visitors to make some gesture of respect to the throne of the Guru Granth Sahib, though not necessarily the full obeisance.
3 Visitors will often find that they are the recipients of generosity or hospitality. It is, for example, rare to leave a Hindu temple without receiving some fruit or nuts, themselves originally an offering from a worshipper. In the Gurdwara, visitors will usually be offered *karah parshad* and perhaps taken off to the kitchen area where they may be offered anything from a full curry dish to a cup of tea and a biscuit.
4 It is not unknown for parties of school children to visit some places of worship and, finding perhaps that the strangeness makes them embarrassed, to collapse into giggles. Teachers need to be on their guard about this.
5 It is always important that teachers make a preparatory visit beforehand and especially so when the place is unfamiliar. This will make the visit a much smoother and more valuable experience.

**Visitors to school**

A very useful source of first-hand experience in RE for pupils can be the visitor. Appropriate visitors could be adherents of different religious traditions, clerical or lay, or possibly representatives of different aid organisations, such as Christian Aid. One school invited the priest organiser of a local church-based night shelter to speak to its Year 3/4 children about his work and its relationship to his faith. This experience, carefully prepared for, had a considerable impact on the pupils who wished afterwards to make regular collections of food, clothes and blankets for the shelter. The visit of the speaker made the work of the night shelter come alive to the pupils. In class the teacher had been able to discuss issues of homelessness and poverty and had considered in this context the work of Mother Teresa in Calcutta and also of others on a more local scale. It was the visitor who was able to come in and fire the children's imagination. This example highlights some important points about visitors to the school or the classroom which should be borne in mind.

First, it is very important that the visit is worthwhile and that it makes an important contribution to the children's learning. Arranging visits is a very time-consuming activity, for the teacher who undertakes it, for the visitor who comes and for the pupils for whom the experience is intended. The visitor should therefore make a contribution which the teacher is unable to make.

Second, it is important that the visitor is a suitable person for the task in hand. The priest organiser of the night shelter was a lively speaker who was able to communicate effectively with children and it was these two qualities which made his visit to the school so successful. Not all potential visitors are so gifted and teachers would be well advised to check this beforehand. Local clergy may, for example, be seen as the most obvious representatives of the local Christian community, but this does not necessarily mean that they are the most suitable people to visit the school to talk about what it means to be a Christian. Some most certainly will be, but it is wise to make enquiries first. Many schools have tales to tell. One school always invites in a retired teacher who is a churchwarden: she brings with her the experience of the Christian local community together with a lifetime's experience of teaching children. Other schools make use of suitable parents. One school serving a multifaith area regularly invites parents from different religious groups in to explain major festivals in their traditions as they come round: a Muslim parent would, for example, explain what happens in a Muslim household at Id, a Jewish parent at Passover, and so on. Parents are a valuable resource often forgotten by schools. Contributions like these from visitors should not be seen as substitutes for normal RE teaching in the school but more as additions which contribute to a more personal and affective dimension of the work.

Third, it is very important that visitors are clear about their brief. This means that when the arrangement is made the teacher needs to explain carefully the nature of the RE work and exactly how the visitor's contribution fits into the overall scheme. This should result in the minimum of duplication and mean that the pupils will receive the full benefit of the special contribution to the learning that the visitor is able to make.

Fourth, it is very important that the pupils should be prepared for any visit that has been arranged. It is particularly useful if the work the children are doing in class can build up to the visit so that it is seen as something special. One school had the privilege of a visit by two Buddhist monks and a Buddhist nun. There was considerable preparation for this so that when the visit took place there was an atmosphere of excited anticipation. Pupils had learnt something of Buddhism, particularly with reference to the life of monks and nuns, their appearance, their chanting and so on. The visit fulfilled all expectations and everyone was delighted with the experience. However the headteacher of a nearby school, on hearing of the Buddhist visit, asked if they could visit his school for a short time after the completion of their visit to the first school. This visit was a disaster. The pupils in the second school, without any preparation for the visit, found the appearance of the visitors with their saffron robes and their shaved heads bizarre – and amusing – and the chanting which was performed for them evoked embarrassed laughter. Far from encouraging understanding and tolerance, this experience reinforced negative stereotypes.

A school's RE coordinator has a particular role, therefore, in identifying and drawing up a list of possible visitors. This list can be drawn up from information gained from colleagues in other schools, from RE advisers and advisory teachers, from staff at RE resource centres and from the faith communities themselves, and should relate to the nature of RE in the school; there is little point in identifying, for example, possible Sikh speakers if Sikhism does not figure in the school RE programme.

RE coordinators in schools often provide guidelines for staff on the role of visitors, as outlined above, with additional guidance as to different cultural mores of visitors from different groups: for example, it is inappropriate for a man to shake hands with a Sikh woman, and an orthodox Muslim man would not normally shake hands with a woman. When offering refreshments, it is wise to bear in mind dietary rules for different groups.

Other issues to bear in mind are expenses – some do have to make a charge even if only to cover expenses – and letters of thanks which, if possible, should be written by the children. There is also the difficult question of whether parents ought to be informed of the purpose of the proposed visit. One rural Church of England primary school invited a representative of another religion to come to talk to the children. Parents learned about this coming visit from conversations with their children and a number wrote to the school requesting that their children should be withdrawn from the session. Such was the response that the school felt that it would have to take the embarrassing step of cancelling, or at least postponing, the session. After a meeting in which the school staff were able to convince the parents that there was no intention to try to convert the pupils to this other religion and that the aims of the enterprise were entirely educational, all the parents withdrew their objections and the visitor came at a later date. It might, however, have been useful to have explained the purpose of the visit beforehand to the parents, perhaps in the regular newsletter which is sent home.

Because a well planned and focused contribution from a visitor can be such an important addition to work in RE, a number of schools build visitors into their programmes.

The headteacher of an infant school describes her school's approach to visitors:

> In our school we take RE seriously but we are aware how little time we can give to it – only 35 hours a year – because of the demands of all the subjects in the National Curriculum. We therefore are very concerned not to waste any time and not to do anything which would lead to that. We do find that visitors can make a unique contribution to aspects of our work and we do build in two every year. We focus on two religions over Key Stage 1, Christianity and Judaism, so most of our RE work draws on these two traditions. In Year 1 we work on the theme of 'Babies' in the Autumn term which leads up very nicely to Christmas. Part of our RE work arising from 'Babies' concerns naming ceremonies especially baptism and every year Father Andrew from the parish church comes in to talk to the children about baptism. Before he comes the children dress up a doll in a christening robe, prepare a bowl of water for the font and light a candle. When Father

Andrew arrives he tells the children stories about baptism, chooses different children to be parents and godparents, and then baptises the doll. The children thoroughly enjoy this, it makes baptism come alive and I know they remember it for a long time.

In Year 2 we do a topic on 'Food' in the Spring term. Part of the RE aspect of the topic focuses upon special foods and the significance of sharing a meal with people. Here we are very fortunate in having in the area a Jewish mother whose children used to attend the school when they were younger. Every year she comes into school to talk about the Sabbath meal shared on the Friday evening at the beginning of the Sabbath. She brings with her the candlesticks, the cloths, the bread, the wine and lays out the table for them. All the time too she emphasises the importance of the whole family gathering together to share the meal and how it welds them together. As with Father Andrew the children find this a memorable occasion and it is not one which we as teachers could do nearly so well.

I do think we are fortunate in having two willing visitors both of whom have such good rapport with the children. We are dreading the day when Father Andrew moves on; the Rector would not be half so good!

# Background

# 18  An introduction to six religions

The 1988 Education Reform Act which was discussed earlier laid down that all agreed syllabuses for RE must 'reflect the fact that the religious traditions in Great Britain are in the main Christian whilst taking account of the teaching and practices of the other principal religions represented in Great Britain'. As the Act did not specify which these other religious traditions might be, early observers were concerned that this absence of guidance might lead to an acrimonious battle between the different religious leaders. In the event nothing like this happened: over the years, five religions, in addition to Christianity, emerged by general consent: Buddhism, Hinduism, Islam, Judaism and Sikhism.

This chapter attempts to give an introduction to these five religions and Christianity, emphasising those aspects of the religions which are perhaps more appropriate for the religious education of children aged 4 to 11 years. These introductions are fairly brief and as such are intended to provide a very basic framework of knowledge and understanding, enough for teachers who are not RE specialists to research further with more confidence. The religions are considered alphabetically.

Although all six religions are described it is not intended that an individual class teacher should teach all of them over the year. Most agreed syllabuses lay down that children in Key Stage 1 should study Christianity and one other religion and in Key Stage 2 Christianity and two others. However, as different agreed syllabuses nominate different religions for the key stages, it is important that all six are included here.

## Buddhism

Buddhism, dating back to the sixth century BC, has about five hundred million followers world-wide. It originated in India but since has spread to a wide range of countries in Asia: Buddhism is the dominant religion in Burma, Thailand and Sri Lanka and there are significant numbers of Buddhists in China, Tibet, Japan, Mongolia, Vietnam, Laos, Cambodia, Korea, Nepal, Sikkim and Bhutan. In recent times Buddhism has spread into Western countries such as Britain and the USA. Like all large religions it is quite diverse with different traditions. The best known of these are the Theravada, the Mahayana and the Zen traditions. The Western Buddhist Order (WBO), formed in the West as recently as 1967, is a movement which seeks to emphasise the essentials of Buddhism and to distinguish these from the many customs and traditions which have grown up over the centuries in the Far East.

### The life of the Buddha

The life of the Buddha is particularly important within Buddhism because not only was he the founder but also his life story and experience encapsulate the teaching of the religion. If one wants to know the essence of Buddhism, it is exemplified in the Buddha's life. The very early Buddhists were more concerned with his teaching so no biography was produced. In later centuries, when interest in details of his life grew, writers collated various disparate written and oral accounts. The resulting account of his life no doubt includes both facts and legendary accretions. The Buddha was born Siddhartha Gautama (sometimes transliterated Gotoma) into a princely family in north India close to the border with Nepal in about 560 BC. The accounts vary slightly but it appears that his father wished him to succeed him as ruler but he feared because of a prophecy that his son might become a religious teacher instead. To protect him from this future his father provided him with a life of luxury and pleasure. He reputedly had three palaces, one for the cold season, one for the hot season and one for the time of the rains. Within this setting he grew to manhood, married and fathered a son. All this time his father ordered that he should not leave the palaces.

However Gautama did not find that this life satisfied him so in search of something more he disobeyed his father and went outside the palace walls into the city. There he saw four sights which shocked and troubled him. He saw a very feeble, old man, he saw a sick man, he saw a corpse and finally he saw a holy ascetic man who had turned his back on the pleasures of life. This was his first experience of suffering, decay and death. He realised that this fate lay ahead for all people. At the age of 29 he left the palace and his family and set off into the world to discover the meaning of life.

Being a Hindu, Gautama naturally went first to the Hindu holy men and joined a group of five ascetics who sought spiritual development through a severe regime of denying the body food, warmth and comfort. It is said that after some time in the ashram he could by pressing his hand on his stomach feel his spine! However this experience did not satisfy his desire to find the meaning of life any more than the other extreme of luxury and ease. He found that both ways were dead ends in the spiritual journey. The middle way between the two extremes must be the right path. Six years after he left home the accounts relate that the Buddha sat down under a tree – the sacred bodhi tree – and meditated for forty-nine days. In the story he was attacked mentally in a vision by the armies of Mara (the devil in Buddhism) and he was even offered all the world's wealth if he would give up his search for the meaning of life. However, calming his mind through meditation and even breathing, he resisted the attacks of Mara and at the end of those forty-nine days seated under the bodhi tree the Buddha was enlightened – and so became the Buddha, the enlightened one. He was released from the pain of decay, sickness and death and from the cycle of birth, death and rebirth.

For the remaining forty-five years of his life the Buddha travelled around India preaching and teaching the meaning of life.

### The teaching of the Buddha

After his enlightenment the Buddha travelled to Banares where, in a deer park, he preached his first sermon to the five ascetics whom he had joined after leaving the palace and who have become known to history as the Five Bikkhus (monks). They were received into and so became the first members of the new order of monks known as the Sangha which was to be the organisation which continued the Buddha's teaching. The Sangha is an absolutely central part of Buddhism; in fact all Buddhists affirm their faith by taking refuge in the Three Jewels of Buddhism: the Buddha, the Dharma (the teaching) and the Sangha (the order of monks and nuns). The Buddha's teaching is summed up in the Four Noble Truths.

### The Four Noble Truths

The Four Noble Truths assert that:

1  Suffering is universal and for most people life is unsatisfactory because it contains suffering and the knowledge that nothing lasts.
2  The cause of suffering is a deep craving or selfish desire for the things of this world and for survival in this world and the next.
3  The only way to cure suffering is to eliminate craving.
4  The way to eliminate craving is to follow the Noble Eightfold Path.

### The Noble Eightfold Path of Liberation

1  The *right view* or understanding of the Buddha's teaching in the Four Noble Truths.
2  The *right intention* to live by the Buddha's teaching, to move away from ill will and spite towards loving kindness and compassion.
3  *Right speech* which is free from lying, malicious gossip and backbiting.
4  *Right conduct* which is free from violence, stealing, fornication and adultery, drugs and alcohol.
5  *Right livelihood* means that certain occupations which cause suffering to others must be avoided. This would include arms trading, selling alcohol or meat or involvement in slavery.
6  *Right effort* means that the Buddhist must make every effort to resist unhelpful states of mind such as hatred or attachment to states which inhibit the road to Nirvana.
7  *Right mindfulness* is the development of meditative states of mind.
8  *Right concentration* or *right contemplation* refers to the Buddhist's capacity to free the mind from unhelpful influences and to achieve a deep calm through meditation upon a chosen object.

The Noble Eightfold Path, properly understood, serves both as a general framework for living and as a way towards Nirvana.

### The Five Moral Precepts

The Buddha laid upon his followers the requirement to follow the Five Moral Precepts:

1  To refrain from killing.
2  To refrain from stealing.
3  To avoid bad contact in sexual matters.
4  To refrain from lying and swearing.
5  To refrain from drugs and alcohol.

### Karma, rebirth (samsara) and Nirvana

Central to Buddhist belief is the concept of Karma, the law of cause and effect. Nothing happens by chance so the actions of earlier life or lives bring people to certain situations. From good actions come happiness and contentment, from bad actions come unhappiness and dissatisfaction. This ties in closely with the Five Moral Precepts. This also means that people take responsibility for their own lives. We remain in this state of dissatisfaction and pain, being reborn (samsara) again and again until we are released into Nirvana or enlightenment, which is a state of deep peace free from the chains of life and existence. If individuals follow the Buddha's teaching as laid down in the Eightfold Path, and through doing this manage to extinguish hatred, greed and the craving for possessions from their lives, then they can attain this state of enlightenment or Nirvana just as the Buddha did.

## The Sangha

The Sangha (the Order), one of the three jewels of Buddhism, and the role of monks and nuns are both central within the religious tradition. Originally monks and nuns were mendicants, going from place to place teaching, but over the centuries monasteries have developed so that now most monks and nuns live a settled life. The monasteries are not cut off from the general population as they are in some religious traditions. Monks and nuns move within the wider community and the wider community has access to the monastery.

A detailed study of monasticism within Buddhism will show that there are different levels of commitment among both monks and nuns and that there are further variations according both to the relevant tradition within Buddhism and to different countries. What follows here is a very general picture of monasticism. There is no doubt that in Buddhism the Sangha is seen as a superior form of life to which people ought to aspire, whether now or in a future life. It provides the right environment for the Noble Eightfold Path to be lived, while the householder and family find that the cares and worries of living distract them in their attempts to follow it.

Monks and nuns own no property except for a few simple, necessary possessions such as a robe, a begging bowl and a mat. Normally they do not eat after midday, wear no jewellery or ornament, do not marry, do not handle money, and avoid places of entertainment such as the cinema. They rely very heavily upon the support of the laity. Each day they walk through the streets carrying their bowl into which people place food. This is an entrenched tradition in a Buddhist society but more difficult in, say, a rural area of Britain. A group of Buddhist monks on a pilgrimage for peace along the Sussex Downs had to arrange for supporters to be at certain places along the way to offer the necessary food. Clearly in such a situation where no food can be expected from the local community, monks and nuns must prepare their own. In a Buddhist environment this tradition works very well: one group teaches the faith and sets an example while the other group gives food and shelter. One gives spiritual food, the other actual food.

Monks and nuns follow a middle way in renunciation – the notion of the middle way is always central to Buddhism. There is real renunciation in that they reject luxury and even normal human comforts but this is not in any way to the degree of the Hindu sadhu. Their major activity is meditation and so the monastic day provides substantial periods of time for meditation and chanting. The central place in the monastery is the meditation room, which would normally have a central image of the Buddha as a focus. In some Buddhist countries all (or probably most) boys become monks for a short period of time. In Burma, for example, in devout families, boys at the age of around 4 are prepared to become monks. In the ceremony, which is a very important one in the life of the family, the boy is first dressed up in prince's clothing to represent the young prince, Gautama. Then the princely clothes are removed to show the shallowness of worldly glamour. Then the boy's head is shaved as a sign of the renunciation of worldly pleasure and he is dressed in the robes of a monk with a begging bowl and mat. He is then taken off to the monastery to live with the monks. The boy remains there only a short time as it is not intended that he should become a monk permanently – if that happened society would collapse – but it is to teach him at an early age the centrality of Buddhist ideals in society.

### Places of worship

There is considerable variation in the style of places of worship within Buddhism, from the very simple to the highly elaborate. Many Buddhists will have their own shrine in their home, perhaps in the corner of a room. Temples and shrines are very likely to have an image of the Buddha as the focus of the building. They may also have a bodhi tree in honour of the Buddha's enlightenment and some will have a stupa (a bell-shaped mound) containing a relic of the Buddha himself or of another holy person who has attained enlightenment. These relics are venerated as many feel that any part of the body of a person who has achieved enlightenment possesses power which can only do good to devotees and bring blessings upon them. Although there are communal gatherings for worship for the laity, most acts of devotion are shown by visiting the shrine or temple, removing the shoes and bringing offerings of food and drink, incense and candles. The principal Buddhist festival which is normally celebrated communally is Wesak, which celebrates the birth, the life and the death of the Buddha.

Pilgrimage is an important aspect of Buddhism. An important centre for pilgrimage is the Doi Suthep Temple near Chiang Mai in Thailand where a tiny bone chip of the Buddha is enclosed in a stupa. Thousands of pilgrims climb the steps to the temple to pray for blessings. Another very popular centre for pilgrimage is in Sri Lanka where the legendary footprint of the Buddha is housed.

### Is Buddhism a religion?

Buddhism is alone among the major world faiths in not being based on the belief in a god. As we have seen, it bases itself upon the Buddha's diagnosis of the human condition and his teaching as to how people can save themselves and through persistence achieve the state of enlightenment or Nirvana which frees them from the chains of existence. It is normally regarded as a religion because, although it has no place for a figure of a god, it differs from secular philosophies in that it sees human life as having a significance beyond the immediate world of the senses.

## Christianity

Christianity, like Judaism and Islam, is based on the belief in one God but conceives him as a Trinity, three persons, or aspects, within the Unity, the Father, the Son and the Holy Spirit. These aspects express the different spheres of God's activity: as creator, as redeemer and as life giver. Christians believe that the most important characteristic of God's nature is love and this is worked out in Christianity's other cardinal doctrine, the Incarnation. Christianity is rooted in the belief that, out of love for the human race, God himself entered humanity and took flesh in the person of Jesus Christ. In the life, death and resurrection of Jesus Christ, Christians believe both that they have seen the nature of God in terms which they can understand, and that they have also been reconciled with and accepted by God. All those who follow Jesus and are baptised constitute the Church, often called the Body of Christ, in which the Holy Spirit dwells.

### Jesus Christ

Absolutely central to the Christian faith is the person of Jesus Christ. Within Christian teaching, he is more than a teacher or a prophet. In the New Testament he is called by many titles; the most enduring have been 'Son of God' and 'Lord'. As one who is the personification of God's love, Christ fills a unique position as the Way, the Truth and the Life. Little really is known of the life of Jesus. Mark, the earliest Gospel, begins with Jesus' appearance at John's baptism. Matthew and Luke give accounts of his birth, though not all Christians would accept these as historical accounts. The four Gospels do not purport to be biographies of Jesus, but rather works with the aim of demonstrating who Jesus is. St John (chapter 20 verse 31) says, 'but these are written that you might believe that Jesus is the Christ, the Son of God'. This helps to account for the selection of material in the Gospels. In Mark, for example, out of sixteen chapters, six are devoted to the final week in Jesus' life, which indicates the significance that Mark attached to these seven days.

Because Jesus is perceived by Christians as the revealer of God's nature, special attention is paid to the Gospels as they contain his words and works. In the Eucharist, when the set passage from the Gospel is read, it is normal for the congregation to stand as a mark of recognition of its significance. As the mediator, Christians address their prayers to God through him, and as Incarnate Lord, Jesus is himself the object of worship.

### The Bible

For all Christians the Bible is a very special book, though different traditions within Christianity disagree as to how exactly it is special. Some Christians see the Bible as the revelation of God – that through the words of scripture, the unseen God reveals his character and his ways to people. Other Christians are more inclined to see the Bible as a record of humankind's experience of God in history. How the Bible is perceived will determine how it is used. Some search the Bible for detailed guidance on the living of daily life, others look for general principles. Some see the Bible as the only source of Christian belief, others will place alongside it the tradition and experience of the church.

The Bible is a book of faith, telling as it does the history of the Jewish people and seeing in it the activity of God. It is interpreted history. The New Testament is the same. In the accounts of Jesus and in the history of the very early church, the hand of God is seen. It is within this overall context that many of the famous stories of Christianity (and of Judaism too) are found: the Creation stories, the heroes (such as Moses, Joshua and Samson) the prophets (such as Amos, Isaiah and Jeremiah), the kings, the Exodus from Egypt, the coming of Christ, his ministry, his death and resurrection, the whole story of the early Christian leaders such as Peter and Paul. The stories, of course, do not finish with the end of the New Testament. The two thousand years of subsequent history have produced many supremely significant events and people, right up to the present time.

Closely tied up with the sacred stories of Christianity are festivals and worship.

### Festivals

As in all religions, festivals are highly important in the Christian calendar. The two principal festivals, Easter and Christmas, arise out of central events in the life of Christ. Others arise out of other events in his life and from the lives of saints. A much fuller account of Christian festivals is found elsewhere in this book.

### Worship

Formal worship has always played a very important part in Christianity. For most Christians the principal service is that which is called the Eucharist, holy communion, Lord's supper, holy mysteries or mass. For some, such as the Quakers or the Salvation Army, the holy communion is never celebrated, and for some other groups, such as the Baptists, it is celebrated less frequently than weekly. Throughout Christendom, for the large majority, though, the Eucharist is the centre of worship. Whatever form it takes – and it can vary from a simple said service to an elaborate sung celebration – the central action of the Eucharist is the taking of bread and wine and the blessing of them. This derives directly from the account of Jesus' last supper with his disciples when he blessed bread and wine and distributed them. In the Eucharist the words of Christ are used and it is believed that in some sense the bread becomes the body of Christ and the wine the blood of Christ which worshippers then receive. The Eucharist brings to mind the life, death and resurrection of Christ and, while a small number of Christians would see it simply as a memorial, most Christians would be more inclined to see the Eucharist as making effective in the present the life-giving sacrifice of Christ.

### Baptism

The rite of entry or initiation into the Christian church is baptism. Although this can be administered at any age, and certain Christian groups such as Baptists will only permit adults to be baptised, most baptisms are of infants. Baptism requires a decision on the part of the one being baptised to turn away from evil and to follow Christ. In the case of infants or young children this decision is taken on their behalf by godparents or sponsors who promise to see that they are brought up in Christian ways. In baptism water is central to the rite: the persons being baptised are immersed in water or (more usually) sprinkled three times, in the name of the Father, the Son and the Holy Spirit, and signed on the forehead with a cross. Often a candle is lit to signify that they have passed from darkness to light. Names given in baptism become Christian names.

### Confirmation

In Western Christendom, in the traditional churches, confirmation is the time when people baptised as infants can take upon themselves the promises made on their behalf by their godparents. This often happens in adolescence, though it can happen at any age beyond that. In the traditional churches candidates for confirmation are brought to the bishop who lays his hands upon them. The candidates are asked the same questions as their godparents were at their baptism and now they take the promises upon themselves. In the Eastern Orthodox churches babies are baptised and confirmed at the same time.

### Marriage

Within the Christian religion, marriage is intended as a lifelong union between a man and a woman, entered into freely. Only one spouse is allowed at any one time and whereas widows and widowers can contract another marriage, the traditional churches have been wary of remarrying those who have been divorced. Weddings normally take place in church, though in the United States of America they may be performed in a variety of other places, such as a house or a garden. Marriage services centre around the making of vows to love, cherish and honour and the receiving of the blessing of God, mediated by the priest or minister.

Marriage customs vary, though it is traditional for the bride to wear a white gown. In the United States bridegrooms normally wear white as well, though in Europe dark clothing is more normal.

Marriages, because they signify a new life for the couple involved, are naturally occasions for rejoicing. They are usually, though not necessarily, accompanied by receptions, often with dances, and by the giving of gifts for the new home.

### Death

Christian funerals are a mixture of rejoicing that the deceased is going to be with God and sadness at the parting and the separation. A traditional funeral would involve the funeral office said in church, perhaps with a requiem mass, followed by the committal of the body to the ground or to burning. Very often now the funeral service takes place at the chapel of the crematorium, or in the USA, in the funeral home.

### Ethics

Christianity has always laid stress upon the importance of this world and of living properly within it. In its infancy, Christianity was often called the Way because it was seen as a way of life which stemmed both from the teaching of Jesus and from Christianity's worship. When pressed by questions, Jesus himself never pointed to an ethical code but rather to an ethical principle: 'love God' and 'love your neighbour as yourself' were the twin pivots of his moral teaching. This notion of loving was seen more in action than in emotional feeling. Loving could be seen as doing to others as you would like them to do unto you. This is reaffirmed in the early Christian literature and to it is added the notion of following the example of Christ, as he is described in the Gospels.

Ethical feeling tends to go beyond the bounds of personal morality of one individual to another. For example there is great concern for the underprivileged, the dispossessed, the hungry and the suffering and there is considerable active work for justice and peace. There is a deep Christian conviction that in serving the poor and needy Christ himself is being served. A mark of Christian missionaries in the nineteenth century, for example, was the building of hospitals and schools where these did not exist before. There is a growing concern among Christians too for ecology, which arises from the belief that the human race is the custodian of the created order.

### The social dimension

The chief social phenomenon created by Christianity is the church. The church is variously described but it is seen primarily as the Body of Christ in the world or as the community of believers. Sometimes the term church is used of the local congregation or gathering, sometimes it is used in a national or international sense. Within the church there are a number of denominations and sects. Each one tends to have its own traditions and emphases.

It is possible to distinguish four main divisions in Christendom:

1  The traditional churches, e.g. the Roman Catholic, the Orthodox and the Anglican.
2  The mainstream Protestant churches, e.g. the Presbyterians, the Baptists and the Methodists.
3  The newer Protestant churches such as the Pentecostals and the Seventh Day Adventists.
4  The fringe Christian sects such as the Jehovah's Witnesses and the Mormons.

During the twentieth century a marked feature of church life was the ecumenical movement, or the move towards church unity. A number of small churches have merged, though in the traditional churches, while relationships are generally warm and cooperative, there have been no such moves as yet.

A particularly significant movement within the church has been and is monasticism. The idea behind monasticism is that men and women join together in religious communities or houses living a life under a rule. Each individual monk or nun after a period of noviceship makes vows of poverty, chastity and obedience. Monasteries have been and are powerful centres of prayer, of culture and of influence. Most monks and nuns are found in the traditional churches, though there is the famous ecumenical monastery at Taize in central France, founded by Brother Roger, a member of the Reformed Church, which is very influential among young people.

## Hinduism

To attempt in any way to describe Hinduism briefly is an almost impossible undertaking, especially for a Westerner. It has no recognised founder, no simple sacred book, and it resists attempts to codify itself too closely. It is a religion of contrasts. It is broad, tolerant and inclusive. It has been described as the religion of Indians who are not members of another religion such as Sikhism, Buddhism or Christianity.

A central idea of Hinduism is what Westerners often call reincarnation or what the Hindu would call *samsara*, which we might interpret as transmigration or rebirth. Life is conceived of as a wheel, a wheel of birth, death, rebirth, a second death and so on, repeated over and over again. According to the merits of the present life, the soul is reborn into another form of life on earth. Good actions lead to rebirth into a higher form of life, bad actions to a lower form of life. This is often called the law of *Karma*. A Hindu would therefore hope for a good Karma and so be reborn into a higher state.

The goal of life is to escape from this wheel of existence and so to be released from it (*moksha*). The soul can then be united with Brahman, the spirit which underlies all creation. This liberation from the wheel of existence can be achieved in many different ways: for example, through meditation, through performing the duties of one's daily life selflessly, and through devotion (bhakti) to a particular god.

### Brahman and the gods or murti

There is a strong impression in the West that Hindus worship many gods – perhaps hundreds or thousands of them. A traveller through India would pass many temples each with its own image of its god so it is not surprising that this view prevails. Most Hindus, though, would see all the deities as manifestations or facets of the one, Brahman. The Rig Veda says: 'He is one but wise men call him by many names.' Brahman, the power underlying creation, is both the source and the sustainer of all things. Brahman is beyond description. The numerous gods or murtis are but windows into Brahman. Hindus do not worship the images or the murti in the temples but they worship that to which they point. They know perfectly well that they are made of clay or metal.

Although there are millions of manifestations of Brahman, there are three which stand above all:

| | |
|---|---|
| *Brahma* | the creator of life |
| *Vishnu* | the preserver of life |
| *Shiva* | the destroyer of life |

*Vishnu* as the preserver of life is thought to have taken human form and entered human affairs at times of special danger in order to preserve righteousness. In Hindu stories his two most famous visitations are in the form of *Rama*, the ideal king, and *Krishna*. Krishna is often pictured with cow girls, in particular one called Radha. Their relationship is seen as a supreme example of the love between Brahman and the human race.

Other popular gods are Kali, the mother goddess, Hanuman, the monkey god, and Ganesha, the elephant god who removes obstacles.

### The sacred books

Hinduism has many sacred scriptures which are classified under two headings: *sruti* – that is, scriptures directly inspired by God (Vedas, Brahmanas, Upanishads); or *dmriti* – books by holy men or prophets (Epics, Puranas, Bhagavad Gita).

The most popular of Hindu scriptures is the *Bhagavad Gita* – usually known as the Gita. It means 'Song of the Beloved' and is a dialogue between Arjuna and Krishna. Arjuna, sitting in his chariot before doing battle with his enemies, who are also his cousins, is appalled by the prospect and argues with his chariot driver Krishna who later begins to teach him. Slowly the truth dawns that this is no ordinary chariot driver but the Lord Krishna. The message of the Gita is complex but much hinges on love – for one's fellows and for God.

### Caste

A mark of the social organisation of Hinduism has been the caste system. In all there are thousands of sub-castes but the classical division is into four main castes:

| | |
|---|---|
| *Brahmins* | the priests |
| *Kshatriyas* | the warriors and rulers |
| *Vaishyas* | the agricultural workers and merchants |
| *Sudras* | the servants |

Traditionally the castes were very separate and people always married within them, but this rigidity is now much less marked. In fact, since 1951 it has been illegal in India to discriminate on the grounds of caste.

Outside the formal caste system were the so-called 'outcasts' or 'untouchables' whose fate it was to do all the unpleasant jobs. They were not allowed to enter any temple and were supposed to live only within touching distance of other 'untouchables '. Gandhi called them the children of God and did much to raise their status in Indian society.

### Worship

As with other religions, Hinduism believes that God cannot be contained in temples or mandirs. However, temples are very prominent in Hinduism because, like images, they are helpful. In one sense the temple is seen as the house of the murti and worshippers will call in to pay their respects. There will also be elaborate ceremonies in the morning and the evening to raise the murti from sleep and to put him/her away for the night. In the morning the image will be washed, anointed and garlanded. Incense will be burned and food placed in their presence. This could all happen in a temple in a remote Indian village or in a British industrial city.

Temples vary much in size and splendour but normally they would have three essential elements: an image of the god/murti, a canopy (normally a roof) to cover the god, and a priest to tend the temple and to make the people's offering. In Britain, a temple may be a former church or a converted hall or house, so it may be quite cramped. Very often there will be the images of a number of murtis spread around the temple. Over the day there is likely to be a constant stream of worshippers visiting the murti bringing gifts.

In temples away from India congregational worship (*puja*) has become an important element in Hindu practice in addition to private devotion. In Britain, for example, Sunday, the day when most are free of work, has become the day when many Hindus gather at the temple to worship together. In the temple there are no chairs or benches so worshippers sit on the floor. They also remove their shoes. Much worship consists of the singing of hymns and, of course, in the larger temples, dancing. The use of fire runs through many of the rituals. An important element is *arti*, a tray with five lights. This is moved slowly in front of the images of the gods. The arti tray is then brought around among the worshippers who pass their hands over the flame and then pass their hands over their own heads. This is symbolic of receiving God's blessing. With Hindu worship we also associate the burning of incense, the offering of flowers and the giving of prasad, a mixture of dried fruit and sugar, which is the gift of God.

Devout Hindus will have a shrine within their homes, perhaps a corner of a room, which will have statues or pictures of gods. This will provide a focus for daily prayers. In India some families will have a priest to perform these ceremonies properly.

### Festivals

There are many festivals in Hinduism; in fact there are so many gods (or manifestations of God) that at almost any given moment there would be a festival of some sort somewhere. Here I will focus on two of the best-known festivals: Diwali and Holi.

**Diwali**, often referred to as the 'Festival of Light', is perhaps the most popular Hindu festival. It lasts for five days and is marked by masses of lights decorating temples, homes, buildings and so on. The festival is associated with the giving of presents and with parties. There are fireworks and there is much enjoyment. There are various stories which are attached to the festival: that Rama returned to his kingdom; that Vishnu's consort, Lakshmi, brought gifts to homes for the coming year; Vishnu's defeat of the demon, Bali; and that it is the birthday of Kali. Whatever the connections it is a time of great exuberance, joy and light.

**Holi** is a spring festival celebrating the end of winter and the beginning of the season of growth. It is associated with bonfires and with coloured water and red powder. People spray each other with coloured water and throw red powder over each other. There is a story associated with it. King Hiranyakapishu, in his pride, ordered that all should worship him and him alone. His own son, Pralhad, defied this edict and continued to worship the Hindu gods. In anger his father tried to destroy him: by having him trampled to death by an elephant, cast into a swollen river, thrown from a mountain and finally thrown into a great fire. None succeeded. Pralhad was unafraid because of his devotion to Vishnu. In his troubles he continued to chant the name of Vishnu. Pralhad survived because he put his faith in God and chanted the divine names within the fire.

This emphasises the importance of simple trust in God. Many consider that the Holi bonfire commemorates that. Others say that it represents the death of the old year.

### A Hindu's life

The life of a Hindu is seen as a series of sixteen steps beginning before birth and ending after death. Each step is sanctified by an act of dedication to God. These sixteen steps divide into four stages. Each of the four stages is marked by suitable and appropriate activities.

- The first stage is one of immaturity and the main task for the individual is to learn the traditions from one's elders.
- The second stage is marked by marriage, by becoming a householder, by the parenting of children and the task of raising and supporting them and playing one's part in society.
- The third stage, with children grown up and independent, is marked by a great freedom from material cares and concerns. There is, therefore, more opportunity to spend time in thought, prayer and meditation. At one time it was not uncommon for people at this stage to leave to live in the peace of the forests.
- The fourth stage is the gradual edging out of life and a turning of heart and mind to meditation. This could be adopting the life of a monk, even perhaps a mendicant.

Many Hindus will, of course, not pass through all four stages. Many will remain in stage two while others will move straight from stage one to stage four. In this latter group are the *guru* who teaches disciples the understanding and techniques to achieve liberation, the *sadhu* who practises the life of sainthood, and the *swami*, the respected monk.

### Initiation ceremonies

After birth a baby is bathed, prayed over by the priest and placed on the father's knee. Then the sacred syllable *AUM* (the divine name) is traced on the baby's tongue with a pointed object dipped in honey and prayers are said over it concerning the future shape of life. For the first ten days the mother and child refrain from most human contact but on the twelfth day the child is named. The child is dressed in new clothes and placed in a swinging cot, twelve lamps are placed under the cot and the priest pronounces the name chosen by the family. Those present sing songs which incorporate the new name. The ceremony is followed by parties and gold and silver ornaments are often bought. Sometimes the child's ears are pierced. Traditionally a boy's name should have an even number of syllables while a girl's should have an odd number.

During the third year (though some authorities say that it should happen just after the first birthday) the child's hair is cut. If this injunction is followed rigidly, the child's head is shaved. However, many parents are content with a short trim. The idea behind this is to make the sign that all bad Karma from a previous existence is removed.

A very important step, the tenth, takes place normally between the ages of 8 and 12 years, according to the caste of the child. It applies only to boys of the three highest castes: the priestly, warrior and merchant. The step is an initiation when the boy is deemed ready to begin a study of the Vedas, the sacred scriptures. This is also an important social event and there is usually a party to celebrate the occasion with the giving of presents. The one who is to be the boy's teacher or guru hangs a sacred thread over the boy's left shoulder and across his chest. The guru now takes responsibility for the boy's spiritual training. Not long after this the boy begins to study the Vedas. Very few boys now undertake the full traditional Vedic training which lasts twelve years. Most do a modified form of training.

### Marriage

The second stage of life is that of the householder and involves the raising and supporting of a family. Marriages in India are usually arranged by the parents of the couple, though this is slowly changing. They will seek to find a suitable match, often in consultation with a priest. Thorough investigations are made. Brides should not be less than 16 years of age and bridegrooms are normally some years older.

The first step is betrothal. The bridegroom's family goes to visit the bride's family and they exchange coconuts as symbols of agreement. The date for the wedding is fixed at this meeting.

On the day of the wedding itself, the festivities begin with the formal giving of the bride by her father to the bridegroom by the bride's hand being placed in the bridegroom's. Presents are exchanged and the bridegroom gives the bride new clothes.

After this stage the guests begin to sing hymns which call down blessings upon the couple. While the singing is going on, two wooden boards are placed near the centre of the hall and a curtain is held between. The couple are garlanded with flowers and brought to stand on the two boards, facing each other but unable to see each other because of the curtain. At the end of each verse the congregation scatters rice over the couple. When the curtain is removed the couple exchange garlands and then sit side by side before the sacred fire.

Before the sacred fire the couple make offerings, and then walk around the fire. Prayers are made for their happiness and for their fruitfulness. The bride's sari is tied formally to the end of the husband's clothes in a knot and he takes seven steps which she follows one by one.

Wedding feasts are as splendid and elaborate as the bride's family can afford. They can also be the cause of debt in many Indian families. After the feast the bride leaves her father's house and travels with her husband to his family home. In the doorway is placed a pot containing wheat. As she enters, the bride kicks this over, spilling the wheat over the floor. This is an expression of hope that the family will never lack an adequate supply of food.

### Death

On death the body of a Hindu is washed, anointed and dressed in new clothes in preparation for cremation. Traditionally this was performed in a Kunda (a cremation spot) near a river and the body would be placed on a pyre. Nowadays many are cremated in modern crematoria. Prayer is offered that the soul of the deceased person now released from the body may go to that stage which its Karma merits.

Often relatives will collect the ashes on the third day and either bury them or place them in a river. So the Hindu dies but unless his Karma is such that he has achieved moksha (release) he is still on the wheel of existence and the round of birth and death will continue.

## Islam

The religion known as Islam began about 1,350 years ago in Arabia. The founder was Muhammad though he is seen only as a prophet, the one through whom God (Allah) spoke. Muslims (*never* to be called Muhammadans, as they follow God not Muhammad) see their religion stretching back long before then, from Abraham through the Old Testament prophets, through Jesus, to Muhammad, the final and greatest of the prophets.

### What do Muslims believe and do?

At the centre of Islam is submission to God. Islam means 'submission' and the true Muslim submits to the will of God.

All Muslims accept five duties:

1   To believe solely in one God and that Muhammad is his prophet.
2   To pray five times each day.
3   To give alms.
4   To fast during the month of Ramadan.
5   To go on pilgrimage to Makkah at least once in one's life (if possible).

These are often called the *Five Pillars* of Islam.

### Allah

There is no God but Allah and Muhammad is his prophet.

Muslims are strictly monotheistic. 'There is no God but Allah' He is 'the One'. He has many other names given in the Qur'an; Muslims talk of the ninety-nine beautiful names of God. He is known as the Lord, the High, the Great, the Creator, the Lifegiver, the Sustainer, the Compassionate, the Merciful. So great is He above all human understanding that all images or pictures of Him are forbidden as they would only diminish Him: hence the absence of human form in much Islamic art. He is seen as supreme over all, the loving provider and the just judge. Soon after birth any baby born into the Muslim community has the sacred text whispered into its ears 'God is most Great'.

### Muhammad

Though in no way divine, Muhammad is regarded as above any other human. As the greatest of the prophets and God's final mouthpiece, Muhammad is held in such respect that when Muslims speak his name they add, 'May the peace and blessings of God be upon him'. It would be unthinkable for him to be depicted in art or in the cinema.

Muhammad was born in AD 570 in the city of Makkah (now in Saudi Arabia). An orphan from an early age, he was brought up by his uncle, and when the time came for him to find employment he became agent to a wealthy widow, Khadijah, fifteen years his senior, whom he later married. During his travels as agent for Khadijah, Muhammad came into contact with other religious groups, Christians and Jews, and was attracted by their religion. From the age of 40 onwards, Muhammad began to have visions of the Archangel Gabriel which he took, after some encouragement, to come from God. The main import of the visions was that he was the 'messenger of God' and that he was ordered to 'recite' the words of God which were coming to him. This recitation was the beginning of the Qur'an (which means recitation), the sacred book.

Muhammad's proclamation gained some converts but evoked considerable hostility from many fellow citizens, so much so that Muhammad and his faithful band had to flee to Madinah (Medina). However, Muhammad re-entered Makkah in triumph in AD 630, two years before his death in AD 632.

### The Qur'an

The sacred book is treated with tremendous respect by Muslims because it is seen as being the words of God. It does not contain the words of Muhammad. He may have spoken them but only as a cypher. He recited God's words and they were heard by his disciples, memorised and later written down. Since the Qur'an was spoken in Arabic, it has remained in that language, as there is a deep fear that the translation of it might change its meaning. Translations are allowed but the Arabic version is the touchstone.

The Qur'an is therefore perceived as the *final* revelation of God's will for the human race and it contains within it the *guidelines* for how life ought to be lived. This tends to be presented in general principles. More detailed instructions appear, in the Traditions, the *Hadith*, which have grown up over a period of time and which therefore do not have the same status as the Qur'an.

Because of the significance attributed to the Qur'an, many Muslims learn the Qur'an by heart in Arabic, and learn Arabic too so as to understand it. Many mosques run schools called madrasahs to help children to learn the Qur'an. Many Muslim children in school in Britain will go to the mosque on several evenings each week to spend a couple of hours studying the Qur'an.

### Prayer

It is laid down upon all Muslims to pray five times each day: just before sunrise, after midday, in the late afternoon, just after sunset and before midnight. Mosques have a chart of clock faces to indicate the exact times for prayer on that day. In a Muslim country a muezzin will mount the minaret of the mosque and call the faithful to prayer, though often today it is a recording. Muslims are therefore reminded constantly of the greatness of God and the need to turn to him in prayer.

Preparation is needed for prayer. Muslims will wash thoroughly hands, mouth, nose, face, arms, head, ears and feet, the outward washing being symbolic of inner cleansing.

In prayer itself, there is a routine of both words and body movements. The set prayers can be said in any place provided it is clean; the worshipper merely unrolls their prayer mat, takes off their shoes and faces Makkah.

Although prayer can be said anywhere, most Muslims prefer to offer it at home or in the mosque.

### The mosque

Mosque means a place of *prostration*, for here Muslims bow their heads to the ground in acts of worship. Mosques as buildings vary considerably. Some in areas where Muslims are recent settlers are converted houses or even factories, others are buildings of considerable splendour. Whatever they are they are basically places of shelter from the climate to enable Muslims to gather for worship, especially on Fridays and on festivals, and places for instruction in the Qur'an for the young.

Mosques tend to be almost completely unfurnished. There are no chairs as this would inhibit the normal means of prayer – only a large floor space, usually carpeted. The only piece of furniture is likely to be a pulpit from which the Friday sermon is preached. Prayers in the mosque are often lead by an imam, a minister employed to lead worship and to teach the faith. In one of the walls, there will be a small alcove (a mihrab) which indicates the direction of Makkah. The sexes are normally separated for prayer. Women are placed in balconies, or at the back of the mosque behind the men, or sometimes in a separate room. The usual reason given is to reduce distractions. Because of the Prophet's strong objection to statues or pictures it is extremely rare to come across any in a mosque.

### Almsgiving

An important teaching of Islam is that all humans are brothers and sisters and one way in which this is recognised is through required almsgiving. All Muslims are required to give 2½ per cent of their earnings to charity – to the poor, needy, widows and so on. This is generally obeyed and in non-Muslim countries Muslims may be giving their donations (zakah) over and above normal income tax.

### Fasting

Fasting is a feature of most religions and is a way of asserting the control of the spiritual over the material in an individual. In Islam, the ninth month of the year, Ramadan, is dedicated to fasting. Muslims can fast at any time but all are required to do so in Ramadan. This means that for the twenty-nine or so days of the month Muslims most not partake of food or drink between dawn and dusk. Ramadan comes at different times of the year and can be a real hardship during summer. Eating is allowed at night and in a Muslim community there is often a party atmosphere after dusk, with sweets and singing. All food and drink required must be consumed at night because at dawn – when it is possible to distinguish a dark thread from a light thread – the fast recommences. Children under 10, the old and sick, pregnant women, travellers and soldiers are exempted.

### Pilgrimage to Makkah

All Muslims are urged to make, once in their lives, the major pilgrimage, the Hajj, to Makkah (Mecca). Because of the expense, many have to deny themselves this privilege. Makkah, because of its associations with the Prophet is the holiest spot on earth for Muslims. The pilgrimage officially lasts for some days, during which the pilgrims visit the Kaaba, a huge cube-shaped building in the centre of the Great Mosque, Mount Safa and Mount Marwa, Mount Arafat and Mina. An interesting and essential feature of the Hajj is that all pilgrims must remove their normal clothing and don special clothing, the ihram. In the case of a male pilgrim the special clothing consists of two pieces of white unsewn cloth, one to go round the waist, down to the ankles, and the other to be placed over the shoulder. For women there is a single piece of cloth which covers the whole body. The only footwear permitted is a backless sandal. The purpose is to stress equality, and brotherhood and self-sacrifice.

### Festivals

The major festivals of Islam are the two Ids: the Id-ul-Fitr and the Id-ul-Adha.

- The *Id-ul-Fitr*, which means technically the lesser festival, is the more popular. It celebrates the end of the month-long fast of Ramadan and is therefore a time of relaxation and rejoicing. It is a day of visiting, having parties, wearing best clothes and exchanging gifts and cards. Often a special sweet pudding made with milk and dates is served. If possible the day also includes visits to the graves of dead relatives.
- The *Id-ul-Adha*, the great festival, commemorates the ending of the Hajj, the pilgrimage to Makkah. It is kept not just by those in Makkah but by Muslims world-wide. It centres around a feast for which animals are sacrificed in the ritual way (halal). An individual family may present a lamb or goat, seven families may come together and provide a cow. Part of the meat is given way, mainly to the poor.

### Birth, marriage and death

#### Birth

When a child is born, whether at home or in hospital, the sacred tenets of Islam are whispered into the baby's ears. Although clearly there can be no understanding, it is felt important that the earliest words heard should concern God and his nature.

#### Marriage

In Islam marriage is often a simple and brief affair. Marriages are normally arranged, though consent from both parties is important. It may well be that the parties go to the mosque and in the presence of four witnesses recite passages from the Qur'an and repeat (three times) their consent to the marriage. In Britain it often happens that only the bridegroom will attend the service in the mosque. The bride will remain at home and be represented by an agent and probably two witnesses who can act on her behalf. They would hear her agreement (made three times) to the marriage and they would repeat this at the mosque when the imam (minister) asked if she was willing. If both sides agree, then they are married. British law requires that there is also a civil ceremony.

Presents are exchanged but, more importantly, the dowry is negotiated and fixed. It is essential that a wife and children are maintained properly and this should be sorted out at the beginning. Divorce is possible but is disapproved of. There are several procedures laid down which are aimed at settling differences before a divorce is permitted.

### Death

There is no one particular set way of burying the dead in Islam though there are common patterns. After death, the body is washed with sweet smelling soaps and spices before being wrapped in the shroud in which it will be buried. Bodies are buried ideally on the day following death in a grave slightly raised above the ground with the face turned to the right and facing Makkah. Relatives and friends meet together for the funeral either at the house or at the mosque. The funeral is generally an ordinary salat but includes prayers for the dead person. Inevitably funeral customs will vary where Muslims are minority groups. It is often not possible in Britain to arrange for the funeral to be on the day after death and most cemeteries insist that bodies are placed in coffins.

## Judaism

The Jewish faith is of ancient origin, claiming such early leaders as Abraham and Moses. It gave birth, in a sense, also to both Christianity and Islam. It is small in numbers of adherents as it is made up largely of Jews born into it through the female line. It does have converts from outside Jewry but while it accepts them it does not especially seek them. By no means all people who are Jewish by birth practise Judaism, and within those who do there are various degrees of observance.

### *Shema*

Judaism is based upon belief in the unity of God. This is summed up in the Shema (Deuteronomy chapter 6, verse 4): 'Hear, O Israel, the Lord our God is *one* Lord'.

This Lord who is one is also Creator and sustainer of the universe, continually active within it. Yet this same Lord is in relationship with the human race. The Shema continues: 'and thou shalt love the Lord your God with all your heart and with all your soul and with all your might'. There is intimacy in the relationship: many Jewish prayers talk to God as *Father*.

Judaism places great emphasis upon faith and trust in the loving purposes of God. More than any other religious group, Jews have suffered over the centuries, especially under the Nazis. Yet many have kept their faith in God's good purposes and lived without bitterness. The *Diary of Anne Frank*, written while Anne, a teenage girl, was in hiding from the Nazis in occupied Holland, is a very powerful example of this.

### The Torah

Judaism believes that its relationship with God is based upon a covenant: 'I will be your God and you will be my people.' The human side of the relationship is to keep God's Law, which finds its central expression in the Ten Commandments:

1  I am the Lord thy God.
2  Thou shalt have no other gods before me.
3  Thou shalt not take the Lord's name in vain.
4  Remember the Sabbath Day to keep it holy.
5  Honour thy father and mother.
6  Thou shalt not murder.
7  Thou shalt not commit adultery.
8  Thou shalt not steal.
9  Thou shalt not bear false witness against thy neighbour.
10  Thou shalt not covet.

By living in this way, Judaism is a vehicle for demonstrating God's righteousness and his justice to the world. The Commandments also show very clearly Judaism's commitment both to loving and serving God and also to one's neighbours.

### The synagogue and the home

The synagogue (literally, place of meeting or gathering) and the home work together in teaching the Law, and consequently the way of holiness.

The synagogue is the focal point of religious training and worship for the Jewish community. The focal point of the synagogue is the *Ark*; this is the receptacle which holds scrolls of the Torah, the five books of Moses. The Ark is placed on the east wall of the synagogue facing towards Jerusalem. In the centre of the synagogue or near to the Ark is a raised platform, the *bimah*, to which the scrolls are brought for public reading. Before the Ark a light burns perpetually. The reading from the scrolls of the Law forms the centre of Sabbath worship and members of the congregation are called up for the honour of reading.

This all emphasises the centrality of the Law in Judaism. Male worshippers usually wear a small skull cap, the yarmulka or kippah, and a prayer shawl called a tallith.

In the home too there is a strong emphasis upon bringing the children up well and Jewish families are traditionally close and warm. The fifth commandment requires children to honour their parents. Parents are expected in return to give their children a good example. Again the emphasis is upon the Law. Many Jewish homes have a *mezuzah* attached to the right-hand doorpost of the house and to those of the living room. The mezuzah is a small case containing a tiny parchment scroll on which the first two paragraphs of the Shema are inscribed. It obeys the command of Deuteronomy chapter 11, verse 20: 'And thou shalt write them upon the door posts of thine house and upon thy gates'. The mezuzah is there as a permanent sign that the Law should be observed in the whole of life. Women occupy a key position in the home and it is there that their powerful influence is felt most. The home too is the place where much of the religion is practised. Festivals such as the Pesach (Passover) are celebrated mainly in the home. The day is (ideally) punctuated three times by prayer in the home: in the morning, at noon and in the evening. As he rises each morning a devout orthodox Jew will put on his yarmulka, the tallith and strap on the phylacteries or tefellin. These are a pair of black leather boxes, one of which is placed on the forehead and the other on the left forearm. They contain the words of the Shema. The practice arises out of the instruction in the book of Deuteronomy chapter 6 verse 8, 'And thou shalt bind them for a sign upon thine head, and they shall be as a frontlet between thine eyes'. This literal interpretation emphasises the importance attached to the subjugation of the mind, the heart and the strength to God in Judaism.

### The festivals and holy days

Judaism has a number of festivals and holy days. Those which are most likely to be discussed in school are probably the Sabbath and the Pesach (Passover).

#### The Sabbath

The fourth commandment orders Jews to keep holy the Sabbath day – the seventh day of the week (Saturday). There should be a cessation of labour, a change from the other six days. This is often seen as a negative thing because it is a day of restrictions (not switching on electric lights and so on) but this misses the heart of the commandment. The Sabbath is intended to be a joy, a delight, a time of moving nearer to God and a respite from worry and concern.

#### Pesach (Passover)

The first of the three pilgrim festivals (the others being Weeks and Tabernacles) is the spring festival which celebrates the freeing of the children of Israel from Egypt. The family and guests gather round for the Passover meal. The youngest person present asks the ancient question, 'Why is this night different from all other nights?', and then the president of the meal replies, 'We were slaves under Pharaoh in the land of Egypt and God brought us forth out of Egypt.' During the meal there are the symbols of the Exodus: the bitter herbs symbolising the anguish of slavery and the unleavened bread which the Israelites had to make quickly and called the bread of affliction.

### The New Year and Day of Atonement

The Jewish New Year inaugurates ten days of penitence: they are described in Hebrew as the 'Ten days of return'. They are to be used for the examination of behaviour and life over the past year, for prayers for forgiveness and for working at restoring harmony in our dealings with God and with our fellows. The New Year begins with an assertion of the Kingship of God and the *shofar* or ram's horn is blown in the synagogue as a call to return to God.

The Day of Atonement (Yom Kippur), the tenth day, is considered the holiest day of the Jewish year. No food or drink is taken. The key notes of the day are true penitence, confession and real reconciliation. Despite this it is not a day of gloom, as symbolised by the white robes of the rabbi. The day ends with the congregation repeating after the rabbi the ancient prayer, 'Hear O Israel the Lord our God, the Lord is One; Blessed be his name whose glorious kingdom is forever and ever.' Then the congregation repeats seven times, 'The Lord, he is God.'

The shofar is again blown as a reminder that the spirit of the Day of Atonement should continue throughout the year.

### Hanukkah

This is a winter festival and falls close to Christmas. It celebrates the victory of Judas Maccabeus in the second century BC. Emperor Antiochus Epiphanes of Syria, whose empire included Palestine, ordered that all his territories should adopt the gods of Greece. To devout Jews this was an impossible demand and they resisted. Antiochus Epiphanes strengthened his resolve and forbade the practice of Judaism. The temple itself was desecrated and in its holiest place was erected a statue of Zeus. Despite the persecutions (described in the Book of the Maccabees in the Apocrypha), many faithful Jews stood firm. Although their numbers were very small against the might of Antiochus, they won through. It was this courageous group who through their faith in God preserved the Faith.

It is said that when Judas Maccabeus and his people repossessed the temple and cleansed it there was only one jar of pure oil remaining, enough to keep the temple candelabrum alight for one night. By a miracle the oil lasted for eight days.

Hanukkah was established to celebrate the cleansing and re-dedication of the temple. Each year in the home and synagogue a light is lit on the first night of the festival and another on each evening until eight are lit. It is not a major festival but has become more popular in Christian countries as it falls close to Christmas.

### Celebrations

#### Barmitzvah/Batmitzvah

Jewish children are normally taught about their religion from an early age and many learn Hebrew because it is the language of the Bible and the prayer books. At the age of 13 a Jewish boy attains religious maturity and is known as Barmitzvah (literally, 'son of the law'). On the Sabbath nearest to his thirteenth birthday he will be called up in the synagogue to recite from the scrolls. In the sermon the rabbi will address him and pronounce on him the Lord's blessing. There is, of course, much social celebrating too at such an event. The boy has become an adult member of the Jewish community. In many places now there is a similar event for girls, the Batmitzvah (literally, 'daughter of the law').

#### Marriage

Family life in Judaism is strongly cherished and marriage is seen as a solemn covenant. Before the ceremony, the bridegroom signs the marriage document in which he promises to be a loving and caring husband. He then stands with his father under the canopy, a large square of embroidered material supported by four poles. Then the bride with her family and attendants enters and joins the bridegroom under the canopy, which represents their future home. The bride and groom drink from a goblet and the bridegroom places a ring on the bride's forefinger. The final act of the marriage is for the bridegroom to break a glass under his foot. This custom is intended to represent that even in the pleasure and joy of life there is pain.

### Death

Although it is a religious duty to preserve life, when death comes it is accepted and the ceremonies which are performed are designed (as in most faiths) to comfort and strengthen the bereaved and to treat the dead with as much dignity as possible.

The body is washed and prepared for burial in a simple coffin. In the case of a Jewish male, the body is wrapped in a simple white shroud and the tallith (prayer shawl). Burial is usually on the day following death or as soon as possible after that. Cremation is permitted by some Jewish congregations. The prayers used are full of praise for God.

Because burial is so soon after death, mourning comes after the funeral. The first week is a time of intense mourning (called shivah) – the family remains at home and is visited by friends who come to commiserate and console. For the first year after death, the family will make a point of being present to join in Kaddish at the synagogue. Kaddish is the act of sanctification made near to the end of the service. It is traditional to observe the anniversary of a death by the lighting of candles in the home and saying Kaddish in the synagogue.

## Sikhism

Sikhism points to *Guru Nanak* (AD 1469–1539) as its founder. Guru Nanak lived in India and was concerned about the rivalry between Hindus and Muslims. His great concern was to enable people to see the truth about God which was to be found in *both* Islam and Hinduism. 'There is but one God, whose name is Truth, the creator, without fear or enmity, deathless, unborn self existent, great, bountiful.' (The Japji) Tradition has it that when Nanak was on his deathbed, both Hindus and Muslims came to claim his body. Nanak instructed them to place fresh cut flowers by him, the Hindus on his right and the Muslims on his left. Whichever flowers remained fresh on the following morning would signify to whom his body belonged. Then, Nanak covered himself with a sheet. Next morning, his body was gone but both lots of flowers were fresh.

Nanak did not intend to found a new religion but inevitably his followers formed a new group and he had to appoint a new guru to succeed him.

A Sikh means 'one who learns', that is, one who learns to know God through the gurus. A guru is a religious teacher.

### *The Guru Granth Sahib*

Nanak was the first of the ten gurus of Sikhism. God is the true Guru; Nanak and his successors are the human instruments through whom he speaks. The tenth guru, Gobind Singh, indicated that after his death there would be no further human gurus. Instead there would be a collection of scriptures, consisting of the teaching of the gurus, the Guru Granth Sahib.

Tremendous respect is accorded the Guru Granth Sahib. It is the central focus of the Gurdwara (temple) (literally 'the door of the guru'). It is placed there on a raised platform on cushions and covered by a canopy. When people enter the Gurdwara, they remove their shoes, cover their head and go straight to the Guru Granth Sahib. There they bow down to a kneeling position, the head touching the ground. Offerings of money or of food are usually made: it is very common to see a bag of apples or a bottle of milk before the platform!

Most Sikh worship consists of the reading of the Guru Granth and the singing of hymns. The reader sits cross-legged behind the Guru Granth, in his hand a chauri, a fan made from animal hairs, which he waves over the sacred book. In every way, the Guru Granth is treated like a living guru. All the important events of life occur before the Guru Granth: the naming of a child, marriage, initiation as an adult.

Some Sikh families have a copy of the Guru Granth at home, though it would not be kept on a bookshelf in the same way as a Bible might. It would normally be kept in a room set aside for the purpose. Sikhs would normally bathe before entering the room and would enter in reverence shoeless and with heads covered. Many Sikh families do not have their own copy because they are not able to give it the proper treatment it should have.

This should act as a caution for teachers who might ask Sikh pupils to bring a copy of the Granth to school. This involves making the classroom into a Gurdwara for the time that it is on the premises; it is much easier to take the children out to the proper Gurdwara.

### The Khalsa (the Brotherhood)

It was the tenth Guru, Gobind Singh, who formed the Sikhs into a soldier brotherhood. This is known as the Khalsa. As a sign of equal brotherhood all males are given the surname *Singh* (Lion) and all females *Kaur* (Princess). A military discipline is imposed upon them: all Sikhs are expected to rise, bathe (normally in cold water) and pray before dawn.

The Brotherhood is to be distinguished by five features of dress. Because all five begin with the letter K they are called the five Ks:

- The *Kesh* (long uncut hair): all Sikhs were ordered not to cut their hair. This symbolises spirituality.
- The *Kangha* (comb): the long hair was not to be unruly but kept clean and in order, symbolised by the comb.
- The *Kirpan* (sword): all Sikhs were to carry a sword, to fight for truth and righteousness. Among Sikhs in the United Kingdom this is almost always now a symbolic sword and may even be a sword brooch.
- The *Kachera* (shorts): these are short trousers worn by men and women, which were much more suited to battle than the long trousers often worn.
- The *Kara* (the bracelet): all Sikhs are supposed to wear a steel band or bracelet on their right wrist. Practically, it may at one time have served as a protection against bow strings. It also has the great symbolism of eternity and unity. It symbolises the eternity and unity of God and also the unity between Sikh and Sikh and Sikh and God.

It may seem odd that what is perhaps the most visible mark of a Sikh male, the turban, does not appear on this list. Nevertheless it is greatly cherished by Sikhs.

The formation of the Khalsa is celebrated each year by the feast of Baisakhi.

### Amrit

All those who wish to be initiated into the Sikh religion and to become members of the Khalsa do so in the Amrit ceremony. This takes place in front of the Guru Granth Sahib. Five members of the Khalsa dressed in yellow tunics with a red or yellow sash over the right shoulder stand with them. These five mix water and sugar in a steel bowl, stirring it with a sword, reciting hymns as they do so. This is the Amrit. Then one by one those wishing to be initiated come forward and kneel. Each one in turn is given the mixture five times to drink, five times it is splashed in the eyes and five times sprinkled upon the head. Then the initiate makes certain vows, for example, not to smoke tobacco or take harmful drugs and always to display the five Ks. By no means all Sikhs undergo initiation.

### Hospitality

The brotherhood of Sikhs is expressed very profoundly by the Gurdwara. Not only are all Sikhs equal before God in the Gurdwara but this is emphasised by the sharing of the *karah parshad* at every service. This is a mixture of flour (or sometimes, semolina), sugar, butter and water which forms a sweet pudding. Each worshipper takes a little in his or her hands and eats it. Attached to each Gurdwara are also kitchens and places to eat (langar). To be hospitable to fellow Sikhs and indeed to all people is very important in Sikhism and many English visitors to a Gurdwara will find that they will be offered tea and biscuits as a minimum, and, if they arrive at the right time, curry and chapattis! During a festival, a Gurdwara may feed many thousands of worshippers.

### Festivals

Anniversaries of the Gurus are called *Gurpurbs*. The principal ones commemorate the birthdays of Guru Nanak and Guru Gobind Singh and the martyrdoms of Guru Arjan and Guru Tegh Bahadar. Normally before each Gurpurb there is a continuous reading of the Guru Granth Sahib (this takes about forty-eight hours), followed on the morning of the Gurpurb by services in the Gurdwara. In India there would normally be a procession of the Guru Granth Sahib through the town drawn on a vehicle decorated with flowers and bunting. This procession does not normally happen in Britain.

Sikhs keep other festivals drawn from Hinduism but often with a different significance, especially Diwali.

### Birth, marriage and death

#### Birth

There are no specific ceremonies associated with birth, but as soon as the mother is well enough she brings her baby to the Gurdwara. There, before the Guru Granth Sahib, the parents make gifts and prayers are said for long life for the child. The concluding prayer contains the following lines:

> I present this child and with Thy Grace
> I administer to him the Amrit.
> May he be a true Sikh
> May he devote himself to the service of his
> Fellow men and his motherland.
> May he be inspired with devotion.

Then Amrit (sugar and water) which has been prepared is offered, a drop is placed on the baby's lips and the remainder is drunk by the mother. Then the Guru Granth is opened at random and the first hymn on the left-hand page read out. Whatever is the first letter of the first word of the hymn should be the initial letter of the baby's name. If it is 'g' the baby may be called Gurdeep, if it is 'm' the baby may be called Malkit. At the end of the service, the karah parshad is shared around again as a sign of brotherhood.

## Marriage

Normally a Sikh marriage is an arranged match. The only essential witness is the Guru Granth Sahib and it is before it that the marriage takes place. It may be in the Gurdwara or in the bride's home. In the Gurdwara, the couple would sit in front of the Guru Granth Sahib, the bride usually dressed in red. The couple and their fathers stand while the Granthi, the leader of the worship, asks for their consent and for the agreement of the gathered congregation. There is a symbolic touch whereby the edge of the bride's sari or her headdress is tied to the bridegroom's sash. The wedding hymn is chanted from the Guru Granth Sahib and then sung, a verse at a time. During the chanting of a verse the couple stand before the Granthi and then while it is being sung they walk around the Guru Granth Sahib slowly in a clockwise direction. This takes place four times, once for each verse. The service concludes, as do all services, with the sharing of the karah parshad.

## Death

Death is seen by Sikhs as the means whereby the faithful pass into the presence of God. Extravagant mourning or wailing is not encouraged, though for ten days after a funeral the family will read through the Guru Granth Sahib, alone and when friends visit them. The normal pattern is for a body to be washed and dressed and then placed in a shroud in preparation for cremation on the same day as death or the next day. If cremation is not possible then the body is buried.

# 19  Christian festivals

This chapter, which looks in some detail at a wide range of Christian festivals, has been included principally for the many church schools, both Anglican and Roman Catholic, which are concerned to reflect Christianity strongly in their RE and in collective worship. It is hoped too that it will be useful, certainly in the material it provides on the major festivals, to all schools.

Like all religions Christianity has many holy days in the course of the year. Of these the most special tend to focus upon events in the life of Jesus Christ. The two principal feasts are Christmas and Easter, both of which have before them a period of preparation (Advent and Lent). There are also many festivals associated with Saints, that is, exceptional followers of Jesus. It should be noted though that there are some traditions within Christianity in which festivals hold comparatively little significance for adherents. In this account what is described relates to what is found in the life of the more ancient and numerically strongest churches of Christendom.

The aim of this chapter is to give some basic information about the festivals and fasts of the Christian year which can be used as a factual starting point both for classroom teaching and for stories told in assembly. Where it is appropriate, relevant passages from the Bible are given. Chapter 13 looks in some detail at the teaching of festivals in the primary classroom, bearing in mind the different ages and stages of the children.

## Advent

Advent marks the beginning of the Christian year and is a period of around four weeks immediately prior to Christmas. It is seen by Christians as a time of preparation and penitence. The message through the Bible readings and the Advent hymns and carols is summed up by the word 'Awake'. Worshippers begin to prepare for the coming of Jesus both as the baby born at Bethlehem and as judge of both the individual and the world.  · The appearance of churches tends to be sober in order to reflect this mood. Altar cloths and vestments tend to be violet or purple in colour and flowers are removed.

Two traditional customs which emphasise the nature of Advent as a period of preparation are the use of the Advent calendar and the Advent corona. With the Advent calendar, the user opens a small numbered door or window on each day of the Advent season. Each one reveals a different picture, culminating, on the final day, with a representation of the Nativity. With the Advent corona one candle is lit on each Sunday of the Advent season.

### Christmas (25 December)

Perhaps the most popular festival of the Christian faith, at least in the Western church, Christmas celebrates the birth of Christ in Bethlehem. Underneath this it is really celebrating the Incarnation, the entry of God into humanity. The well known Christmas stories are recorded in St Matthew chapter 1 verses 18–25 and St Luke chapter 2 verses 1–24 and concern the census, the birth in the stable and the visit by the shepherds. A reflection on the significance of the events is given in St John chapter 1 verses 1–14.

Churches tend to be richly decorated with flowers, the Advent colours are replaced with whites and golds and many churches are ablaze with candles, symbolising the entry of the Light into the world. An extremely popular service is the midnight mass. Many churches also erect a crib, depicting the scene in the stable with Mary, Joseph and the shepherds. The figure of Father Christmas or Santa Claus arises from St Nicholas, patron saint of children, who traditionally brought them gifts of toys on his own feast day in December.

### Epiphany (6 January)

Also called Twelfth Night, Epiphany ends the Christmas season: hence the old tradition of clearing away all the Christmas decorations by this date. Epiphany means (literally) 'Manifestation' and it is associated with the manifestation or showing forth of the infant Christ to the Gentiles, in the figures of the wise men or magi who followed the star.

The story is told in Matthew chapter 2 verses 1–12. In the popular mind it is elided with Christmas but in the church's year it is used to emphasise this universal aspect of the coming of Jesus. Many churches which have cribs will remove the shepherds and replace them with images of the magi bearing their symbolic gifts of gold, frankincense and myrrh. Hymns associated with this festival are 'We three kings of orient are' and 'Bethlehem of noblest cities'.

### Candlemas (2 February)

Candlemas is the abbreviated way of describing the feast otherwise known as 'The Purification of the Blessed Virgin Mary' or 'The Presentation of Christ in the Temple'. This commemorates the event when Mary and Joseph in observation of the law brought the infant Jesus to the temple to present him to God and make a thanks offering. While in the temple, two old and devout Jews, Simeon and Anna, recognised the specialness of Jesus and Simeon spoke the famous hymn, the Nunc Dimittis. In this he hailed Jesus as the 'Light to lighten the Gentiles and to be the glory of thy people, Israel'. The story is found in Luke chapter 2 verses 22–35. It is this theme of Jesus who will bring the light of the knowledge of God to the whole world which is emphasised, and in its full form the Candlemas ceremonies include a procession of the whole congregation around the church carrying lighted candles.

**Lady Day (25 March)**

More fully entitled 'The Annunciation of Our Lord to the Blessed Virgin Mary', this feast celebrates the announcement of the future birth of Christ. According to the account in Luke chapter 1 verses 26–38, the angel Gabriel comes to Mary, a young engaged woman in Nazareth and announces that she has been chosen to bear a son, Jesus, through the operation of the Holy Spirit. The account concludes with Mary's acceptance: 'Behold the handmaid of the Lord; be it unto me according to thy word.'

**Lent**

As Advent is the period of preparation for Christmas, so Lent is for Easter. It is also longer, lasting forty days, and is more widely observed. It is a period of penitence in which the faithful attempt to work harder at their religion. Three key ideas of Lent are prayer, almsgiving and fasting. So in Lent Christians try to spend more time in prayer and study, often reading more of their Bibles or studying a religious book either singly or in groups.

There is an effort too to think more of others and this self-denial underlies both almsgiving and fasting. This is the background to the old custom of giving up something luxurious that one enjoys for Lent and then giving the money saved to charity. Fasting, as well as being a form of self-denial, is also a way of bringing the body under the control of the spirit. In the early centuries the Lenten fast was very strict; only one meal a day was allowed and no meat or fish. This has gradually been relaxed and now in, for example, the Roman Catholic Church, only Ash Wednesday and Good Friday are fast days in this sense.

Churches also express the same note of penitence and self-denial. The hangings and vestments are purple or violet and as Good Friday approaches crucifixes and statues are often veiled.

**Ash Wednesday**

The first day of Lent, and a solemn day, Ash Wednesday is intended to be kept as a day of fasting. Its name comes from the ancient and widespread practice of ashing. At the beginning of the Ash Wednesday Eucharist worshippers come forward to have a cross marked with ash on their forehead. As the priest places the mark there he speaks the words, 'Remember, O man, that dust thou art and unto dust shalt thou return.' This is intended to set the mood for Lent.

The day immediately prior to Ash Wednesday is Shrove Tuesday. This term comes from the old verb 'to shrive' (to confess) when the faithful made their confessions and were given absolution. The day is better known today for its pancakes and its pancake races. This tradition comes from the custom of eating up all the food in the house which would be forbidden in Lent.

## Mothering Sunday

Mid-Lent Sunday or the Fourth Sunday in Lent has traditionally been called Mothering Sunday. The probable reason for this is that it was the day when children who had left home returned to visit their mothers. Traditionally they would bring with them bunches of flowers and sometimes a simnel cake. This custom is continued in many churches and children come up during the service to receive little bunches of flowers which they give to their mothers. It is also called Refreshment Sunday, probably because the day was a relaxation in the self-denial of Lent.

## Holy Week

Holy Week is the week stretching from Palm Sunday to Easter Day which includes Maundy Thursday, Good Friday and Holy Saturday.

### *Palm Sunday*

Palm Sunday commemorates the entry of Christ into Jerusalem on a donkey to the acclamation of the crowds who placed palm leaves and garments in his path. Christ entered the city and then went to the temple (Mark chapter 11 verses 1–13). The symbolism for Christians is that here Christ is entering the holy city and its temple as King. The day is marked by the blessing and distribution of palms (small crosses made out of palm leaves) and there is usually a procession of both priest and people to the singing of a hymn, often 'All glory, laud and honour to thee Redeemer King'. In some parishes, a donkey, where one is available, is added to the procession. It is a bitter-sweet occasion because although the service begins with this joyful procession it later contains a long reading of the Passion and Death of Christ.

### *Maundy Thursday*

This is the Thursday before Easter when Christ met in the upper room with his disciples for the Last Supper (Mark chapter 14 verses 12–31, John chapter 13 verses 1–15). This was the occasion of the institution of the Eucharist, when Jesus blessed and broke bread. Jesus also washed his disciples' feet as an example of how they ought to treat each other. After the meal, Jesus and the disciples went to the Garden of Gethsemane (Mark chapter 14 verses 32–52)). Here Jesus endured a period of mental agony during which his disciples slept. Judas then betrayed Jesus to the soldiers and Jesus was arrested and led away.

On Maundy Thursday, worshippers are torn between giving thanks for the Eucharist and being aware of the awful context in which it is taking place. For this reason the main focus for thanksgiving for the Eucharist tends to be the Feast of Corpus Christi in early summer.

In many churches a feature of the services is the washing of feet, following in the example of Christ. Each year, for example, the Pope washes the feet of beggars in St Peter's, Rome. The English custom of the sovereign distributing Maundy money is a survival of the ancient footwashing. Originally the sovereign did wash the feet of beggars but this was transmuted into the giving of money.

After the end of the Eucharist, it is very common for churches to be stripped of hangings, cloths, crosses and so on to make them as bare as possible to symbolise the dereliction of Good Friday. In many churches too a small altar is prepared covered with flowers, called the Altar of Repose. This symbolises the Garden of Gethsemane and worshippers can watch with Christ in his agony.

### Good Friday

Good Friday is so called only because its effects are good for the world. It commemorates the crucifixion of Jesus, his death and hurried burial. It is the most solemn day of the Christian year.

It is recorded in all four Gospels, each of which give it their own emphasis: Matthew chapter 27 verses 24–66, Mark chapter 15, verses 15–47, Luke chapter 23 verses 26–56, John chapter 19 verses 1–42. Churches are bare of any ornament from the stripping of the previous evening. For the Christian, it is a distressing day. It is observed in a variety of ways. Many churches offer a Three Hours' Devotion, timed from 12 noon to 3 p.m., the last three hours on the cross, which is a series of devotional addresses interspersed with hymns. Others abbreviate this to one hour. Others celebrate the liturgy for the day which includes acts of devotion to the cross of Christ. Pilgrims in Jerusalem will follow the traditional path which Jesus took on his way from his condemnation to Golgotha. According to tradition he stopped fourteen times on this journey, the Via Dolorosa (Way of Sorrow), and each spot is marked. These are called the Stations of the Cross and many churches go through these using representations and pictures.

A traditional custom on Good Friday is eating hot cross buns.

### Easter Eve

Easter Eve, the Saturday between Good Friday and Easter Sunday, is the one complete day in which Jesus lay in the tomb. In practice churches cannot be left as they were on Good Friday because it takes time to decorate them with flowers and greenery for the splendour of Easter Day.

In the evening it is traditional for the Easter Eve vigil to be held. This begins with the kindling of the new fire, usually a small bonfire outside the church, which symbolises the new light, life and energy of the resurrection of Jesus. From this fire the great Paschal (Easter) candle is lit and carried into the dark church. Three times the deacon who is carrying the candle sings, 'The Light of Christ', and each time the people reply, 'Thanks be to God'. Then is sung the 'Exultet' which lays out the significance of the night and why it is the reason for universal joy. Then there are nine readings and a sermon. The congregation then moves to the font for the blessing of the baptismal waters and any who have been prepared for baptism are baptised at this point. The whole congregation then renew their own baptismal vows. After this there is normally the first Eucharist of Easter. This is particularly significant among the Orthodox churches of the East.

### *Easter Day*

Easter Day is the celebration of the resurrection of Christ from the dead and the new life which is promised to his people. It is the oldest and the greatest of all Christian festivals. Churches are usually decked with flowers and it is traditional for arum lilies to be in evidence. Many churches have Easter gardens which depict the three empty crosses and the empty tomb with the folded grave clothes.

The accounts of the resurrection are found in all four Gospels: Matthew chapter 28 verses 1–20, Mark chapter 16 verses 1–20, Luke chapter 24 verses 1–49, John chapters 20 and 21. All accounts are agreed that: (1) on the Sunday the stone covering the mouth of the tomb had been rolled back and that not only was the tomb empty but also the grave clothes were neatly folded; (2) the disciples were not expecting to find the tomb empty; and (3) the disciples met with Jesus. Particularly memorable stories are that of the two disciples walking to Emmaus who met with Jesus along the way but only recognised him in the breaking of bread (Luke chapter 24 verses 13–35), and the story of Mary Magdalene weeping by the tomb and finding that the man she had supposed to be the gardener was Jesus (John chapter 20 verses 11–18).

It is an old custom to give eggs at Easter – often chocolate ones. In some places eggs are hard-boiled, dyed and decorated and sometimes these are rolled down hills. Here the symbolism is in the rolling away of the stone from the mouth of the tomb. Usually, though, the symbolism is one of new life: out of the hard, lifeless egg bursts forth the fresh new life of the chick.

The date of Easter Day varies from year to year, though it always falls within the limits of 21 March and 25 April. This is because its date is determined by the date of the Jewish feast of Passover and that in turn is determined by the moon.

### Ascension Day

Ascension Day celebrates the end of Christ's resurrection appearances and his exaltation into heaven. According to Acts chapter 1 verse 3, it happened forty days after Easter. An account is given in Acts chapter 1 verses 3–9. Theologically it is regarded as the feast of the Lordship of Christ over all creation.

### Whitsunday (Pentecost)

This is celebrated as the birthday of the church. The account is found in the Acts of the Apostles chapter 2 verses 1–4 when the Holy Spirit came upon the church. It is central to the Christian faith that the church is guided, inspired and sustained by the Spirit of God. The real name of the feast is Pentecost but it is commonly known as Whitsunday. It falls fifty days after Easter.

### Harvest

This is an unofficial but very popular festival, especially strong in Britain, in which thanks are given for the fruits of the earth. It is usually held on a Sunday in September or October after the harvest has been gathered.

It may be associated with a parish harvest supper. People bring along fruit or vegetables and the church is decorated with these. In some urban industrial areas, harvest festivals include items made in factories and workshops in the area.

## All Saints and All Souls (1 and 2 November)

All Saints Day celebrates and gives thanks for the lives of all Christian saints (that is, Christians who have been 'lights of the world in their several generations'), known and unknown. It is also, less commonly, called All Hallows Day. With it is associated Halloween (the Eve of All Hallows) on 30 November. The notion was that the celebration of so much goodness on All Saints Day naturally brought out all the forces of evil, and as forces of evil are associated with darkness, so the night before All Saints was full of the symbols of evil – witches, wizards, sprites, goblins, ghosts and so on. With the dawn of All Saints Day, the goodness and the light drove them from the scene. Once a time of real fear, Halloween is now a party time, with children and adults dressing up as witches and wizards.

All Souls Day follows All Saints and brings to mind all the dead. At the requiem on that day, long lists of names of departed members of churches and of families are read out and prayers are offered for their rest. In some countries it is the custom at this season for families to light lamps on the graves of their departed members.

## Major saints days

Throughout the year, special saints have their own days. Here is a list of some of the most prominent.

| | |
|---|---|
| 25 January | St Paul (Acts chapter 9 verses 1–22) |
| 19 March | St Joseph, husband of the Blessed Virgin Mary (Matthew chapter 1 verses 18–25) |
| 11 June | St Barnabas (Acts Chapter 11 verses 19–30) |
| 29 June | St Peter (Matthew chapter 4 verses 12–20) |
| 22 July | St Mary Magdalene (John chapter 20 verses 11–18) |
| 25 July | St James the Apostle (Mark chapter 10 verses 35–45) |
| 21 September | St Matthew the Apostle (Matthew chapter 9 verses 9–13) |
| 30 November | St Andrew (Matthew chapter 4 verses 12–20) |

Other saints popular among children are:

| | |
|---|---|
| 1 March | St David, patron of Wales |
| 17 March | St Patrick, patron of Ireland |
| 23 April | St George, patron of England |
| 26 May | St Augustine of Canterbury |
| 27 May | Venerable Bede |
| 22 June | St Alban, the first British martyr |
| 4 October | St Francis of Assisi |

# Index

191846

191846